SCIENTIFIC AND ENGINEERING APPLICATIONS USING MATLAB

Edited by **Emilson Pereira Leite**

Scientific and Engineering Applications Using MATLAB
Edited by Emilson Pereira Leite

Published by InTech
Janeza Trdine 9, 51000 Rijeka, Croatia

Publishing Process Manager Davor Vidic

Technical Editor Teodora Smiljanic

Cover Designer InTech Design Team

Additional hard copies can be obtained from orders@intechopen.com

Scientific and Engineering Applications Using MATLAB, Edited by Emilson Pereira Leite
p. cm.
ISBN 978-953-307-659-1

For EU product safety concerns:
IN TECH d.o.o., Prolaz Marije Krucifikse Kozulić 3, 51000 Rijeka, Croatia,
info@intechopen.com or visit our website at intechopen.com.

Meet the editor

Dr. Emilson Pereira Leite is a Professor at the Institute of Geosciences, University of Campinas, Brazil. He received his PhD in Geophysics from University of São Paulo in 2005. He has published around 20 articles in peer-reviewed journals, conferences and popular science magazines. He has been working with MATLAB® for the last decade and is the Editor of the book entitled "Matlab - Modelling, Programming and Simulations", published by Sciyo in 2010.

Contents

Preface

The purpose of this book is to present 10 scientific and engineering works whose numerical and graphical analysis were all constructed using the power of Matlab® tools. The first five chapters of this book show applications in seismology, meteorology and natural environment. Chapters 6 and 7 focus on modeling and simulation of Water Distribution Networks. Simulation was also applied to study wide area protection for interconnected power grids (Chapter 8) and performance of conical antennas (Chapter 9). The last chapter deals with depth positioning of underwater robot vehicles. I always tell my students that by using interactive software like Matlab®, they can focus their efforts on learning and applying difficult concepts rather than in details of programming. Therefore, this book is a collection of interesting examples of where this computational package can be applied. As the Editor of this book, I would like to thank InTech - Open Access Publisher for all the support during the publishing process and authors for their efforts in order to produce high quality works.

Dr. Emilson Pereira Leite
Institute of Geosciences, University of Campinas,
Brazil

1

Ground Motion Estimation During Strong Seismic Events Using Matlab

Margaret Segou
Earthquake Science Center, Menlo Park, United States Geological Survey (USGS), United States of America

1. Introduction

This chapter presents the implementation of seismological and earthquake engineering principles and the development of innovative computer code using Matlab platform. Since earthquakes remain the greatest natural disaster for modern society, causing loss of life and millions of damages to the urban environment, the efforts of earth scientists and engineers lie in providing the tools for quick and adequate assessment of potential damage.
The foundation of seismic hazard analysis is based on the accurate scientific estimation of anticipated ground motion at a site following the occurrence of a strong earthquake. The seismic parameters involved in this estimation are the magnitude of the earthquake, the distance between the epicenter and the site in question, the description of the site's geological formations and additional characteristics of the earthquake's rupture style. Nowadays, knowledge about the level of the anticipated shaking near cities or villages is directly linked with past observations. In scientific practice the above statement describes the development of elaborate empirical mathematical models, which are based on the available seismological data. Seismological data collection and analysis is a demanding time-consuming task, related with Digital Signal Processing and Data Archiving. The goal of this chapter is two-fold; firstly to provide an insight of the necessary Digital Signal Processing steps, easily performed through Matlab, leading to the derivation of earthquake engineering parameters and secondly testing traditional regression analysis and optimization in order to develop empirical equations modeling the aforementioned parameters.

2. Data processing

According to modern data acquisition practice once an earthquake, exceeding a specific threshold occurs, ground motion time-series recorded by digital seismometers or accelerometers, usually at a sampling frequency equal to 200 samples-per-second, are transmitted to the data analysis center. No matter the progress of modern technology, scientists in earthquake prone countries cannot simply ignore the older analog acceleration time series, which in many cases can be irreplaceable. Matlab through *resample1* function provides the necessary tool to produce an equally sampled time series at a given sampling interval. After this processing stage, the main objective is to remove the undesirable long period and high frequency noise, which can be attributed to various sources like the mechanical hysteresis of the instrument or exposure to wind gasps and industrial environment (Segou et al., 2008). The subsequent processing steps are related with:

1. Visualization of time series and calculation of the peak ground acceleration parameter
2. Computation of Fourier amplitude spectrum
3. Filter design of the appropriate Infinite Impulse Response filter for the specific time series
4. Phase Preserving Implementation of the -previously designed- filter in the frequency domain
5. Graphical comparison of the Fourier amplitude velocity spectrum for the filtered and unfiltered time series, to determine whether the noise of the record has been successfully removed
6. Computation of the response acceleration spectra
7. Calculation of earthquake engineering parameters, like spectrum intensity (SI), useful to assess potential structural damage.

For the aforementioned steps a number of Matlab functions such as *fft* and *ifft* for domain conversion and *butter* for Infinite Impulse Response (IIR) filter design of Butterworth type have formed the core of Proschema software (Segou & Voulgaris, 2010), developed in Matlab R2009a version.

The visual inspection of the time series at the beginning of strong motion processing allows to determine the quality of the recording, decide whether removal of spurious spikes, known as *despiking,* is needed or if any other pre-processing steps are required. Figure 1 displays the time series of acceleration through the *plot* function using *linspace* function to derive the time line of the horizontal axis based on the sampling rate of the instrument in the field. Peak ground acceleration value (PGA) represents the maximum absolute amplitude of this acceleration time series (Amp) and it can be calculated using the *max* and *abs* functions.

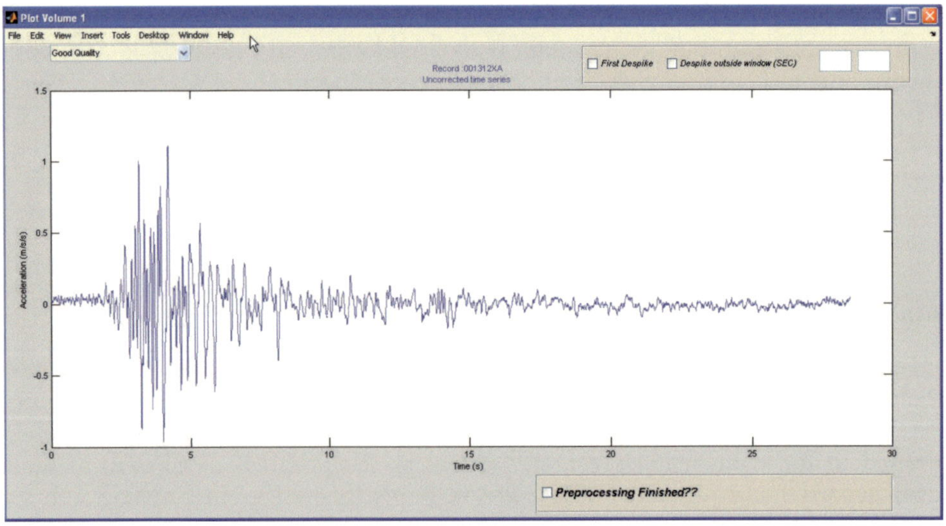

Fig. 1. Time series of acceleration.

In strong motion processing it is usual to implement a phase-preserving IIR filter in order to avoid phase delays, which will eventually distort the onset of the earthquake. Figure 2 presents a comparison between causal and phase-preserving filtering during strong motion processing. Figure 3 presents the uncorrected acceleration and filtered acceleration time series using five different pairs of cut-off frequencies combined in a phase preserving pass-band Butterworth filter's implementation.

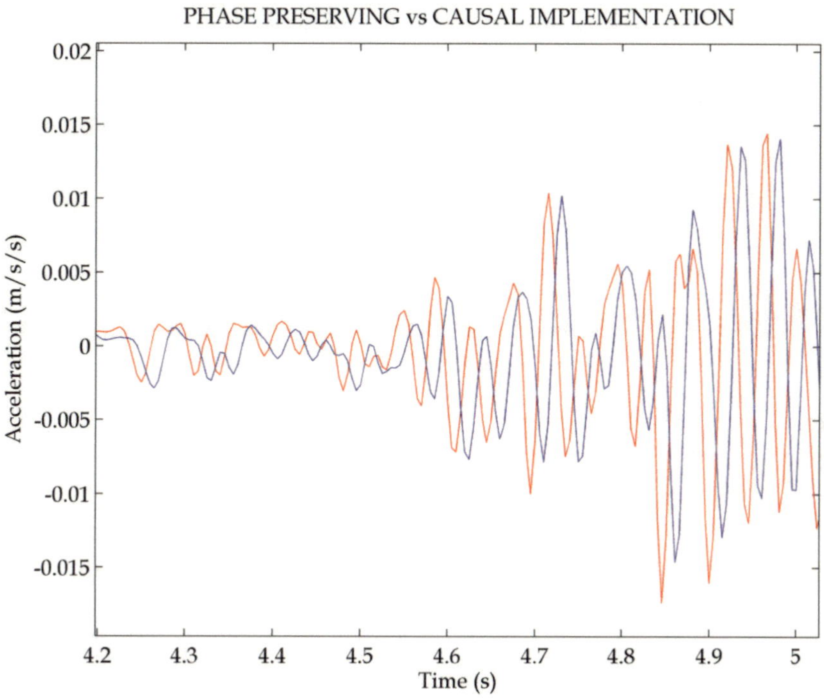

Fig. 2. Comparison between phase-preserving (in red) and causal (in blue) implementation of an IIR filter.

Another important aspect is the integration of a sinusoidal signal, such as the acceleration time series in this case study (Figure 1). This computation in the frequency domain corresponds to the convolution of Fourier amplitude spectrum with the frequency response of the perfect integration operator, equal to $1/i\omega$, whereas for differentiation the frequency response of the operator is just the inverse of the perfect integrator, simply $i\omega$ (Karl, 1989). After convolution the user can easily select the real part of an array of complex numbers, such as the Fourier amplitude spectrum, by using the *real* function.
Immediately after filtering the acceleration time series the inspection of velocity and displacement time series (Figure 4), calculated after single and double integration respectively, is required in order to determine whether the high-frequency and long period noise has been removed adequately from the records.
In more elaborate mathematical calculations, related with the response of a single degree of freedom (SDOF) harmonic oscillator $\ddot{u}$ of a specific damping level ζ subjected to an acceleration time series x (Equation 1a), the computational effort required is greater. In order to calculate the response spectral acceleration S_A at a given period ω, the user should define the maximum of the oscillator time series (Equation 1b) for this specific period.

$$\ddot{x} + 2\zeta\omega\dot{x} + \omega^2 x = \ddot{u}(t) \tag{1a}$$

$$S_A(\omega_n, \zeta) = \max_t \left| \ddot{x}(t) + \ddot{u}_g(t) \right| \tag{1b}$$

The calculation of the response spectral acceleration of the damped SDOF harmonic oscillator over a range of periods and various damping levels provides the response acceleration spectrum (Figure 5), which describes the shaking of typical structures during an earthquake. Figure 5 is the output of Proschema software using the *Plot Pseudo Spectral Acceleration* option.

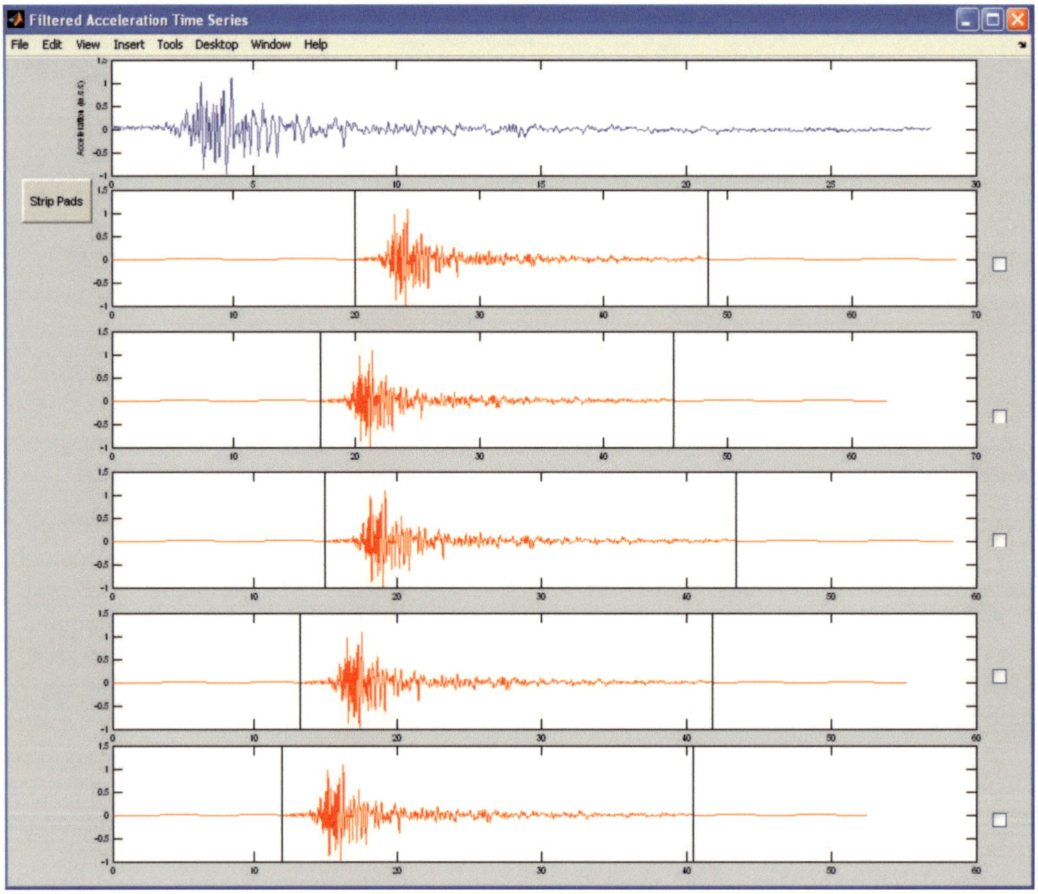

Fig. 3. Uncorrected (in blue) and filtered acceleration (in red) time series.

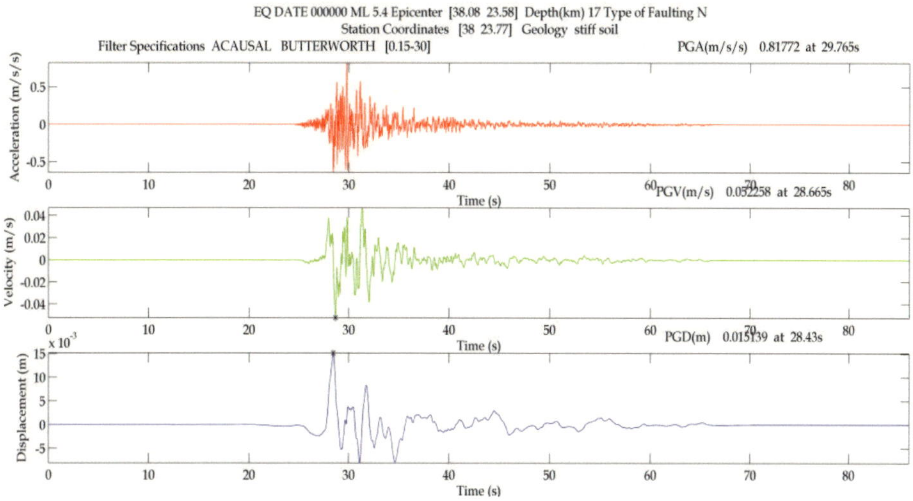

Fig. 4. Filtered acceleration, velocity and displacement time series.

Once the response acceleration spectrum is computed the calculation of more sophisticated earthquake engineering parameters, such as spectrum intensity (SI) follows. Spectrum intensity is defined as the integral of pseudo-velocity spectrum of 5% damping level between 0.1 s and 2.5 s. The critical issue behind the derivation of SI, and other parameters, is related with the common problem of calculation the area under the graph of an unknown function. Matlab makes possible the approximation of this unknown mathematical function, corresponding to the graph, using the boundary integral method (Liggett & Salmon, 1981) through a spline curve using chord-length parametrization and cubic spline interpolation. The above can be implemented through the combined use of *diff* function for calculating differences and approximate derivatives, at points ($SV_{(\omega,\varsigma)}$, T) between 0.1 s and 2.5 s (Figure 6), the cumulative sum function *cumsum* and the cubic spline approximation function *csapi*. After the determination of the unknown function, through cubic spline approximation, it is straightforward to calculate the area of interest under response spectrum by evaluating the cubic spline function in the interval of interest. In Figure 6 the example illustrates the cubic spline approximation for computing the engineering parameter SI, using the response spectrum of a corrected strong motion record after the removal of high frequency and long period noise.

After computing so many parameters, either single value (1X1), such spectrum intensity (SI) and peak ground acceleration (PGA), or one dimensional arrays (1XN) like the acceleration time series (Amp) or even multi-dimensional arrays (NXM), the problem of minimizing storage requirements arises. To overcome this problem the desirable parameters e.g. PGA, can be assigned as fields of a structure array. Assigning fields in a structure array called e.g. Output Data Structure (OPD) can be achieved through Command Prompt lines e.g OPD. pga=[pga].

At this point the calculation of engineering parameters, such as PGA, corresponds to the observations (OBS) of the natural system, reaches to an end. In the next section the development of an empirical model, aiming to predict the anticipated peak ground acceleration (PGA) during a strong earthquake, is briefly described.

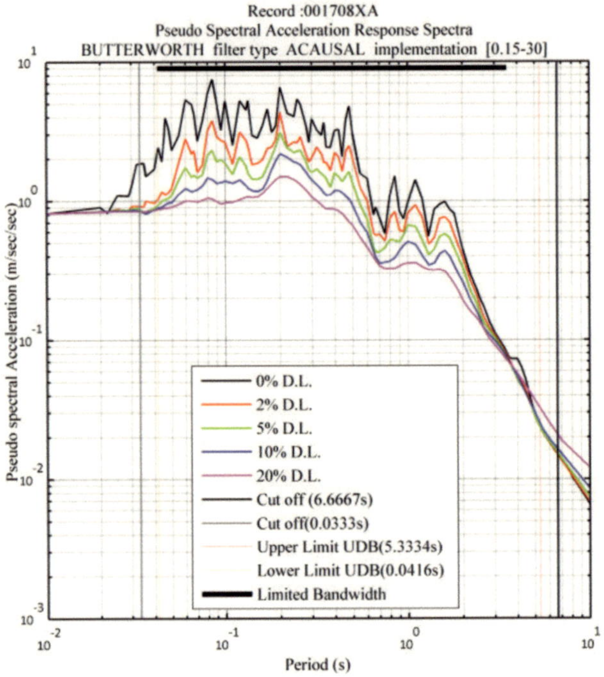

Fig. 5. Response acceleration spectrum for various damping levels (0%, 2%, 5%, 10% and 20% of the critical damping) over two hundred period estimators ranging between 0.01 s and 10.00 s.

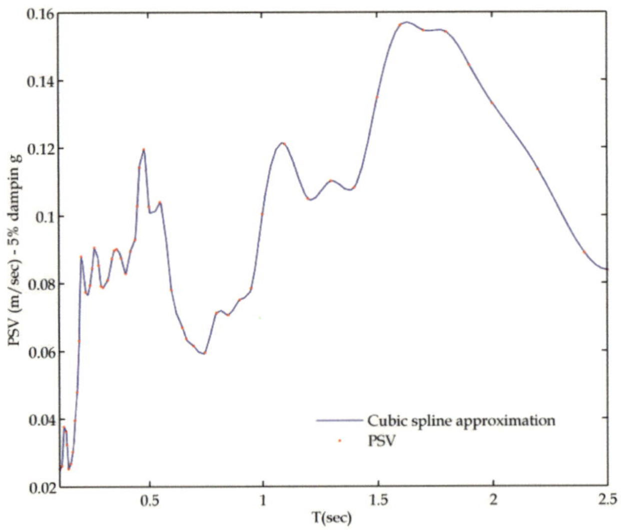

Fig. 6. Engineering parameter calculation after an important earthquake aided by cubic spline approximation.

3. Regression analysis versus stochastic optimization

The mathematical expression of an empirical model that is frequently used in ground motion modelling is given below:

$$\log_{10}(\text{PGA}) = \text{a} + \text{bM} + \text{cM}^2 + (\text{d} + \text{eM})\log_{10}\sqrt{\text{R}^2 + (\text{H} - \text{h})^2} + e + f \tag{2}$$

In Equation (2) the seismic magnitude M, distance R (km) and depth H (km) are considered to be the independent variables of the model (Equation 2). Random variables were introduced in Equation (2) for modeling soil site conditions (e) and style of faulting (f). From this point on the scientific effort focuses in solving equation (2), corresponding to the determination of the coefficients [a, b, c, d, e, f, h].

The traditional method to determine the coefficients of Equation (2) corresponds to regression analysis whereas modern techniques of mathematical optimization are developed over the last decades. The contribution of optimization to geophysics has been interestingly growing the last decades due to its efficiently in modelling complex natural systems by determining the best solution from a set of alternative solutions (Goldberg, 1989). But which is the main advantage of optimization? The answer to this question would be its ability to reach the optimal solution for any system even under extreme computational environments, either when data-sets are limited but also when vast data-sets of high diversity require the determination of a solution describing sufficiently all the samples given. In the following section the advantages of optimization versus regression would be analysed and the best solver for optimization process would be selected through a test involving a number of important deterministic and stochastic algorithms.

3.1 Regression analysis

Using the *nonlinfit* function the implementation of mixed effects technique can be a first approach to modelling using regression analysis, leading to the determination of the coefficients of Equation (2). The results however revealed that this method was not successful in determining coefficients e and f, corresponding to the random effects terms of the model, due to the poor representation -in the database- of different types of soils and styles-of-faulting, respectively.

3.2 Optimization

In theory, traditional regression analysis -discussed in previous paragraph- is expected to provide one possible solution for any given equation. Nowadays optimization addresses the necessity for determining the best solution for data-sets of complex physical systems. As described previously the effort lies in determining the optimal solution for the mathematical model of Equation (2), which leads to the implementation of constrained optimization techniques. The mathematical problem corresponds to the minimization of misfit represented by the sum of squares of the residuals, between the logarithms of observed and predicted values (Equation 3). Constrained minimization problems have some basic pillars which are briefly given as: (1) the existence of a candidate theoretical solution, to initiate optimization (2) the existence of an objective function, to evaluate whether minimizing the misfit is achieved (3) a set of linear constraints serving as bounds for the coefficients' determination and (4) the determination of convergence criteria (Rothlauf, 2006).

$$OF = \sum_i (pred_i - obs_i)^2 \quad (3)$$

It should be noted that for consistency in this example the same objective function, linear constraints and convergence criteria have been used during the implementation of the aforementioned solvers.

Techniques used during optimization to exhaust the search space are classified generally in three classes: (1) Calculus based techniques (2) Guided Random search techniques and (3) Enumerative techniques (Filho et al., 1994). In this paper calculus based versus guided random search techniques will be test through comparison of different solvers whereas enumerative algorithms will be discarded since "they cannot compete to the robustness race" when compared with the aforementioned techniques mainly due to the characteristics of their search domains (Said, 2005).

3.2.2 Optimization using calculus based techniques

Calculus based techniques are further divided in Direct and Indirect Search methods (Filho et al., 1994). Indirect Search methods as Non Linear Least Squares -in this example- is the most common approach in data fitting problems in earth sciences corresponding to the implementation of the maximum likelihood criterion (Draper & Smith, 1987) for determining the best solution setting the value of the objective function in Equation (3) to zero.

Pattern Search, on the other hand, is a Direct Search method used broadly in its generalized form in optimization of non-continuous and non-differentiable functions (Hookes & Jeeves; 1961; Dolan et al., 2003). An initial population of possible solutions serves as set of starting points. During optimization the available search space is either increasing or decreasing, depending on a gradient, in the effort to improve the solutions suggested previously (Audet & Dennis, 2003). The latter are then evaluated, for their effectiveness to minimize the misfit between predicted and observed values, using an objective function (Equation 3). Direct search methods are considered to be the simplest variation of deterministic algorithms used in optimization criticized for their efficacy to search sufficiently large solution spaces (Goldberg, 1989).

3.2.1 Optimization using guided random search techniques

Guided random search techniques are classified in Genetic Algorithms and Simulated Annealing (Filho et al., 1994). Both algorithms use information in order to guide their search for the optimal solution of the system. The development however of Genetic Algorithms is based on natural selection principles whereas Simulated Annealing relies on thermodynamic processes.

Fogel et al. (1966) developed Genetic Algorithms (GA), alternatively known as evolutionary programming, as "a technique in which candidate solutions to given tasks were represented as finite-state machines, which were evolved by randomly mutating their state-transition diagrams". Holland (1975) focused on how genetic operators observed in nature, such as survival-of-the-fittest, crossover and mutation could be introduced into evolutionary computing. During the last decades Genetic Algorithms applications has been described in the works of De Jong (1975), Grefenstette (1986), Goldberg (1989), Davis (1991), discussed in Mitchell (1996) thourougly, pointing out their strength in determining solutions for complex natural systems. The robustness of Genetic Algorithms in geophysics has been only recently described by researchers (Stoffa & Sen, 1991; Tavakoli & Pezeshk, 2005), making the aforementioned solvers known for their application in constrained minimization problems (Goldberg, 1985). GA's are not limited by restrictive assumptions, concerning the continuity, the existence of derivatives and the unimodality of the function in terms of computational geometry. This is an advantage over regression analysis which often determines local minima as the solution of a given equation (Goldberg, 1989), while at the same time the suggested solution is highly dependent on a single point of initialization.

In the following paragraph we focus on the initialization, the process of improvement and the destination of constrained minimization by using stochastic solvers such as GAs. By keeping the analogy to biological systems a number of chromosomes/strings form the genetic prescription for the development and the operation of the organism. In our case the chromosomes/strings are composed by six genes/characters, representing the set of coefficients of Equation (2).

GAs start with a possible solution or a set of possible solutions corresponding to a theoretic attenuation curve and continues with optimization in order to determine the optimal solution for the given data set. In this study both initialization options have been tested, corresponding either to a single starting point (Simple Genetic Algorithm) or multiple random-generated starting points (Genetic Algorithm with initial Population Develoment), forming an initial population of candidate solutions each one satisfying the given linear constraints for the determination of the coefficients of Equation (2). In order to ensure well-dispersed and random initial population development, for the adequate representation of the search space, Latin Hypercube sampling was used (Diaz-Gomez & Hougen, 2006). The technique was elaborated by Iman et al. (1981) as stratified sampling without replacement, whereas in recent years risk analysis software employs Latin Hypercube sampling in preference of Monte Carlo approach for population development.

During optimization every candidate solution/string satisfying the given linear constraints is evaluated, through the objective function of Equation (3), for its effectiveness in minimizing the misfit, hence bringing the response value of the system near a desired value. Within a generation (group of solutions) fitness scaling serves the purpose of ranking each candidate solution to facilitate the selection of the best solutions that should surviving in the next generation. In that way, mimicking nature, the fitter solution survives and can be a parent individual to the next generation whereas worst fit solutions are penalized.

In the present study a number of 200 generations is considered, each one with population size of 600 individuals/solutions. Stochastic operators like the cross-over, mutation and survival-of-the-fittest guarantee diversity of the population (Pan, 1995) forcing the GA to search the solution space intensively, thereby reducing the possibility that the algorithm will return a local minimum (Goldberg, 1985). In terms of survival, 2 elite individuals/solutions are guaranteed to survive to the next generation in this study. A crossover fraction equal to 0.8 specifies the percentage of individual/solutions, other than elite children, produced by crossover in the next generation. Crossover mimics natural recombination between two parent chromosomes/solutions during which the offspring chromosome/solution has changed values of specific genes/numbers with respect to the parent genes/numbers. In this example two point cross-over has been implemented where the selected string is divided into 3 segments and then 2 segments are exchanged with the corresponding segments of another string. Mutation, on the other hand, alters a randomly selected character/coefficient within a string/solution to create a new possible solution. Adaptive mutation, used in this example, generates new directions in the search space, with respect to the last successful or unsuccessful generation, bounded by the linear constraints set for the coefficients.

By combining the aforementioned stochastic operators, three versions of GAs, aim to test the relation between diversity of the population and performance, corresponding to

1. Simple Genetic Algorithm (SGA)
2. Genetic Algorithm with initial Population Development (GADP)
3. Hybrid Genetic Algorithm (HGA).

It is noted that Hybrid Genetic Algorithm (HGA) introduces the solution, determined a priori by a Simple Genetic Algorithm (SGA), to a deterministic solver, which requires the existence of derivatives, in order to provide local optima once the Genetic Algorithm has determined the neighborhood of the global optima (Il-Seok et al., 2004). The author included this enhanced evolutionary algorithm in the comparison to test the efficiency of the interaction between stochastic and deterministic solvers.

Simulated Annealing is a meta-heuristic algorithm proposed by Kirkpatrick, et al. (1983) and Cerny (1985) for the determination of global minima. It mimics the physical process where metals are slowly cooled so that eventually their crystal structure is frozen. The latter state corresponds to the determination of the optimal solution, using a minimum energy configuration during its implementation (Bertsimas and Tsitsiklis, 1993).

In this study optimization starts from a randomly generated initial population and a hypothesis for a parameter, known as Temperature, slowly decreasing from 100° C by a factor of 0.0059° C in the process of determining the optimal solution. During implementation each new possible solution is evaluated, for its effectiveness in minimizing the objective function (Equation 3), then in case of a lower misfit value the suggested solution is adapted. Simulated Annealing, an important solver in stochastic minimization problems (Bohachevsky et al., 1986), has been reported to successfully determine global minima however the author agree with the results of Ingber (1993) that this algorithm requires fine tuning to specific problems relative to other solvers.

4. Selecting the optimum solver

In order to test the efficiency of the optimization solvers a subset of the database was used, corresponding to rock site conditions, with the purpose of determining the coefficients of Equation (2) for peak ground acceleration and unspecified style-of-faulting. The solvers implemented for this test correspond to: (1) Simple Genetic Algorithm (SGA), (2) Genetic Algorithm with initial Population Development through Latin Hypercube sampling (GADP) (3) Hybrid Genetic Algorithm (HGA), (4) Simulated Annealing algorithm (SA) (5) Non Linear Least Squares (NLLSQ) (6) Non Linear Least Squares with initial population development (NLLSQDP) and (7) Pattern Search algorithm (PS). Although the author provided some basic principles of the solvers in the previous section, details and theoretical comparison between the solvers can be found in recent literature (Wetter and Wright, 2003; Gabere, 2007; Alander, 2009; El-Mihoub et al, 2006; Solomatine, 1998 among others).

Before evaluating the performance of these solvers it is meaningful to describe their relative computational efficiencies. The major difference between the two main categories of stochastic solvers (GAs, SA) is that GAs can either automatically produce a starting point (SGA) or they can be enhanced by initial population development (GADP), whereas Simulated Annealing requires a priori definition of initial conditions (Davis, 1987). The latter requirement applies for deterministic algorithms (NLLSQ, NLLSQDP, PS) as well. The difference however between Simulated Annealing (SA) and deterministic solvers (NLLSQ, NLLSQDP, PS) is that the latter depend on the existence of derivatives in order to continue their iterations.

The evaluation of the performance of optimization solvers follows a qualitative and quantitative method. Analytically by qualitative criteria the authors refers to inability of the solver to determine a possible solution (1) within the given number of generations (2) satisfying the linear constraints and (3) in a timely manner. When the above criteria failed, optimization was implemented again with different starting points, which is acknowledged to be the main source of error that could lead to a solver's failure. The alternative solution, that of relaxing convergence criteria in the case of a solver's fail, was not considered since it would jeopardize the final comparison between different solvers. In the event of a solver's failure to produce a possible solution for second time, it was excluded from the quantitative comparison. In that sense Non Linear Least Squares (NLLSQ) solver failing the (2) criterion has been implemented again using this time multiple starting points (NLLSQDP). After the second failure to determine a feasible solution by returning the initial conditions -describing only the theoretical ground motion prediction equation, which was subjectively set by the programmer- Non Linear Least Squares (NLLSQ, NLLSQDP) have been excluded from the comparison from this point forward.

Table 1 presents the results of the quantitative comparison of the optimization solvers together with the coefficients of Equation (2) together with the numerical details used during optimization, such as the linear constraints introduced in the form of lower and upper bounds. It is noted that convergence criterion, alternatively known as tolerance, was set to 1E-06 for the purpose of this test. The quantitative comparison has been based in two criteria (1) the standard error, in logarithm base 10, and (2) the average sample log-likelihood (LLH) value (Scherbaum et al., 2009) of the resulting ground motion prediction equation as derived by a specific solver.

The standard error (σ_k) has been calculated as the mean of absolute residuals between observed and predicted by the model g_k (where k denotes the index of the solver) ground motion values described in the equation below:

$$\sigma_k = \frac{1}{N}\left|obs_i g_k(x_i)\right| \tag{4}$$

Assuming that the set of observations adequately describes nature, the likelihood $L(g_k \mid x)$, of the model g_k given the set of observations x, would represent how close model g_k describes reality. According to Scherbaum et al. (2009) the average sample log-likelihood (LLH) estimator has been calculated as the mean of log-likelihood values over N number of x samples

$$\left\langle \log\left(L\left(g_k|x\right)\right)\right\rangle = \frac{1}{N}\sum_{i=1}^{N}\log\left(g_k\left(x_i\right)\right) \tag{5}$$

It is noted that the sigma value is calculated as the standard deviation of the residuals in log 10 units, for consistency with Equation 2, using the *std* function. It is noted that the calculation of log-likelihood estimator of Equation 5 has been made through the function *normlike*.

Initial Points	1.00000	0.15000	0.00300	-0.50000	0.01000	0.01000		
Lower Bounds	1.00000	0.01000	0.00100	-1.50000	0.00010	0.00100		
Upper Bounds	3.00000	0.50000	1.00000	-0.00010	1.00000	2.00000		
	a	**b**	**c**	**d**	**e**	**h**	**σ**	**LLH**
NLLSQ	1.70166	0.35714	0.00100	-1.22962	0.00010	0.00100		
NLLSQDP	1.70166	0.35714	0.00100	-1.22962	0.00010	0.00100		
GA	1.82357	0.32641	0.00279	-1.27552	0.00755	0.00116	0.3464	1.8184
GADP	2.62122	0.11622	0.01568	-1.47212	0.03988	0.00136	0.3426	1.8044
HGA	1.70170	0.35713	0.00100	-1.22961	0.00010	0.00100		
PS	1.50000	0.01000	0.00100	-0.00010	0.00010	1.00100		
SA	1.73819	0.32360	0.00608	-1.25514	0.00264	0.55508	0.3484	1.8259

Table 1. Initial and boundary conditions for the seven solvers used in constrained minimization problem. Successful solvers are presented in bold.

The graphical comparison of the most successful solvers of Table 1 is shown in Figure 7. Matlab through the Optimization Toolbox provides core functions for solving minimization problems, using a number of suggested solvers such as the deterministic non-linear least squares (*lsqcurvefit* function) and Pattern Search (*patternsearch* function), the stochastic Genetic Algorithm (*ga* function) and Simulated Annealing (*simulannealbnd* function). Especially in the case of Genetic Algorithms the development of initial population of possible solutions is achieved through Latin Hypercube sampling using the *lhsdesign* function. The adjustment of stochastic operators, such as the survival-of-the fittest, mutation and cross-over, for Genetic Algorithms' implementation can be achieved through the *gaoptimset* function whereas for Pattern Search *psoptimset* function is required.

5. Conclusions

Two major conclusions can be drawn from the results of this study: firstly, deterministic algorithms, such as Non Linear Least Squares (NLLSQ, NLLSQDP) fail to determine the whole set of coefficients since the values of the coefficients c, e and h (Table 1) remain fixed to their lower boundary value. The above remark emphasizes the weakness of deterministic algorithms leading to the determination of local minima instead of returning a global solution for the minimization problem. Secondly, the effectiveness of GAs in solving minimization problems, even in their simpler parameterization (SGA), is supported by their ranking following the LLH criterion. Thus, the use of Genetic Algorithms aided by initial Population Development (GADP) by Latin Hypercube sampling for the constrained minimization problem set in Equation (2) is suggested.

Once the final set of coefficients is determined the seismologist can assess the expected ground motion at any given site, located at distance R from the epicenter of a strong earthquake with magnitude M. Figure 8 presents the estimated ground motion after a magnitude M5 and M6 earthquake at a rock site for various distances using stochastically derived ground motion prediction equation using Genetic Algorithm with initial Population Developement.

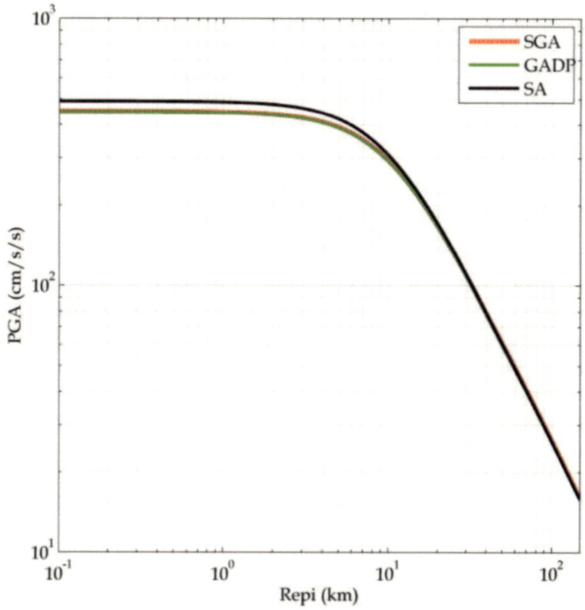

Fig. 7. Graphical representation of ground motion prediction equations (see Equation 2) as a result of constrained minimization using different solvers for the case of an M6 event at rock site for unspecified style of faulting.

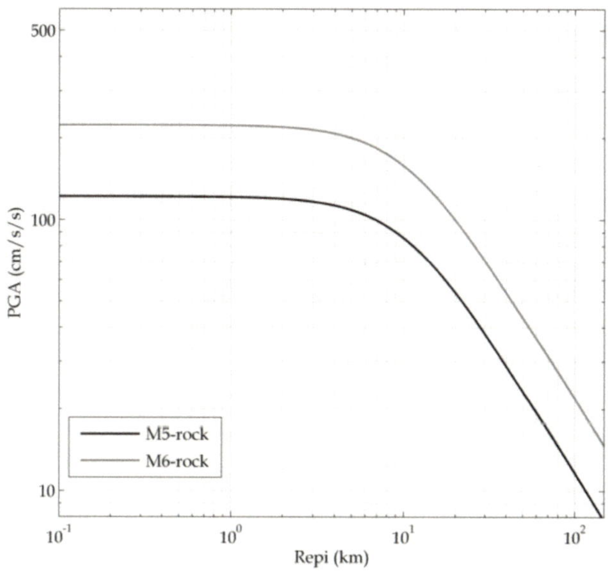

Fig. 8. Attenuation of peak ground acceleration (PGA) over a wide range of distances from the seismic source.

Ground motion prediction equations are an important tool for the scientific and engineering community to forecast anticipated ground motion and predict potential economical losses and structural damages. Another important application of ground motion prediction equations lies in developing possible scenarios for the planning short and long term emergency response.

This chapter describes how Matlab can be used in scientific research for Digital Signal Processing, Data Archiving but also for modeling complex natural systems through Optimization. Since the number of graduate students writing computer codes from scratch, in order to expand the frontiers of their research, continue to grow, core Matlab functions can be used to develop new software packages in the future. The application examples of this chapter clearly show that in seismological practice, demanding mathematical procedures can be implemented and their results can be easily visualized through Matlab.

6. References

Alander, J.T. (2009). *An Indexed Bibliography of Genetic Algorithms and Simulated Annealing: Hybrids and Comparisons*, Report for the Department of Electrical Engineering and Automation, Vaasa, Finland.

Audet, C. & Dennis, J.E. (2003) Analysis of generalized pattern searches. *SIAM Journal on Optimization*, Vol. 13, No. 3, pp. 889–903.

Bertsimas, D. & Tsitsiklis, J. (1993). Simulated Annealing, *Statistical Review*, Vol. 8, No. 1, pp. 10-15.

Bohachevsky, I.O., Johnson, M.E. & Stein, M. L. (1986). Generalized Simulated Annealing for Function Optimization, *Technometrics*, Vol. 28, No 3, pp. 209-217.

Cerny, V. (1982). A thermodynamical approach to the travelling salesman problem: An efficient simulation algorithm, *Journal of Optimization Theory and Applications*, Vol. 45, pp. 41-51.

Davis, L. (1991). *Handbook of Genetic Algorithms*, Van Nostrand Reinhold, New York.

Goldberg, D. E. (1989). *Genetic Algorithms in search, optimization and machine learning*, Addison Wesley Longman, Reading, Massachusetts.

De Jong, K. A. (1975). An analysis of the behavior of a class of genetic adaptive systems. Dissertation Abstracts International, Vol. 36, No. 10, 5140B.

Diaz-Gomez, P.A. & Hougen, D.F. (2006). Genetic Algorithms for hunting snakes in hypercubes: Fitness function and open questions, *Proceedings of the Seventh ACIS International Conference on Software Engineering, Aritificial Intelligence, Networking and Parallel/Distributed Computing*, Las Vegas, 2006.

Dolan, E.D., Lewis, R. M. & Torczon, V. (2003). On the local convergence of pattern search, *SIAM Journal on Optimization*, Vol. 14, No. 2, 567-583.

El-Mihoub, T.A., Hopgood, A.A.,Nolle L. & Battersby, A. (2006). Hybrid genetic algorithms: A review, *Engineering Letters*, Vol. 13, No. 2, pp. 124-137.

Filho, J.L., Treleaven, P.C. & Alippi, C. (1994). Genetic-Algorithm programming envirinments, *Computer*, Vol. 27, No. 6, pp. 28-43.

Fogel, L.J., Owens, A.J., & Walsh, M. J. (1966). *Artificial intelligence through simulated evolution*, John Wile, New York.

Gabere, M.N. (2007). *Simulated Annealing Driven Pattern Search*. Algorithms for Global Optimization, Msc Thesis, School of Computational and Applied Mathematics, University of the Witwatersrand, Witwatersrand.

Grefenstette, J.J. (1986). Optimization of control parameters for genetic algorithms, *IEEE Transactions SMC*, Vol. 16, pp. 122-128.

Holland, J. H. (1975). *Adaptation in natural and artificial Systems: An introductory analysis with applications to biology, control, and artificial intelligence*, A. Arbor (editor), University of Michigan Press, MIT press, Cambridge.

Hookes, R. & Jeeves, T.A. (1961). 'Direct search' solution of numerical and statistical problems, *Journal of the Association for Computing Machinery* (ACM), Vol. 8, No.2, pp. 212–229.

Il-Seok O., Jin-Seon L. & Byung-Ro M., Hybrid Genetic Algorithms for Feature Selection, *IEEE Transactions on Pattern Analysis and Machine Intelligence*, Vol. 26, No.11, pp. 1424-1437.

Iman, R. L., Helton, J. C., & Campbell, J. E. (1981). An approach to sensitivity analysis of computer models, Part 1. Introduction, input variable selection and preliminary variable assessment, *Journal of Quality Technology*, Vol. 31, No.3,pp. 174-183.

Ingber, L. (1983). Simulated annealing: Practice versus theory, *Journal of Mathematical Computational Modelling*, Vol. 18, No.11,pp. 29-57.

Karl, J. H. (1989). *An introduction to digital signal processing*. Academic Press Inc., San Diego, California.

Kirkpatrick, S., Gelatt, Jr. C.D, & Vecchi, M.P. (1983). Optimization by simulated annealing, *Science, Vol.* 220, No.4598,pp. 671-680.

Kramer, S. L., 1996. Geotechnical Earthquake Engineering. Prentice Hall International Inc., New Jersey, pp652.

Liggett, J.A. & Salmon, J.R. (1981). Cubic spline boundary elements, *International Journal for Numerical Methods in Engineering* , Vol.17,pp. 543-556.

Mitchell, M. (1996). *An Introduction to Genetic Algorithms*, MIT Press, Cambridge.

Rothlauf, F. (2006). *Representations for Genetic and Evolutionary Algorithms*, Springer Verlag, Berlin Heidelberg New York.

Pan, Z., Chen, Y., Kang, L. & Zhang, Y. (1995). Parameter estimation by Genetic Algorithms For nonlinear regression, *Proceedings of International Conference on Optimization Technique and Applications*, G.Z.Liu (editor).

Said, Y. H. (2005). Genetic Algorithms and their applications. *Handbook of Statistics 24*, Calyampudi Radhakrishna Rao, Edward J. Wegman, Jeffrey L. Solka (editors),pp. 359-390.

Scherbaum, F., Delavaud, E. & Riggelsen, C. (2009). Model selection in seismic hazard analysis: An information-theoretic perspective, *Bulletin of Seismological Society of America*, Vol.99,pp. 3234–3247.

Segou, M., Voulgaris, N., Makropoulos, K. C., & Stavrakakis, G. N. (2008). A review of the Greek strong motion database: needs, improvements and future development, in *Proceedings of the 31st general Assembly of the European Seismological Commission*, Hersonissos, Crete, Greece, 7-12 September 2008.

Segou, M. and Voulgaris, N. (2010). Proschema: A Matlab application for processing strong motion records and estimating earthquake engineering parameters, *Computers & Geosciences*, Vol.10,pp. 977-986.

Solomatine, D. P. (1998). Genetic and other global optimization algorithms - comparison and use in calibration problems, *Proceedings of the 3rd International Conference on Hydroinformatics*, Balkema Publishers, Copenhagen, Denmark.

Stoffa, P. L., & Sen, M. K. (1991). Nonlinear multiparameter optimization using genetic algorithms: Inversion of plane wave seismograms, *Geophysics*, Vol. 56, No.11,pp. 1794-1810.

Tavakoli, B., & Pezeshk, S. (2005). Empirical-stochastic ground-motion prediction for eastern North America, *Bulletin of Seismological Society of America,* Vol. 95,pp. 2283-2296.

Wetter, M. & Wright, J. (2003). Comparison of generalized pattern search and a genetic algorithm optimization method, *Proceedings of the Eighth International Conference on Building Simulation (IBPSA),* Eindhoven, Netherlands.

2

Aftershock Identification Through Genetic Fault-Plane Fitting

F.A.Nava, V.H.Márquez and J.F.Granados
Seismology Dept., Earth Sciences Division, CICESE
Mexico

1. Introduction

Since the earlier times of documented seismological observations, it was noticed that an earthquake (usually a large one) was followed by a sequence of many smaller earthquakes, originating in the epicentral region; the first, larger, earthquake is called the *mainshock*, or *main shock* or *main event*, and the following, smaller, earthquakes are called *aftershocks*. These sequences, and their spatial and temporal distributions, depend on the characteristics of the mainshock and on the physical properties and the state of stress, strain, temperature, etc., of the region of occurrence (Kisslinger, 1996).

The observation that in many aftershock sequences the magnitude of the largest aftershock is about $\Delta M \approx 1.2$ less than that of the mainshock is known as Båth's law (Helmstetter & Sornette, 2003; Richter, 1968); it implies an energy ratio $E(M_{aft}) / E(M_{main}) \sim 0.007$ between largest aftershock and mainshock. An earthquake following some mainshock but not small enough to be considered an aftershock by the Båth's law criterion is often considered to be a mainshock in its own right and to constitute, together with the mainshock, a *multiple event* or *multiplet*. A large event followed by an even larger one is demoted from mainshock to *foreshock*; a probabilistic calculation, based on the observation that aftershocks follow the Gutenberg-Richter relation (Gutenberg & Richter, 1954; Kisslinger & Jones, 1991; Shcherbakov et al., 2005), indicates that for $\Delta M = 1.2$ the seismicity following a given mainshock has a $\sim 6.3\%$ probability of including a "daughter" event larger than the mainshock (Helmstetter et al., 2003; Holliday et al, 2008).

Thus, the simple definition of aftershock as an earthquake occurring after a mainshock and in its epicentral region, although implying some causal relation with the mainshock, is partly semantic and largely circumstantial. Indeed, smallish earthquakes that constitute the *background seismicity* occur all the time in a seismic region in the absence of large events, and continue occurring whether or not a large earthquake occurs, so that not all earthquakes occurring in the region after a mainshock are necessarily aftershocks.

If aftershocks are a result of the occurrence of the mainshock, then they should be related in a physical way with its rupture process. The aftershock-producing mechanism is not yet known, but it is conceivably related with adjustments to the post-mainshock stress field (Lay & Wallace, 1995) possibly through viscolelastic processes or through fluid flow (Nur & Booker, 1972); whichever the actual process, aftershocks should be related with the rupture plane of the mainshock. Kisslinger (1996) qualitatively defines three kinds of aftershocks:

Class 1 is those occurring on the ruptured area of the fault plane or on a thin band around it. Class 2 is events that occur on the same fault but outside of the co-seismic ruptured area. Class 3 is events occurring elsewhere, on faults other than the one ruptured by the mainshock; these events, whether in the same region or not, will not be considered here as aftershocks, but rather will be classified as *triggered earthquakes.*

The number of aftershocks decreases with time after the mainshock according to the modified Omori relation (Utsu, 1961, 1969, 1970) as

$$N(t) = \frac{k}{(t+c)^p}, \tag{1}$$

where t is time measured from that of the mainshock, and k, c, and p are positive parameters which vary with the lithologic, tectonic, and other conditions of the study area. Commonly, p ranges from 0.9 to 1.8, with most instances between 1.1 and 1.4 (Utsu, 1961); values which do not show dependence on the magnitude of the mainshock (Utsu, 1962).

Aftershocks occurring within 24 to 48 hours after a large earthquake locate mostly over the co-seismic rupture area, and provide a good estimation of it (Lay & Wallace, 1995), which indicates that seismicity at the time is mostly class 1; over longer times the aftershock area increases (Felzer & Brodsky, 2006; Helmstetter & Sornette, 2002; Mogi, 1968; Tajima y Kanamori, 1985; Valdés *et al.*, 1982), including at the edges class 2 events.

Among other reasons why aftershock identification is important, we can mention the following few examples. Aftershocks can give important information about the rupture area; also, from estimations of co-seismic slip on the fault plane by inversion of seismic waves, several authors have found that aftershocks are scarce in areas of maximum slip and concentrate around their edges (Dreger *et al.*, 1994; Engdahl *et al*, 1989; Hauksson *et al.*, 1994; Mendoza & Hartzell, 1988), so that aftershocks give information about the rupture process of the mainshock. Aftershocks can also yield information about the properties of the epicentral region (Knopoff et al., 1982; Kisslinger, 1996; Kisslinger & Hasegawa, 1991; Figueroa, 2009), and about possible triggering mechanisms (Roquemore & Simila, 1994).

Since aftershocks can be large enough to contribute to the damage (particularly after structures have been debilitated by a mainshock), it is important to estimate the hazard associated with aftershock activity (Felzer et al., 2003; Reasenberg & Jones, 1989).

It has been proposed that, since aftershock activity depends among other factors on the stress status of the region, there is research on whether some characteristics of the aftershock activity from intermediate-sized earthquakes can be useful as precursory data for large earthquake hazard estimation (e.g. Jones, 1994; Keilis-Borok et al., 1980; Wyss, 1986).

Finally, for some studies concerned with large earthquakes, aftershocks can be considered as noise, and have to be eliminated from the catalogs (e.g. Gardner. & Knopoff, 1974; Habermann & Wyss, 1984).

In order to use or eliminate aftershocks it is first necessary to identify them. Many methods have been used, ranging from visual inspection (Molchan & Dmitrieva, 1992) to sophisticated numerical techniques. A common method identifies aftershocks as those shocks locating within temporal and spatial windows having lengths which usually depend on the magnitude of the mainshock (Gardner & Knopoff, 1974; Keilis-Borok *et al.*, 1980; Knopoff *et al.*, 1982). More sophisticated methods identify aftershocks as belonging to a spatial cluster, consisting of events within a given distance of at least one other event belonging to the cluster, which includes the mainshock (Davis & Frohlich 1991a,b; Frohlich

& Davis, 1985). A variation of the window method considers events from larger to smaller magnitudes with the size of the spatial windows a function of the magnitude, and density of events (Prozorov & Dziewonski, 1982; Prozorov, 1986). Other methods include recognizing some statistical property (e.g. Kagan & Knopoff 1976, 1981; Vere-Jones & Davies 1966) or interpreting the relations between events according to some statistical chain or branching model (Molchan & Dmitrieva, 1992; Reasenberg, 1985).

Our method includes some of the above mentioned techniques used to discard events which cannot be aftershocks, and then proceeds to identify aftershocks based on the physical model of a rupture plane and on recognized statistical relationships. An early unsophisticated application of the rupture plane model, which proved that this principle of aftershock identification was feasible, was part of an unpublished MSc. thesis (Granados, 2000).

2. The method

We work with seismic catalogs containing occurrence time (days), hypocentral x (East), y (North), and z (up), and, optionally, horizontal and vertical location uncertainties u_h and u_v, all these in kilometers. If location uncertainties are not included in the catalog, optional horizontal and vertical uncertainties are assigned equally to all events.

Any events occurring before the event with the largest magnitude $M_{\max}$, the mainshock, are eliminated. All spatial coordinates are then referred to those of the mainshock.

A rough time cutoff, eliminates events occurring after more than an optional cutoff time (default is $n_{yr} = 4\,\text{years}$), because after a few years it is difficult to distinguish aftershock activity from background seismicity.

The extent of the aftershock area depends on the energy, i.e. on the magnitude, of the mainshock (Utsu, & Seki, 1955), as does the rupture area. A first rough spatial discrimination, based on an average of the empirical magnitude M vs. source-length r (km) relationships of Wells and Coppersmith (1994):

$$r_f = 10^{(M_{\max} - 5)/1.22} \tag{2a}$$

or (Kagan, 2004):

$$r = 20 \cdot 10^{(M-6)/2}; \tag{2b}$$

eliminates events farther away from the hypocenter than 1.5 times the r_f length estimated by (2).

Next, a spatial clustering analysis, where events separated by no more than a given critical distance r, of the order of hundreds of meters to a few kilometers, depending on the spatial coverage of the catalog, are considered to be related, is used to eliminate events which do not relate to the mainshock or to other possible aftershocks.

The parameters in the modified Omori's law (1) are not known a priori; they are estimated from the statistics of the aftershocks (Davis & Frohlich, 1991b; Guo & Ogata, 1997; Ogata, 1983), which we do not yet have. However, this relation tells us that for long enough times after the occurrence of the mainshock the number of aftershocks decreases until seismic activity in the epicentral region returns to its background level (Ogata & Shimazaki, 1984).

When aftershock occurrence shows gaps comparable to those characterizing the background seismicity, we can consider that the aftershock activity is, if not ended, at least scarce enough to be comparable to the background activity and can no longer be distinguished from it. The critical gap length depends on the region and the magnitude threshold of the observations; we use a default critical gap length $t_{gap} = 10\,\text{days}$. The gap is measured as the average of a given number of inter-event times (default $n_{gap} = 10$). Events occurring after a critical gap are discarded from the possible aftershocks.

Weights, based on relation (1), are optionally assigned to the remaining events, using typical values for c (default $c \approx 2$) and p (default $p \approx 1.0$) and by setting $k = c^p \;\Rightarrow\; N(t=0) = 1$, so that those events which have a large likelihood of being aftershocks have weights ~1, while later events have smaller weights:

$$w_i = \frac{c^p}{(t_i + c)^p}. \tag{3}$$

Next, plane fitting is carried out iteratively; at each iteration, a plane that passes through the mainshock hypocenter is fitted to all remaining events, through a genetic scheme described below, and fit outliers (events too far away from the plane) are discarded. Iteration continues until the goodness-of-fit criterion is met (successful fit) or until a preset maximum number of iterations is attained (unsuccessful fit).

The t_{gap}, c, and p values can be refined using the final results of a first, tentative aftershock determination, to do a second one.

The genetic plane search for the plane, characterized by its azimuth ϕ and dip δ, which minimizes the L1 norm of the perpendicular distances from the fault plane to all events, is as follows. An initial set of equispaced ϕ_j and δ_j values, covering the acceptable ranges, is built and the fit to the aftershock candidates is evaluated for each pair of values.

To estimate the error of fit for each candidate plane, for each azimuth ϕ_j and dip δ_j pair, event coordinates (x,y,z) are rotated as:

$$\begin{pmatrix} x'_i \\ y'_i \\ z'_i \end{pmatrix} = \begin{pmatrix} \cos\phi_j \sin\delta_j & -\sin\phi_j \sin\delta_j & \cos\delta_j \\ \sin\phi_j & \cos\phi_j & 0 \\ -\cos\phi_j \cos\delta_j & \sin\phi_j \cos\delta_j & \sin\delta_j \end{pmatrix} \begin{pmatrix} x_i \\ y_i \\ z_i \end{pmatrix}, \tag{4}$$

and in the (x',y',z') coordinate system the equation of the plane is $x' = 0$, so that the L1 fit error for the j'th parameter pair is easily computed as

$$\varepsilon_j \equiv \varepsilon(\phi_j,\delta_j) = \sum_{i=1}^{N_a} | x'_i(\phi_j,\delta_j)\, w_i \,| \;/\; \sum_{i=1}^{N_a} w_i\,, \tag{5}$$

where N_a is the number of remaining aftershock candidates.

The parameter pairs corresponding to the best N_p fits are chosen as the parents of the next generation; they are sorted by the absolute value of their respective errors, so that parent number 1 is the best fit and parent number N_p has the largest error ε_{N_p}. The standard deviations of the parent's parameters, σ_ϕ and σ_δ, are evaluated.

Next, $N_p(N_p-1)/2$ children are constructed with parameters which are averages of those of each pair of parents; other N_c children are constructed for each parent j by randomly modifying one or the other of the parameter values, according to

$$\begin{aligned} \phi_{jN_p+k} &= N\left(\phi_j, \sigma_\phi^m \varepsilon_j / \varepsilon_{N_p}\right) \\ \delta_{jN_p+k} &= N\left(\delta_j, \sigma_\delta^m \varepsilon_j / \varepsilon_{N_p}\right) \end{aligned} ; \quad k = 1, \ldots, N_c, \tag{6}$$

where N designates the normal distribution, $\sigma_\phi^m = \max\{\sigma_{\min}, \sigma_\phi\}$, $\sigma_\delta^m = \max\{\sigma_{\min}, \sigma_\delta\}$, and $\sigma_{\min}$ is a minimum allowable value that ensures significant variations.

Errors are computed for the children and the N_p best fits among the whole population, parents plus children, are chosen as the parents for the next generation. The process is repeated until the goodness of fit criterion is met (and the process ends) or until a preset number of generations is attained.

For the current iteration the best fit is for the plane corresponding to parent number one, $\phi = \phi_1$ and $\delta = \delta_1$; using these values event coordinates are rotated as in (4) and the standard deviation, σ, of the x' distances is evaluated. Those events with

$$x_i' > f_\sigma \sigma + u_i, \tag{7}$$

where f_σ is a damping factor (default is 1.25) and u_i is the location uncertainty, adjusted for the plane dip as

$$u_i = \sqrt{(u_{hi} \sin\delta)^2 + (u_{vi} \cos\delta)^2}, \tag{8}$$

are eliminated as outliers.

This method has been implemented as a Matlab program, *aftplane.m,* which allows the user to interactively set most parameters, 3D plots the input hypocenters, identifies the aftershocks of one mainshock, optionally plots the aftershocks and/or independent shocks (in different colors), and optionally outputs the corresponding catalogs. A definite advantage of using Matlab for this algorithm is that both data and trial models are handled as matrices, so that rotating, sorting, and identifying values is done more efficiently and with less lines of code than would be possible in other programming languages like FORTRAN or BASIC.

A variation of this method is used as a function by program *cleancat.m* which identifies and eliminates the aftershocks of all mainshocks in a catalog. For each event not previously identified as an aftershock, aftershocks are identified following the same steps described above, except that, after fitting the plane a search is made for events with magnitudes $M > M_{main} - \Delta M$, which will not be considered as aftershocks, and if any are found, the aftershock list is cut so as to exclude all events beginning with the first of these non-aftershocks. Thus, for mainshocks occurring at times t_i, instead of the total Omori number of aftershocks (Utsu, 1970; Ogata, 1983)

$$N(t) = \sum_i H(t - t_i)\, K_i (t - t_i + c_i)^{-p},$$

where $H(t)$ is the Heavyside function, we are actually evaluating

$$N(t) = \sum_i \chi\left(\frac{t_i}{t_k - t_i}\right) K_i (t - t_i + c)^{-p} , \tag{9}$$

where

$$\chi(t) = \Pi(t - 1/2) = \begin{cases} t & 0 \le t \le 1 \\ 0 & \text{other } t \end{cases} ,$$

$\Pi(t)$ is the boxcar function, and $t_k > t_i$ is the time of the succeeding event occurring along the same fault plane and cluster or the time when the gap criterion is met ($t_k = \infty$ if no such event or gap occur). An event at t_k may "inherit" some of the aftershocks from the one at t_i, but they will be identified as aftershocks and be duly eliminated. Båth's law indicates that ΔM should be 1.2, but this criterion results, for most catalogs, in too many mainshocks; our default value is thus $\Delta M = 1.0$, which means that we accept as aftershocks those with energy ratio $E(M) / E(M_{main}) < \sim 0.016$, but this ΔM value can be easily changed by the user. The largest events in the catalog are plotted vs. time above the initial and resulting event densities, to illustrate which aftershocks were eliminated. The program iterates the whole process, as many times as needed, until no more aftershocks are found

In *cleancat*, parameters are not set interactively, but can be easily adjusted in a list of adjustable parameters at the beginning of the code.

The program optionally outputs a catalog excluding identified aftershocks.

3. Application

We will now show some examples of the application of the method. The *aftplane* program will be used to identify fault planes and aftershocks from three mainshock-aftershock sequences from two different parts of the world featuring different tectonic environments. The *cleancat* program will be used to clean the catalog of a fault system.

3.1 Aftplane: transcurrent regime, Joshua Tree and Landers earthquakes

In 1992, two large earthquakes, the Joshua Tree, April 23 M_W 6.2, 33.9°N, 116.3°W and the Landers, June 28 M_W 7.3, 34.2°N, 116.5°W, occurred close together on a line previously unrecognized as a potential throughgoing seismogenic fault (Nur et al., 1993). We chose these events as illustration because, although both events have mainly strike-slip mechanisms, they have slightly different strikes and dips, so that we wanted to test whether the method could identify these small differences.

Figure 1 shows the location of the study area in souther California, USA, and its recent seismicity; the faults ruptured during the Joshua Tree and Landers earthquakes are located within the red diamond.

For both events we used maximum allowable horizontal and vertical location uncertainties of $u_h^{\max} = 0.2$ km and $u_v^{\max} = 0.5$ km, respectively; a priory cutoff times $n_{yr} = 4$ years; maximum distance for spatial clustering $r = 1$ km; maximum permissible time gap $t_{gap} = 10$ days estimated as the average of $n_{gap} = 10$ inter-event times; Omori weighting parameters $c = 2.0$ days and $p = 1.0$; aftershock magnitude criterion $\Delta M = 1.0$; fit criterion maximum error ε_{max} km.

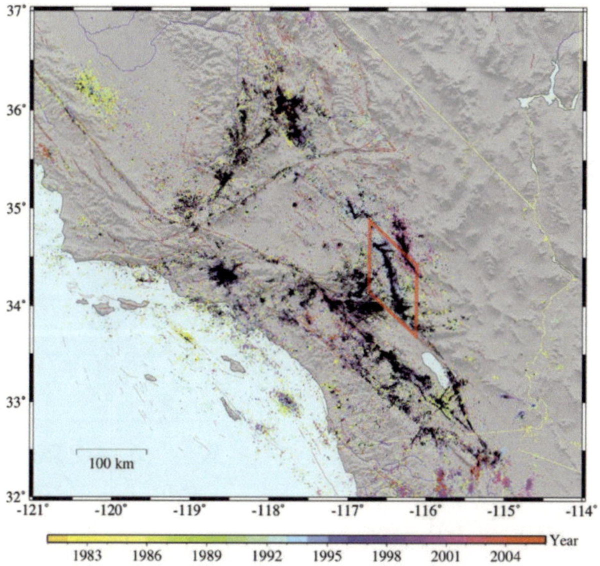

Fig. 1. Seismicity map of southern California showing the location of the Joshua Tree and Landers faults (both within the red diamond.) (Modified from Lin et al, 2007.)

3.2 Aftplane: Joshua Tree earthquake

The catalog for the Joshuea tree earthquake contained 5075 events spanning 66.30 days (~0.182 yr). Figure 2 (left) shows the 3497 remaining events after the first rough elimination by acceptable uncertainties and by an estimated expected fault length of ~7.97 km corresponding to a critical distance of 11.96 km. Figure 2 (right) shows as blue circles the 3379 shocks identified as clustering with the main event.

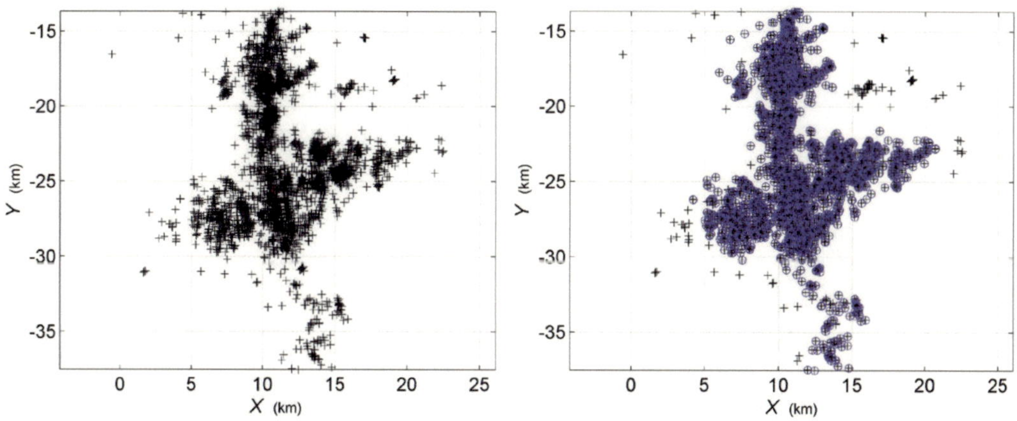

Fig. 2. Joshua Tree mainshock plus 3497 acceptable aftershock candidates (left) and Joshua Tree mainshock plus 3379 clustered aftershock candidates (right).

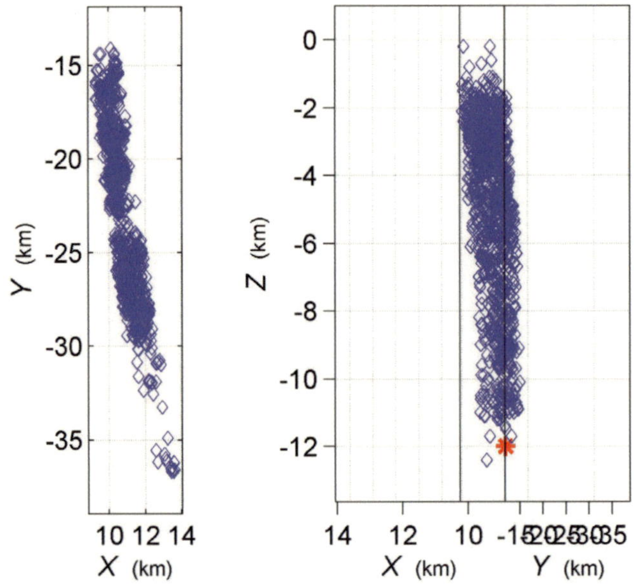

Fig. 3. Joshua Tree mainshock (red asterisk) plus 1094 aftershocks (blue diamonds); left: plan view showing 171.6° faultplane azimuth; right: view along faultplane azimuth clearly showing the 86.6° dip.

The main Joshua Tree shock and the identified 1094 aftershocks are shown in figure 3, both in a plan view (left) which clearly shows the resulting 171.6° faultplane azimuth, and a cross section along the fault plane azimuth (right) which shows the resulting 86.6° faultplane dip. The values found by aftplane agree extremely well with those estimated by Velasco et al. (1994) of strike 171°, dip 89°. Figure 4 shows a cross section parallel to the fault plane, illustrating aftershock concentrations.

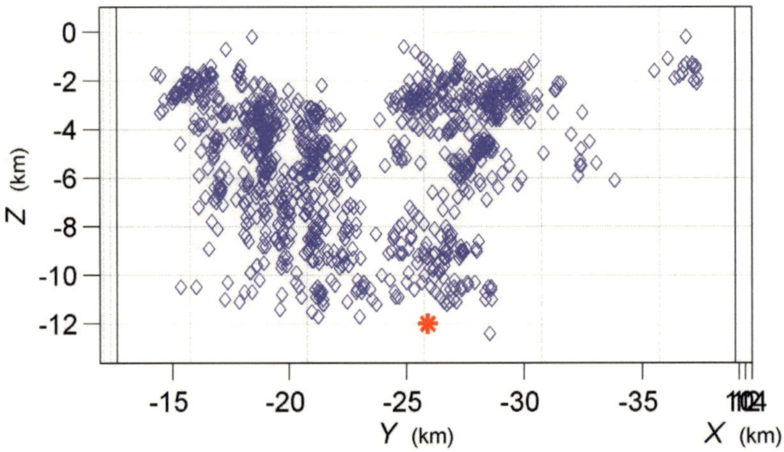

Fig. 4. Joshua Tree mainshock (red asterisk) plus 1094 aftershocks (diamonds), cross section seen along azimuth 81.6°, perpendicular to the 171.6° faultplane azimuth.

3.2.1 Aftplane: Landers earthquake

The catalog for the Landers earthquake contained 49,605 events spanning 4,932.52 days (~13.514 yr). Figure 5 (left) shows the 17,553 remaining events after the first rough elimination by acceptable uncertainties and by an estimated expected fault length of ~76.78 km corresponding to a critical distance of 115.17 km. Figure 5 (right) shows as blue circles the 12,834 shocks identified as clustering with the main event.

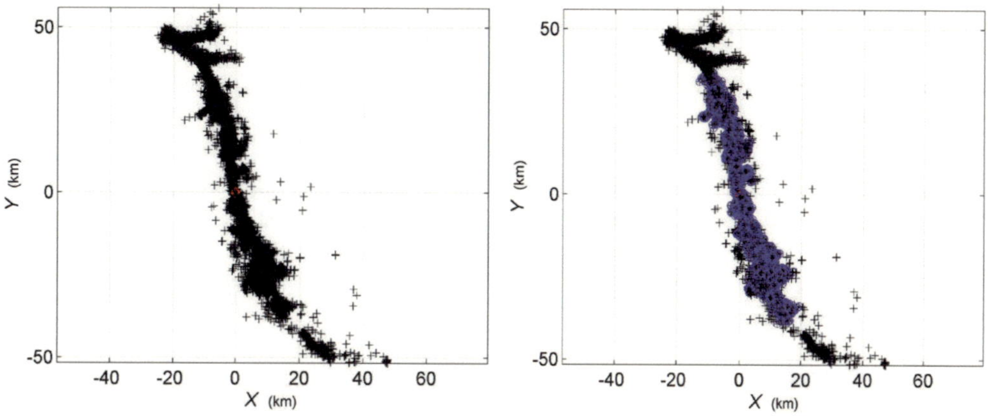

Fig. 5. Landers mainshock plus 17553 acceptable aftershock candidates (left) and Landers mainshock plus 12834 clustered aftershock candidates (right).

The main Landers shock and the identified 3,225 aftershocks are shown in figure 6, in a cross section seen along the determined 340.6° fault plane azimuth, which shows the resulting 70.1° faultplane dip. The values found by aftplane agree extremely well with those estimated by Velasco et al. (1994) of strike 341°°, dip 70°. Figure 7 shows a cross section parallel to the fault plane, illustrating aftershock concentrations.

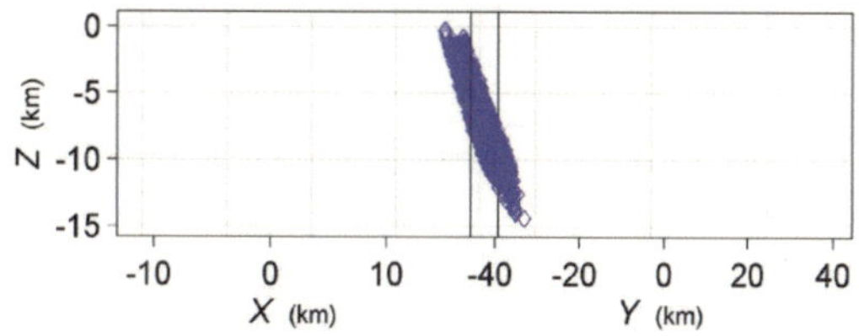

Fig. 6. Landers mainshock (red asterisk) plus 3225 aftershocks (blue diamonds), view along 340.6° faultplane azimuth. The location of the mainshock hypocenter is obscured by those of the aftershocks. Dip 70.1°

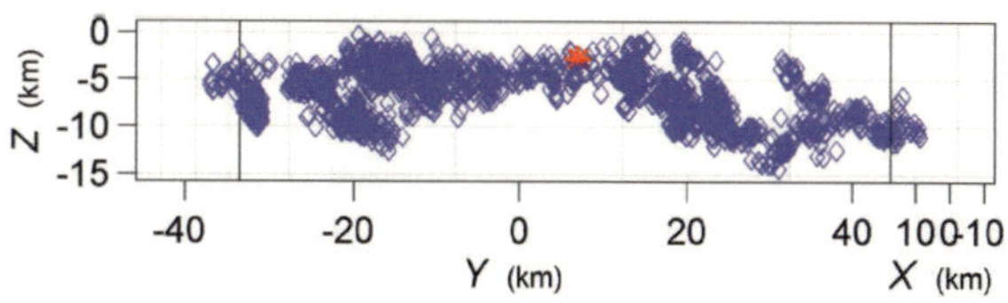

Fig. 7. Landers mainshock (red asterisk) plus 3225 aftershocks (blue diamonds), view along azimuth 70°, perpendicular to 340.6° faultplane azimuth.

3.3 Aftplane: subduction regime, Armería (Tecomán, Colima) earthquake

The Armería M_W 7.4 earthquake, also known as the Tecomán or Colima 2003 earthquake, occurred on January 22, 2003, on the subduction zone along the boundary of the Northamerican and Pacific plates in central-western Mexico.

Figure 8 shows the location of the study area, the mainshock epicenter (red star) and the subsequent seismicity recorded and located by the Colima Seismic Network (RESCO).

Nuñez et al (2004) and Yagi et al (2004) estimated a fault plane with a 300° strike and a quite shallow 20° dip, which agrees with the 20° to 30° dip of the subduction zone determined by Andrews et al (2010).

For aftplane we used the RESCO catalog with the same parameter values mentioned above, except for horizontal and vertical location uncertainties of $u_h = 0.075$ km and $u_v = 0.50$ km, and maximum distance for spatial clustering $r = 4$ km;

The catalog for the Armería earthquake contained 11,475 events spanning 1,529.9 days (~4.192 yr). Figure 9 (left) shows the 10,275 remaining events after the first rough elimination by acceptable uncertainties and by an estimated expected fault length of ~92.73 km corresponding to a critical distance of 139.09 km. Figure 9 (right) shows as blue circles the 7,109 shocks identified as clustering with the main event.

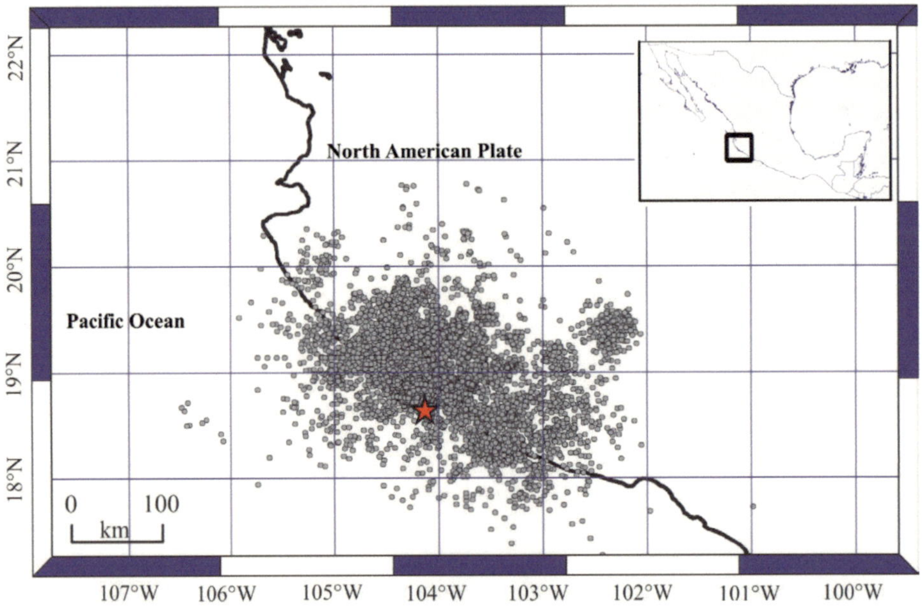

Fig. 8. Location of the Armería, 22 January 2003, MW 7.3 earthquake; the star indicates the epicenter of the main shock, circles are located events following the mainshock, located by the RESCO network.

The main Armería shock and the identified 460 aftershocks are shown in figure 10, in a cross section seen along the determined 86.2° fault plane azimuth, which shows the resulting 33.2° faultplane dip. The values found by aftplane agree extremely well with the above mentioned estimates strike 300° and 20° to 30° (Nuñez et al., 2004; Yagi et al., 2004; Andrews et al., 2010). Figure 11 shows a cross section parallel to the fault plane, illustrating aftershock concentrations.

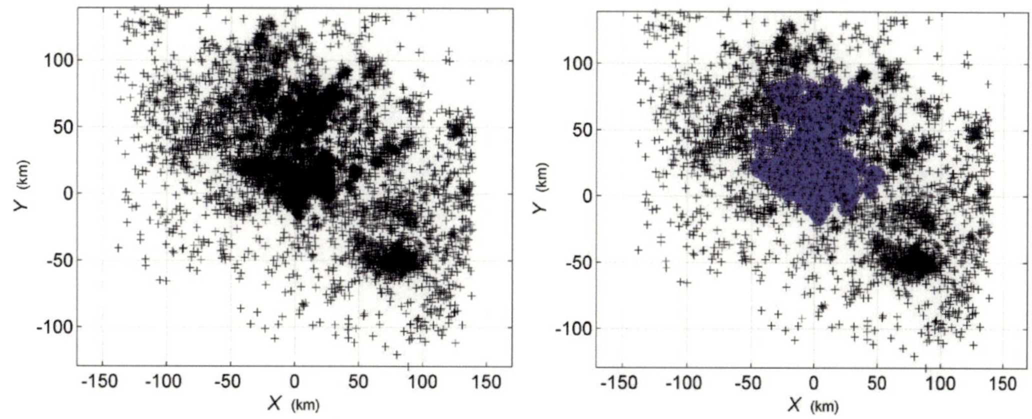

Fig. 9. Armería mainshock plus 10868 acceptable aftershock candidates shown as black crosses (left) and Armería mainshock plus 7109 clustered aftershock candidates shown as blue circles (right).

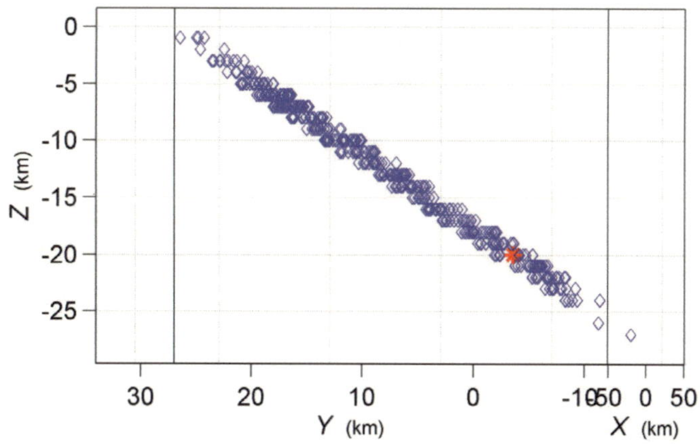

Fig. 10. Armería mainshock (red asterisk) plus 460 aftershocks (blue diamonds), view along 86.2° faultplane azimuth.

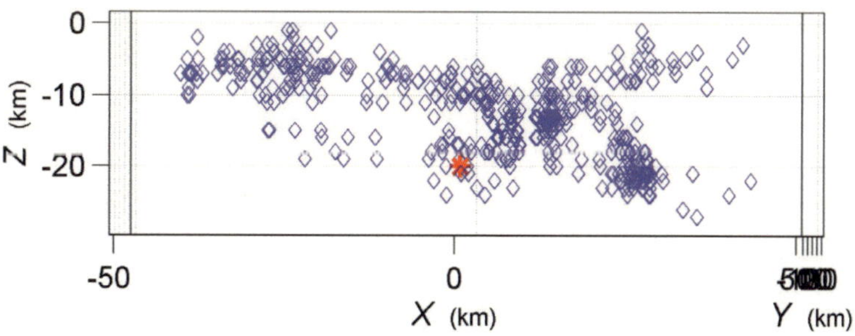

Fig. 11. Armería mainshock (red asterisk) plus 460 aftershocks (blue diamonds), view along azimuth 356.2°, perpendicular to 86.2° faultplane azimuth.

3.4 Cleancat: whole Joshua Tree-Landers fault system

To illustrate the use of program *cleancat* we chose the catalog covering the whole Joshua Tree-Landers fault system (Figure 1), because this is a system with many close-lying, subparallel, faults, which gives scope to the iterative aftershock recognition scheme of the program.

The parameters used are $u_{h,h}^{max} = 0.2$ km and $u_v^{max} = 0.5$ km; a priory cutoff times $n_{yr} = 4$ years; maximum distance for spatial clustering $r = 2$ km; maximum permissible time gap $t_{gap} = 30$ days estimated as the average of $n_{gap} = 10$ inter-event times; Omori weighting parameters $c = 2.0$ days and $p = 1.0$; aftershock magnitude criterion $\Delta M = 1$; fit criterion maximum error $\varepsilon_{max} = 0.35$ km.

Figure 11 shows all events in the catalog (black crosses), and identified aftershocks as yellow circles. Total processing consisted of 10 iterations which identified and eliminated 11,665, 4,212, 1,702, 86, 94, 30, 80, 18, 49, and 1 aftershocks, respectively, for a total of 17,937 aftershocks.

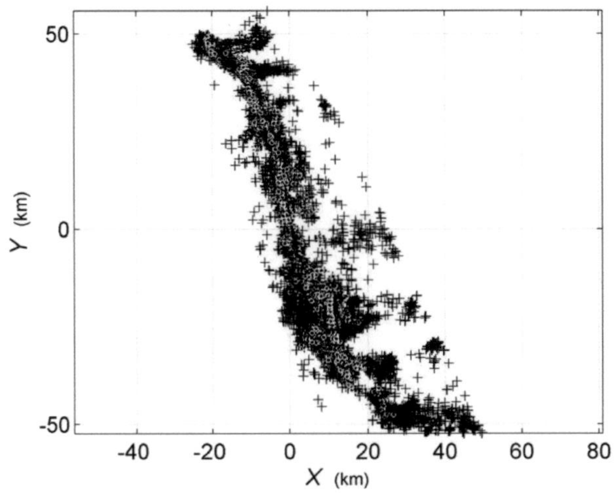

Fig. 11. Joshua Tree- Landers fault system seismicity (black crosses) and identified aftershocks (yellow circles).

Figure 12 shows the occurrence times and magnitudes of the largest events in the catalog (top), and below them (middle) is plotted the ocurrence density (per $\Delta t = 46$ day) vs. time (blue line); peaks in the occurrence rate after large shocks aftershocks are clearly seen. The bottom panel of figure 12 shows the occurrence density after aftershock elimination using $\Delta M = 1.0$ (red line); although densities are much lower than before filtering, the peaks coinciding with the occurrence of the Joshua Tree and Landers earthquakes indicate that many aftershocks are not being identified.

Use of $\Delta M = 0.9$ (Fig.13) effectively diminishes the troublesome above mentioned peaks to background seismicity level; the seismicity rate peak around $t \sim 7.25\,10^5$ days is associated with distributed seismicity with events about the same size. Thus, we see that Båth's law is not appropriate for the mainshock-aftershock relationships in the seismicity of the Joshua Tree-Landers fault system; a small (0.1 unit) change in the magnitude criterion can make a large difference in the aftershock recognition capability.

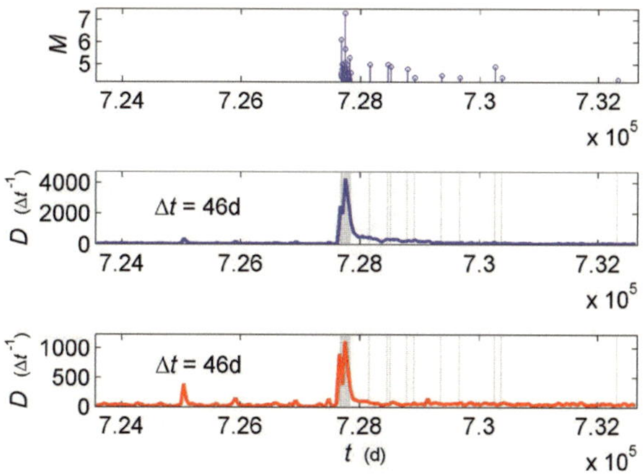

Fig. 12. Joshua Tree-Landers fault system seismicity versus time. The top panel shows the largest events in the period (blue circles with vertical lines). The middle and bottom panels show seismicity rates, for 46 day-long time intervals, before (middle) and after (bottom) processing by cleancat, respectively; note the different vertical scales.

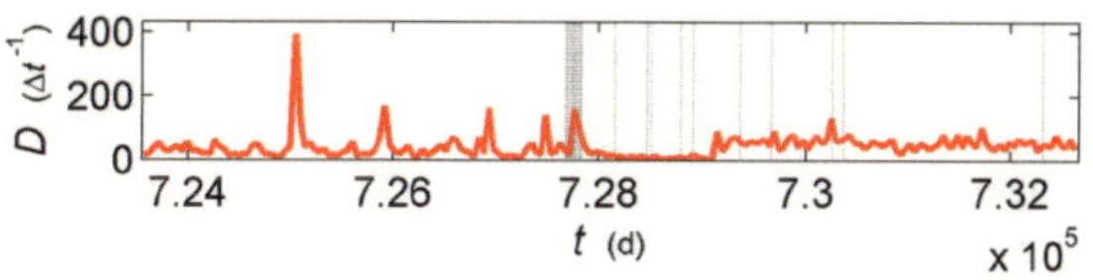

Fig. 13. Joshua Tree-Landers fault system seismicity rates, for 46 day-long time intervals, after processing by cleancat, with $\Delta M = 0.9$.

4. Conclusions

We present a simple method for identification and/or elimination of aftershocks, based on the generally accepted assumption that aftershocks are related to the fault rupture of the mainshock. The method has been tried on various catalogs with good results and, when aftershocks are numerous enough, good estimates of rupture planes that agree very well with those reported in the literature.

A variation of the method used for eliminating all aftershocks from a seismicity catalog ("catalog cleaning") uses, iteratively, a variation of the same principle. Using the seismicity occurrence time rate as illustration and criterion of the effectiveness of the method, indicates that the required difference between mainshock and aftershocks ΔM is a key parameter for correct aftershock identification, and that $\Delta M = 1.2$ (Båth's law) may be too strict for some geographic areas and/or seismo-tectonic settings.

5. Acknowledgements

Many thanks to José Frez, Juan García A., and María Luisa Argote for useful criticism and comments. We are grateful to RESCO and Gabriel Reyes, and to the SCEC for the use of their catalogs. We also thank Mr Davor Vidic of Intech for the kind invitation to participate in the present book.

6. References

Andrews,V., Stock, J. Ramírez-Vázquez,C., & Reyes-Dávila, G. (2010). Double-difference Relocation of the Aftershocks of the Tecomán, Colima, Mexico Earthquake of 22 January 2003. *Pageoph*, DOI 10.1007/s00024-010-0203-0.

Davis, S. D. & Frohlich, C. (1991a). Single-link cluster analysis, synthetic earthquakes catalogues and aftershock identification. *Geophys. J. Int.* 104, 289-306.

Davis, S. D. & Frohlich, C. (1991b). Single-link cluster analysis of earthquake aftershock: decay laws and regional variations. *J. Geophys. Res.* 96, 6335-6350.

Dieterich, J. (1994). A constitutive law for rate of earthquake production and its application to earthquake clustering. *J. Geophys. Res.* 99, 2601-2618.

Dreger, D., Pasyanos, M., Loper, S., McKenzie, R., Gregor, N., Uhrhammer, B., & Romanowicz, B. (1994). Source process of the 17 January 1994 Northdridge earthquake. *EOS*, 75(16), 103. (abstract)

Engdahl, E. R., Billington, S., & Kisslinger, C. (1989). Telesismically recorded seismicity before and after the May 7, 1986, Andreanof Islands, Alaska, earthquake". J. Geophys. *Res.* 94, 15481-15498.

Felzer,K., Abercrombie,R., & Ekstrom,G. (2003). Secondary aftershocks and their importance for aftershock forecasting. *Bull. Seismol. Soc. Am.* 93, 1433-1448.

Felzer,K., Abercrombie,R., & Ekstrom,G. (2004) A common origin for aftershocks, foreshocks, and multiplets. *Bull. Seismol. Soc. Am.* 94, 88-98.

Felzer,K. & Brodsky,E. (2006). Decay of aftershock density with distance indicates triggering by dynamic stress. *Nature* 441, 735-738.

Figueroa, A. (2009). Analysis of inter-event time in aftershock sequences for identification stress relaxation status., MSc Thesis, UNAM, 89pp (in Spanish).

Frohlich, C. & Davis, S. D. (1985). Identification of aftershocks of deep earthquakes by a new ratios method. *Geophys. Res. Lett.* 12, 713-716.

Gardner, J. & Knopoff, L. (1974). Is the sequence of earthquakes in Southern California with aftershocks removed Poissonian? Yes. *Bull. Seismol. Soc. Am.* 64, 1363- 1367.

Granados,J. (2000). *Identification of seismic aftershocks in catalogs.* MSc.Thesis in Earth Sciences, CICESE, 145pp (in Spanish).

Guo, Z. & Ogata, Y. (1997). Statistical relations between the parameters of aftershocks in time, space, and magnitude. *J.Geiphys.Res.*102(B2), 2857-2873.

Gutenberg, B. & Richter, C. (1954). *Seismicity of the Earth and associated phenomena.* Princeton Univ. Press, 310pp.

Habermann, R. and Wyss, M. (1984). Background seismicity rates and precursory seismic quiescence: Imperial Valley, California, *Bull. Seismol. Soc. Am.* 74, 1743–1755.

Hauksson, E., Hutton, K., & Kanamori, H. (1994). The M_w 6.7 Northdridge, California, earthquake of January 17, 1994 and its aftershocks. *Program Northdridge Abstr., 89th Annu. Meet. Seismol. Soc. Am.*, unpublished abstract.

Helmstetter, A. & Sornette, D. (2002). Diffusion of epicenters of earthquake aftershocks, Omori's law and generalized continuous-time random walk models. *Phys.Rev.E* 66, 061104.

Helmstetter, A. & Sornette, D. (2003). Båth's law derived from the Gutenberg-Richter law and from aftershock properties. *Geophys.Res.Lett.*30, 2069.

Helmstetter, A., Sornette, D., & Grasso, J. (2003). Mainshocks are aftershocks of conditional foreshocks: How do foreshock statistical properties emerge from aftershock laws. *J.Geophys.Res.* 108(B1), 2046.

Holliday, J., Turcotte, D., & Rundle, J. (2008). A review of earthquake statistics: fault and seismicity-based models, ETAS and BASS. Pageoph 165, 1003-1024.

Kagan, Y. & Knopoff, L. (1976). Statistical search for non-random features of the seismicity of strong earthquakes. *Phys. Earth planet. Inter.* 12, 291-318.

Kagan,Y. (2004) Short-Term Properties of Earthquake Catalogs and Models of Earthquake Source. *Bull. Seismol. Soc. Am.* 94, 1207–1228

Keilis-Borok, V., Knopoff, L., & Rowain, I. (1980). Bursts of aftershocks long term precursors of strong earthquakes. *Nature.* 283, 259- 263 p.

Kisslinger, C. (1996). Aftershocks and fault-zone properties. *Advances in geophysics,* 38, 1-36.

Kisslinger, C. & Hasegawa, A. (1991). Seismotectonics of intermediate-depth earthquakes from properties of aftershocks sequences. *Tectonophysics* 197, 27-40.

Kisslinger, C. & Jones, L. M. (1991). Properties of aftershocks sequences in southern California. *J. Geophys. Res.,* 96, 11947-11958.

Knopoff, L., Kagan, Y., & Knopoff, R. (1982). *b*-values for foreshocks and aftershocks in real and simulated earthquake sequences. *Bull. Seismol. Soc. Am.* 72, 1663-1675.

Jones, L. M. (1994). Foreshocks, aftershocks, and earthquake probabilities: Accounting for the Landers earthquake. *Bull. Seismol. Soc. Am.,* 84, 892 - 899 p.

Lay, T. & Wallace, T. (1995). *Modern global seismology.* Academic Press, Inc., 521pp.

Lin, G., Shearer, P. M., & Hauksson, E. (2007). Applying a three-dimensional velocity model, waveform cross correlation, and cluster analysis to locate southern California seismicity from 1981 to 2005. *J. Geophys. Res.* 112, B12309, doi:10.1029/2007JB004986.

Lomnitz, C. (1966). Magnitude stability in earthquake sequences. *Bull. Seismol. Soc. Am.* 56, 247- 249.

Mendoza, C. & Hartzell, S. H., (1988). Aftershock patterns and mainshock faulting. *Bull. Seismol. Soc. Am.* 78, 1438-1449.

Mogi, K. (1968). Development of aftershock areas of great earthquakes. *Bull. Earthquake Res. Insti., Tokyo Univ.,* 46, 175 - 203.

Molchan, G. M. & Dmitrieva, O. E. (1992). Aftershock identification: Methods and new approaches. *Geophys. J. Int.* 109, 501-516.

Núñez-Cornú, F. J., Reyes-Dávila, G. A., Rutz-López, M., Trejo-Gómez, E., Camarena-García, M. A., & Ramírez-Vazquez, C. A. (2004). The 2003 Armería, México Earthquake (M w 7.4): Mainshock and Early Aftershocks, Seism. Res. Lett. 75, 734-743.

Nur, A. & Booker, J. (1972). Aftershocks caused by pore fluid flow? *Science,* 175, 885-887.

Nur,A., Ron,H. & Beroza,G. (1993). The nature of the Landers-Mojave earthquake line. *Science* 261, 201-203.

Ogata, Y. & Shimazaki, K. (1984). Transition from aftershock to normal activity: the 1965 Rat Islands earthquake aftershock sequence. *Bull. Seismol. Soc. Am.* 74, 1757-1765.

Ogata, Y. 1983. Estimation of the parameters in the modified Omori formula for aftershock frequencies by the maximum likelihood procedure. *J. Phys. Earth,* 31, 115 -124.

Prozorov, A. & Dziewonski, A. (1982). A method of studying variations in the clustering property of earthquakes: application to the analysis of global seismicity. *J. Geophys. Res.* 87, 2829-2839 p.

Prozorov, A. (1986). Dynamic algorithm for removing aftershocks from the world earthquake catalog. *Comp. Seism.* 19, 58-62., Eds. Keilis-Borok, V. & Levshin, A., Nauka, Moscow.

Reasenberg, P. A. & Jones, L. (1989). Earthquake Hazard after a mainshock in California. *Science,* 243, 1173-1176.

Richter, C. (1958). *Elementary seismology*. W.H. Freeman & Co., USA, 768 pp.

Roquemore, G. R. & Simila, G. W. (1994). Aftershocks from the 28 June 1992 Landers earthquake: Northern Mojave Desert to the Coso Volcanic Field, California. *Bull. Seismol. Soc. Am.* 84, 854–862.

Shcherbakov, R., Turcotte, D., & Rundle, J. (2005). Aftershock statistics. *Pageoph* 162, 1051-1076.

Tajima, F. & Kanamori, H. (1985). Global survey of aftershock area expansion patterns. *Phys. Earth Planet. Int.* 40, 77-134.

Utsu, T. & Seki, A., (1955). Relation between the area of aftershock region and the energy of the mainshock. *Zisin,* 7, 233-240.

Utsu, T. (1957). Magnitudes of earthquakes and occurrence of their aftershocks, *Zisin Ser. 2,* 10,: 35-45.

Utsu, T. (1961). A statistical study on the occurrence of aftershocks, *Geophys. Mag.,* 30, 521-605.

Utsu, T. (1969). Aftershocks and earthquake statistics (I). *J. Fac. Sci. Hokkaido Univ., Ser. VII,* 2, 129-195.

Utsu, T. (1970). Aftershocks and earthquake statistics (II)- Further investigation of aftershocks and other earthquake sequences based on a new classification of earthquake sequences. *J. Fac. Sci. Hokkaido Univ., Ser. VII, 3,* 197-266.

Valdés, C., Meyer, R., Zuniga, R., Havskov J., & Singh, K. S. (1982). Analysis of the Petatlan aftershocks: numbers, energy release and asperities. *J. Geophys. Res.* 87, 8519-8527.

Velasco, A., Ammon, C., & Lay, T. (1994). Empirical green function deconvolution of broadband surface waves: Rupture directivity of the 1992 Landers, California (Mw = 7.3), earthquake. *Bull. Seismol. Soc. Am.* 84, 735-750.

Vere-Jones, D. & Davies, R. (1966). A statistical survey of earthquakes in the main seismic region of New Zealand. Part II. Time series analysis. *New Zealand J. Geol. Geophys* 9, 251-284.

Wells, D. L. & Coppersmith, K. (1994). New Empirical Relationships among Magnitude, Rupture Length, Rupture Width, Rupture Area, and Surface Displacement. *Bull. Seismol. Soc. Am.* 84, 974 -1002.

Wyss,M. (1986) Seismic quiescence precursor to the 1983 Kaoiki (MS = 6.6), Hawaii, earthquake. Bull.Seismol.Soc.Am. 76, 785-800.

Yagi, Y., Mikumo, T., Pacheco, J., & Reyes, G. (2004). Source Rupture Process of the Tecomán, Colima, Mexico Earthquake of 22 January 2003, Determined by Joint Inversion of Teleseismic Body-Wave and Near-Source Data, Bull. Seism. Soc. Am. 94, 1795–1807.

3

Sea Surface Temperature (SST) and the Indian Summer Monsoon

S. C. Chakravarty
Indian Space Research Organisation (ISRO)
Bangalore,
India

1. Introduction

Every year during the summer months (June-September), the southern part of Asia, in particular the Indian subcontinent receives continuous and widespread rains due to the monsoon (meaning seasonal change of wind direction) more specifically known as the summer or South-West (SW) monsoon. The phenomena in summer takes place due to the cross hemispheric reversal of winds bringing in considerable amount of water vapour from the high pressure regions over the relatively colder Indian and Pacific oceans and the Arabian sea to the low pressure system over heated land mass areas. Due to large geographical coverage and high inter annual variability in terms of associated rainfall it constitutes one of the important elements of the global climate system (Mooley & Parthasarathy, 1984). Also the overall mean monsoon precipitation distribution significantly depends on the intra-seasonal oscillations of dry and wet spells (Waliser et al., 2003). The sudden onset of monsoon is characterised by a highly energised pattern of lightning, thunderstorm, cloud burst and incessant rainfall over a large area of southwest coastal region of the Indian Kerala state (Soman & Kumar, 1993). Normally the first episodic rain of the monsoon occurs over Burma and Thailand in the middle of May and then extends to the northwest over most of India within a month. The northward progression of monsoon is symptomatic of a large-scale transition of deep convection system (called the tropical convection zone) from the oceanic-equatorial to tropical-continental regions (Sikka & Gadgil 1980).

While the SW monsoon period (June-September), accounting for about 80% of the total rainfall is vital to meet the Indian agricultural and hydrological requirements, the winter monsoon flowing from North East direction during October-November contributes only marginally albeit meeting the ground water requirement of some areas falling in the shadow region of the summer monsoon cover. Many oceanic and atmospheric parameters like the El Nino and Southern Oscillation (ENSO), Eurasian snow cover in winter/spring, northern hemispheric temperature in winter etc. influence the year-to-year variability of the monsoon rainfall over India (Rajeevan et al., 2004). Hence the inter annual variations severely affect the ground water resources of not only India and neighbouring countries like Sri Lanka, Bangladesh and Pakistan but also on small scales, the equatorial Africa, northern Australia, and south-western United States.

The monsoon rainfall intensity has intra- and inter- annual variation at different spatial scales impacting on the availability of water for agriculture and other uses. As a result almost half of the world's population living in monsoon region suffer from food and water insecurity. The detailed scientific reasons of such variation in monsoon rainfall conditions are not clearly understood. Effort directed to make accurate prediction of the overall monsoon rainfall of the season averaged over the whole country as such is quite useful for farming activity. More desirable objective of such forecasts is to predict the prospects of seasonal rainfall with finer details of its spatial distribution so that the peasants may decide about the sowing activity at district or even village levels for better crop yields.

There are three major monsoon variables: (i) the yearly onset date of monsoon over India (it first enters the coastal Kerala state by 1st June ± 8 days and later progresses to cover the whole country), (ii) total seasonal rainfall during June-September (the area weighted summer monsoon long term average rainfall for the whole country as estimated by India Meteorological Department (IMD) is about 88 cm with a coefficient of variation of 10% which in real terms may lead to widespread drought/flood) and (iii) seasonal rainfall distribution over different Indian meteorological sub-divisions (prediction of this is the most difficult). To gain an early knowledge of the amount of seasonal monsoon rainfall or determination of its trend has been a challenging scientific problem for long. A number of empirical, statistical and dynamical/general circulation models have been developed for the purpose by various groups the world over (Munot & Kumar, 2007). For the Indian region mainly the statistical models have been used on an operational basis with partial success. For example the statistical model could not forecast the recent rain deficient years of 2002, 2004 and 2009. Moreover the variations of the 2 monsoon indices namely the time of onset and the total amount of monsoon rains are not directly correlated to the rainfall distribution in different parts of the country which would follow the dynamics of meteorological parameters at local or micro levels.

The Asian–Australian monsoon (another name of the same Indian summer monsoon in a regional context) is a coupled geophysical phenomenon the intensity of which is regulated through negative feedbacks between the land, ocean, and atmosphere. Indian Ocean heat transport calculations using 41-yr (1958–98) data revealed that the Indian Ocean heat transport possesses strong variability at all time scales from intra seasonal (10–90 days) to inter annual (a biennial signal is significant). The amplitude of the intra seasonal variability is similar to the seasonal cycle, and the amplitude of the inter- annual variability is about one-tenth of the seasonal cycle (Chirokova & Webster, 2006).

According to IMD's definition of monsoon transition, at the surface the onset is recognized as a rapid, substantial, and sustained increase in rainfall over a large spatial scale while the withdrawal marks the return to dry, quiescent conditions. The criterion is that the rainfall amounts over Kerala district increase from below 5 to over 15 mm/day during the onset (Anathakrishnan and Soman, 1988). A different condition that assesses the onset and withdrawal dates of the Indian monsoon has also been derived from variability in the large-scale hydrologic cycle. The hydrologic cycle is chosen as a key physical basis for monitoring the monsoon due to the essential roles played by zonal and meridional gradients in water vapour, clouds, and rainfall in driving the large-scale monsoon circulation. Lateral transports of water vapour are required for the sustenance of monsoon rains. To diagnose onset and withdrawal, vertically integrated moisture transport (VIMT) is considered more representative by some authors instead of rainfall, which over the large scale is often poorly measured and modelled. An index, named the hydrologic onset and withdrawal index (HOWI), is thus formed from those regions where VIMT variability is pronounced at the beginning and end of the monsoon season respectively. Analysis of inter annual variability in monsoon onset and withdrawal dates based on the HOWI reveals robust associations that are weak and insignificant when assessed using other onset criteria. The HOWI criterion shows strong correlations between total rainfall and both onset and withdrawal of monsoon (Fasullo & Webster, 2006). But these indices have a drawback of being determined retrospectively and hence their less predictive potentials.

While the tropical day-to-day weather conditions have a restricted predictability of 2-3 days, the seasonal (June-September) mean monsoon circulation in the tropics is potentially more predictable (Rajeevan, 2001). This is understandable as the low frequency or longer period oscillatory features of the tropical variability is caused by slowly varying boundary conditions and forcings due to sea surface temperature (SST), land surface temperature, soil moisture, snow cover, etc. (Charney & Shukla, 1981). But a considerable fraction of monsoon variability results from internal dynamics at higher frequencies (intra seasonal) often due to local/regional effects of environmental factors including aerosol distribution, atmospheric pollution, orography, forest dynamics etc. This intra seasonal variation is the main limiting factor of the monsoon predictability at subdivision level. Still, overall it makes sense in estimating and forecasting the likely onset date of the summer monsoon as well as the total seasonal rainfall in three categories of normal (~area weighted average value of ~88 cm, excess (~97 cm) and deficient (~79 cm). This information is very important for macro level planning of 'Kharif' crop cultivation with paddy as the main crop. The 'Kharif' crops such as paddy, sugarcane, groundnut, maize, pulses etc., need timely and adequate water either through rains or through artificial irrigation system. Indian agriculture still depends heavily on monsoon rains and sowing times differ with locations and with crop-type during April-July months. It would therefore be ideal to get early alerts at micro level, a difficult proposition at present but may be realized in future. In absence of this, the accurate predictions of the monsoon onset dates (date over Kerala governs onsets over other regions following a climatological pattern of monsoon progress as shown in Fig-1 for the south Asian region and over India) and the integrated seasonal rainfall, help in managing the agricultural output to a large extent.

Efforts for accurately predicting the onset date and the overall strength of seasonal precipitation have been continuing for a long time using synoptic data analysis, empirical, statistical and dynamical modelling by the IMD (Hastenrath & Greischar, 1993; Raghu Kant &. Iyengar, 2003). Out of a number of parameters SST anomalies of the Pacific/Indian ocean related to the strong El Nino and La-Nina events and associated circulation like ENSO have been correlated with delayed/weak and early/strong monsoon rainfall over India (Joseph et al, 1994; Nakazawa, 1988; Philander, 1990).

Due to the availability of all-weather and homogenized SST data sets since 2002-03 from microwave sensor (AMSRE) of AQUA satellite, it has been possible to carry out a quantitative assessment of SST anomalies with 3-day temporal and 0.25^{o}x0.25^{o} lat-long grid (pixel unit) resolutions. Hence a more detailed investigation of the effect of SST on the monsoon can be tested both for variations in the onset dates and also the total seasonal rainfall over monsoon fed regions. As a demonstration to utilizing the satellite data for monitoring the SST vis-à-vis the monsoon system over India, a study has been carried out to develop a real time model and the preliminary results published (Chakravarty, 2009).

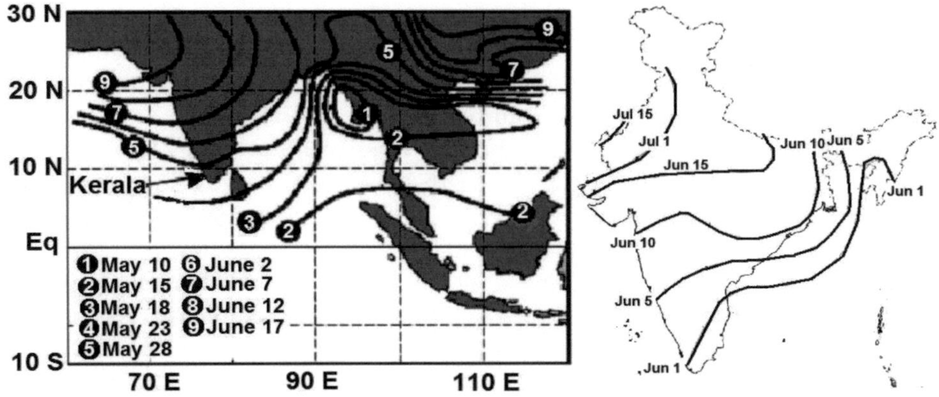

Fig. 1. Climatological dates of the onset of the south Asian summer monsoon (adapted from Fasullo and Webster, 2002). The monsoon onset date contours are also shown over India.

In addition to SST data from satellites, upper air balloon and rocket experiments have been regularly conducted from Thiruvananthapuram, the capital of the Kerala State to detect any changes in the temperature and wind fields up to ~70 km owing to monsoon circulation. A special campaign called ROMEX (Rocket Monsoon Experiment), involving balloon and rocket borne wind measurements was carried out during April-June, 2007 for real-time monitoring of middle atmospheric zonal/meridional winds to study the prognostic potential of early reversal of upper winds for the possible date of setting in of summer monsoon over the Kerala coastal region (Chakravarty & Namboodiri, 2007). The essential statistics for such prediction was built up using voluminous data already collected between 1971-90 using balloon/rocket flights from Thumba Equatorial Rocket Launching Station (TERLS) of the Indian Space Research Organisation (ISRO), Thiruvanathapuram. The results showed distinct potential of upper tropospheric and stratospheric wind reversal parameters (circulation indices) being used for predicting the monsoon onset day from the climatological trends of these circulation indices and 2007 campaign data used as a test case.
In the background of the above summary providing the present status of the various observational and modelling aspects and their applications to predict the prospects of seasonal monsoon rainfall, the main purpose of this chapter is to (a) review and carry out further studies on the development of a real time model using SST as the main parameter over a region covering central/western Pacific ocean and the Indian ocean to predict at regular intervals the prospects of possible onset date and total rainfall over India (b) as a collateral and supporting information to (a) above, demonstrate possible use of upper air parameters like the troposphere/stratosphere circulation indices for predicting the monsoon onset and strength for the ensuing season, (c) possible operationalisation of the MATLAB programme with features to provide periodic updates on the monsoon rainfall during April-September with built in graphics for various plots to show the monsoon trends. This assumes that the AQUA/AMSRE satellite type SST and other data would continue to be available.

2. Data and method of analysis

The Southern Oscillation Index (SOI) is calculated from the monthly or seasonal fluctuations in the air pressure difference between Tahiti and Darwin. Sustained negative values of the

SOI often indicate El Niño episodes. These negative values are usually accompanied by sustained warming of the central and eastern tropical Pacific Ocean, a decrease in the strength of the Pacific Trade Winds, and a reduction in rainfall over eastern and northern Australia. Though there are departures as the strong El Niño event of 1997/98 had only marginal effect on Australia. But severe droughts resulted from the weak to moderate El Niño events of 2002/03 and 2006/07. Positive values of the SOI are associated with stronger Pacific trade winds and warmer sea temperatures to the north of Australia, popularly known as a La Niña episode. Waters in the central and eastern tropical Pacific Ocean become cooler during this time. Together these give an increased probability that eastern and northern Australia will be wetter than normal. The strong and preceding El Niño/La Niña episodes are also used mainly to parameterise a statistical correlation coefficient. This aspect is further dealt in this chapter. The method used by the Australian Bureau of Meteorology is based on the Mean Sea Level Pressure (MSLP) difference between Tahiti and Darwin. It is calculated as follows:

$$SOI = 10\frac{[P_{diff} - P_{diffav}]}{SD(P_{diff})}$$

where P_{diff} = (average Tahiti MSLP for the month) - (average Darwin MSLP for the month), P_{diffav}=long term average of P_{diff} for the month in question, and $SD(P_{diff})$ = long term standard deviation of P_{diff} for the month in question. The multiplication by 10 is a convention. Using this convention, the SOI ranges from about –35 to about +35, and the value of the SOI can be quoted as a whole number. The SOI is usually computed on a monthly basis, with values over longer periods such as year being sometimes used. Daily or weekly values of the SOI do not convey much in the way of useful information about the current state of the climate and can fluctuate markedly because of daily weather patterns, and should not be used for climate purposes. The monthly average SOI data are used to calculate the annual and pre-monsoon period (Jan-April) mean SOI values for 1970-2010 period. The monthly average SOI contours are generated with respect to the different years to identify El Nino and La-Nina episodes. The official monsoon onset dates over Kerala for different years are taken from daily weather bulletins, Met. Center, Thiruvananthapuram, Kerala for correlation studies with ENSO, SST etc.

The global daily SST data from AQUA satellite's TMI/AMSRE sensors are produced by Remote Sensing Systems and sponsored by the NASA Earth Science REASoN DISCOVER Project and the AMSR-E Science Team. Data since 2002-03 are available at their official website (www.remss.com). The daily global SST values for the period 2003-11 are examined during the pre-monsoon as well as monsoon months. A MATLAB computer program is developed to read daily binary AMSRE files of global SST (3 days aggregate values at a fixed morning time every day) and generate global contour plots. After going through a large number of day's data of all these years a part of Pacific Ocean region bounded by -20° to 10° in latitude & 80° to 240° in longitude is selected as test site for further analysis. This oceanic region (ignoring a small part of land area) is termed Nino-Broad Pacific or Nino-BP to distinguish it from other existing Nino region definitions. Fig-2 shows the areas bounded by existing Nino regions and the new Nino-BP region used in the present analysis. The program then can focus on any Nino area and produce time series of SST pixel (25 km x 25km area) number values distributed in the selected 27-31 °C temperature bins with a resolution of 1 °C separately for the years 2003-11. Total number of pixels within this test region is 65,000. Using MATLAB graphics, the SST contours and bar charts (at weekly intervals) are automatically plotted separately for each year covering Jan-May and June-September months. The programme with the regular input of TMI/AMSRE data can thus be used to follow the trends for prospects of monsoon strength on real time basis.

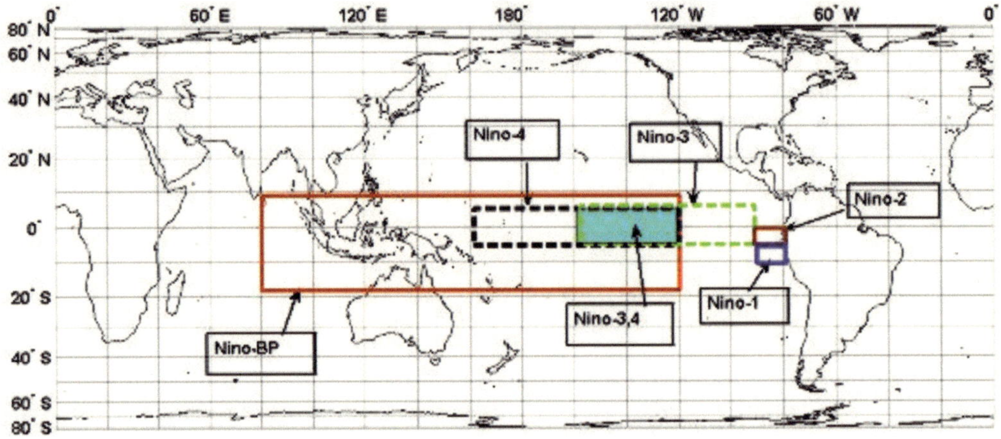

Fig. 2. Oceanic regions called Nino-1, Nino-2, Nino-3, Nino-4, Nino-3, 4 for carrying out different sensitivity analysis and the new Nino-BP region defined here for association with Indian monsoon sensitivity.

3. Results

The results obtained are categorised in the following sub sections: (a) variations of annual average, pre-monsoon and monthly averages of SOI and its correlation with onset and strength of monsoon rainfall, (b) global and Nino-BP region maps of SST, (c) variations of pixel-based structure of SST in the Nino-BP and Nino-4 regions and efficacy of a real time model for monitoring the monsoon system and (d) upper air indices of monsoon circulation.

3.1 SOI and onset of monsoon

Every 3 to 7 years, SST off the South American (SA) coast suddenly warms up compared to the temperatures of the western Pacific region. This phenomenon is known as an El Nino, or 'warm event'. It is initiated by a decrease in easterly trade winds reducing the upwelling near SA coast with consequent warming. This lowers atmospheric pressure over the eastern Pacific, causing the trade winds to be further reduced. Gradually, if this process continues, an El Nino develops. In strong El Nino situations, warmer than normal waters cover nearly the entire eastern and central tropical Pacific. The area of strong convection (large rain clouds) usually shifts eastward as waters in those areas warm up. In the western Pacific, easterly trade winds often reverse and blow from the west, reducing ocean temperatures and increase in atmospheric pressure and decrease in cloud formation. The whole process of El Nino or La Nina (reverse of El Nino) is found to have some influence on SW monsoon variability though not clearly quantified.

The annual means and the means of pre-monsoon months (Mar-May) of SOI data (or ENSO index) for the period 1970-2010 are plotted in Fig-3. The figure also shows the variability of

SOI smoothened by taking 12 months running means of the monthly average SOI data for the same period. A high value of correlation coefficient (~0.84) is found between the annual average and pre monsoon months average values indicating that the effect of these events during pre monsoon months normally continue in a similar manner of warming or cooling for a longer period of the year. Fig-4 shows the contour plot of the monthly mean ENSO index values for the period. It is seen that the El Nino and La Nina events take place in an alternating manner both having periodicities of ~5-6 years. The darkest (black) shades indicate occurrence of El Nino and lightest (white) shades La Nina episodes. Other grey shades indicate different intermediate states of these events including the normal condition of neither being present. There are higher frequency seasonal structures within the episodic year that can be seen in the contours.

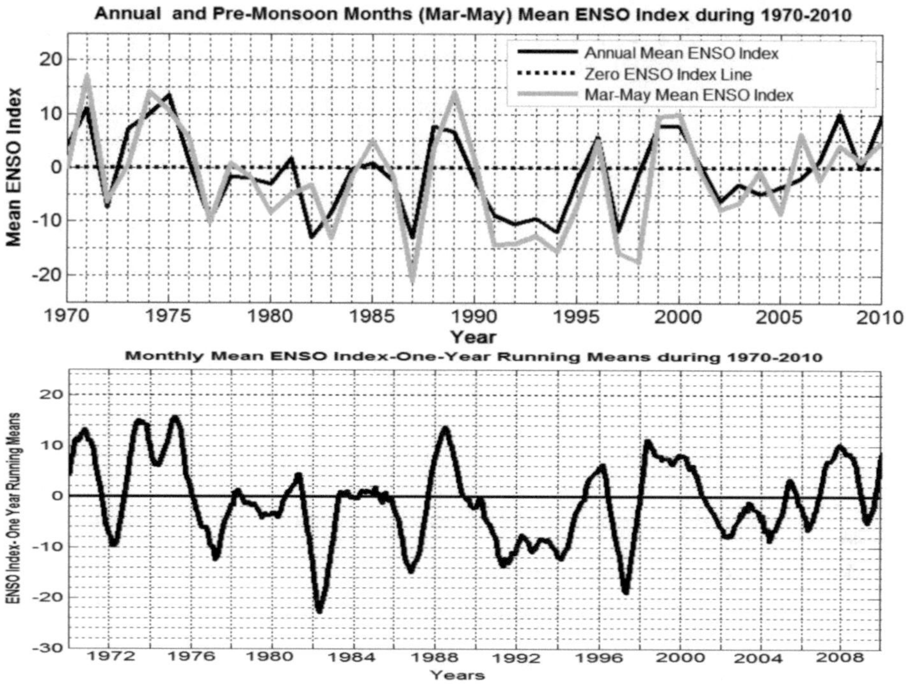

Fig. 3. Variation of ENSO index during the period 1970-2010. Top panel shows the annual and pre monsoon months (Mar-May) average values and the bottom panel 12 months running means.

The determination of the monsoon onset date over Kerala is normally announced and later slightly modified based on the event definition by IMD. Since there is another criterion of the hydrologic onset and withdrawal index (HOWI) mentioned earlier, a comparison is made by plotting these two sets of dates in Fig-5. The HOWI index data is available only during 1970-2000. The figure shows some major differences between the onset dates with a correlation coefficient of ~0.61. Hence the studies related to the causes of variations of onset dates would have less meaningful results if there were a change in the definition itself. It is found that a burst of rainfall due to non-monsoon reasons may happen locally to mimic an early onset of monsoon applicable to both the data sets with differing degrees.

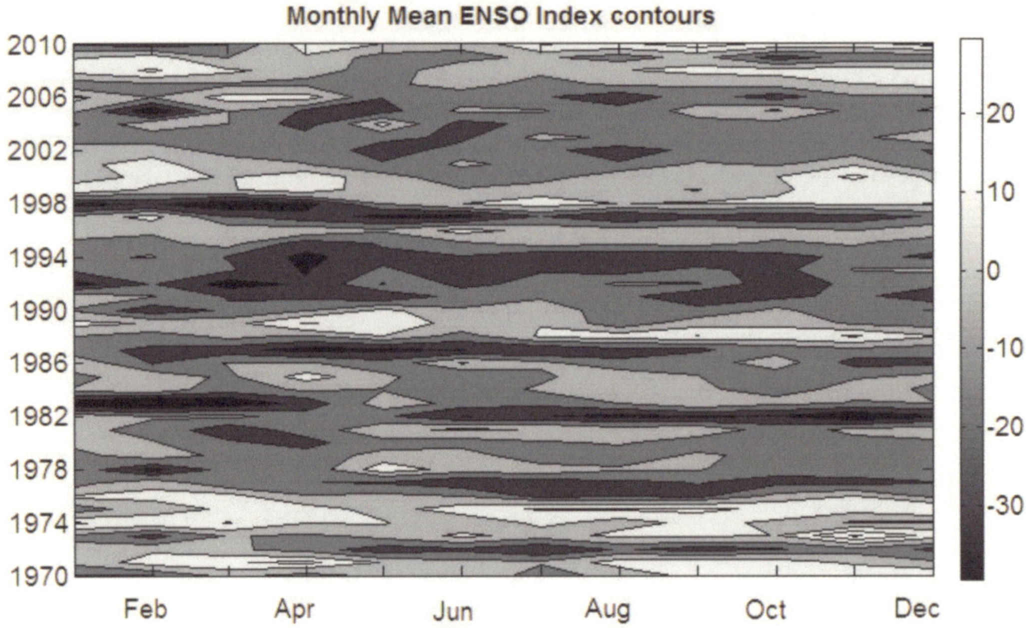

Fig. 4. Contour plot of monthly mean ENSO index during 1970-2010. The darker shades show El Nino and the lighter La Nina episodes.

Notwithstanding the imperfect way the monsoon onset is defined, it may still be helpful to examine any direct influence of the El Nino/La Nina events on the monsoon onset dates over Kerala coast. The annual and pre-monsoon period means of SOI are plotted with respect to the onset dates of each year during 1970-2010 in Fig-6. From the distribution it is

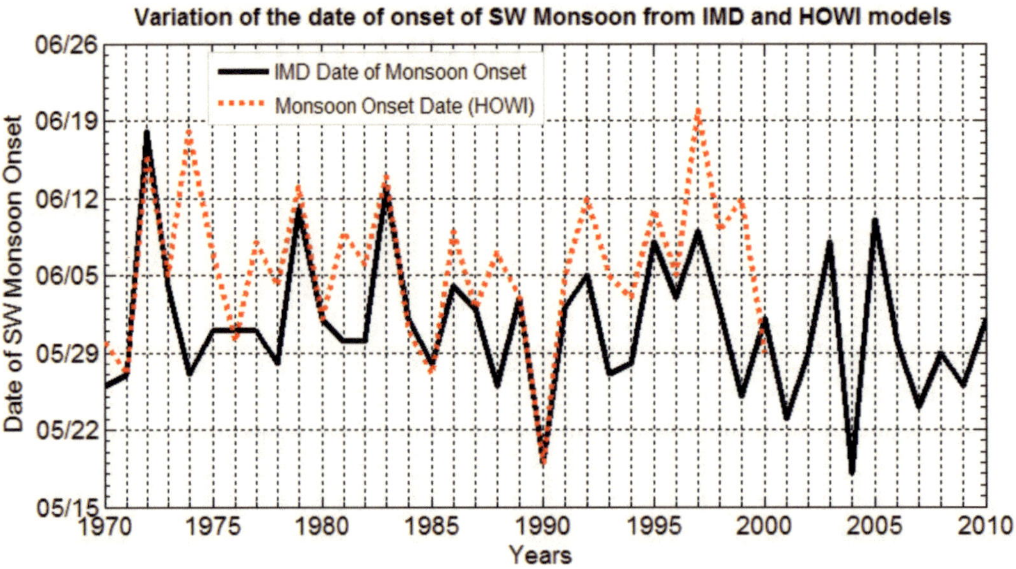

Fig. 5. Comparison of monsoon onset days using IMD and HOWI data sets.

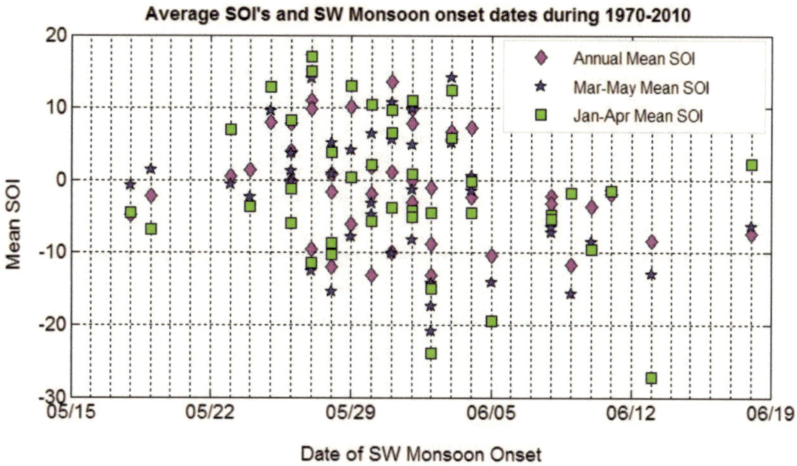

Fig. 6. Scatter plot of mean values of SOI and monsoon onset dates for the years 1970-2010.

clear that only in 4 cases out of 40 years of data, the SOI exceeded 15 in the negative scale (strong El-Nino event) and for all of these years the monsoon onset dates were delayed, i.e., beyond the normal onset date of 1 June. For all other values of SOI ranging between –14 and +15 the correlation is very poor. There have been much more delayed onset for smaller negative values of mean SOI. It may be noted that at least for positive values of SOI the onset has taken place within 4 June. So from normal conditions to La-Nina events provide a better prognosis that the monsoon would be timely compared to the El Nino events association with delayed monsoon. Apart from the onset date the other parameter is the % deviations of total area weighted seasonal (June-September) rainfall from long term mean value over India. Table-1 shows a few selected years of strong El Nino or La Nina events and associated SOI indices, onset dates and % deviations of rainfall. It is noted that there is a better correlation of negative and positive association to rainfall index with strong El Nino and La Nina events respectively.

Year	Annual Average SOI	Mar-May Average SOI	SW Monsoon Onset Date	% Deviation of Total seasonal rain
		El Nino Years		
1982	-13.1	-3.2	30-May	-13.6
1987	-13.1	-20.9	02-Jun	-18.0
1991	-8.8	-14.3	02-Jun	-7.5
1992	-10.4	-14.1	05-Jun	-7.6
		La Nina Years		
1971	11.0	17.0	27-May	3.9
1975	13.6	10.7	31-May	13.1
1988	7.8	3.7	26-May	13.1
2010	9.8	4.9	01-Jun	2.0

Table 1. Selected years of strong El Nino and La Nina events, associated SOI values, Monsoon onset date and percentage deviations (from long term mean) of monsoon seasonal rainfall.

From the above analysis it is noted that the mere presence of El Nino/La Nina events does not in itself provide any definite clue to the prospects of the ensuing monsoon (onset date in particular). However the normal conditions of oceanic state and mild La Nina situations appear to be favourable for a better monsoon. It is not possible to quantify these effects on the basis of these events. Hence it is necessary to deal with the oceanic state in a more quantitative manner. The sea surface temperature variations can be studied in more details using regular satellite data at a high resolution. The main parameter which is responsible for rainfall under monsoon system is the evaporation from the ocean surface which is closely linked to cloud formation and rainfall while being transported away from the source region.

3.2 Global and regional SST maps from satellite data

NASA's AQUA satellite launched during 2002 to an orbit of about 700 km has been broadcasting all the data on X-Band. Remote Sensing Systems (RSS), Santa Rosa, California produces Level 3 TMI/AMSR-E Ocean Products, *i.e.*, SST, sea surface wind (SSW) speed, atmospheric water vapor, and cloud liquid water. Data is visualised as daily, 3-day, weekly and monthly aggregates. As against daily maps with gaps in total coverage, the 3-day aggregate data covers the entire globe and represents the values on the present and past two days taken together. The microwave sensors produce all weather data with a high spatial resolution or pixel dimensions of 25 km x 25 km. The products are optimally interpolated and corrected for diurnal variations finally providing data normalised to a daily minimum SST, defined to occur approximately at 8 AM local time. The core MATLAB code uses the daily binary files of global SST data available on near real-time basis and converts these SSTs into global/regional maps. An example of such a global SST map on 9 April 2007 is shown in Fig-7. There are overall 1440 x 720 temperature points in the map; each presenting the average temperature value of pixel area 25 km x 25km. The map shows that the eastern/central Pacific Ocean temperatures are colder and there was no El Nino in progress. A sequence of such maps for following days would help monitoring appearance of any anomalous change in SST (allowing for the usual seasonal variation).

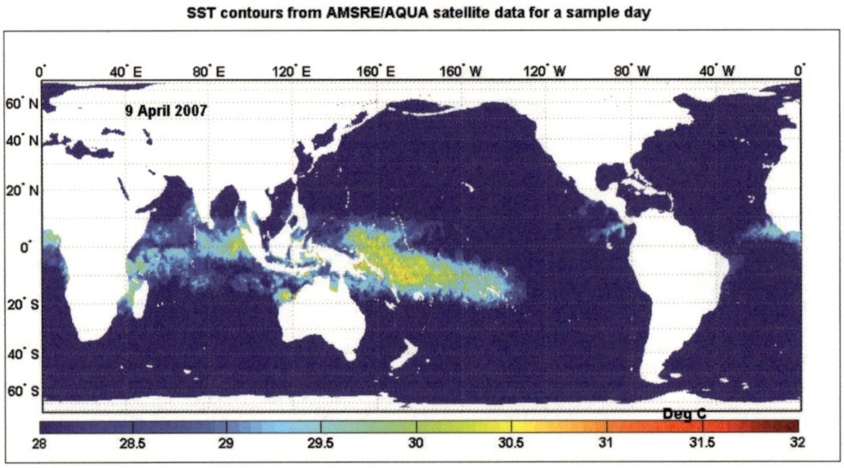

Fig. 7. Global SST contour map using AQUA data On 9 April 2007. Blue to red colour coding is to distinguish low and high temperature pixels. There are no measurements over the land areas and these are shown in white. Concentration of high temperature pixels in the Indian and western Pacific oceans is a nominal phenomena for April month.

The same programme can be employed to focus on the specific Nino regions of interest and map the SST values for different days. As an illustration for the Nano-BP region the SST maps are drawn on 3 days in the pre monsoon months (Mar-May) for two years of 2004 and 2008. Fig-8 shows these 2 sets of SST contours for comparison. The year 2004 had an early monsoon onset on 18 May and year 2008 a near normal onset on 29 May. The total seasonal rainfall over India for 2004 was 12% deficient and 2008 almost normal. It can be noted from the figure that the SSTs were generally higher during 2004 compared to 2008 for the same days of the year. The figure also shows that there is a larger region in the eastern Pacific Ocean which is colder during 2008 with a gradual decrease in the size of this area as the days progress compared to those during 2004. More quantification of these results is required and this has been attempted in terms of the distribution of SST values at pixel levels.

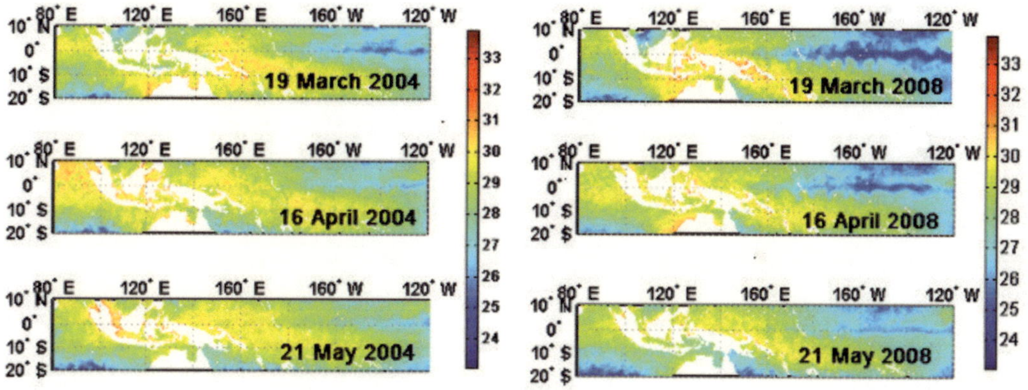

Fig. 8. SST contours of 3 selected days during pre-monsoon period for the years 2004 and 2008 over the Nino-BP region. Red/blue colours indicate cold/hot regions. White areas are landmasses.

3.3 Sensitivity analysis of SST at pixel level

The AQUA satellite data is available from 2003 and hence the detailed investigation at pixel levels is carried out for the period 2003-11. The data up to 30 April 2011 has been analysed to get an idea about the prospects of the monsoon of the coming season, i.e., June-September, 2011. The study shows that both the trend of the average temperature over the Nino-BP region and distribution of number of temperature bins between 25-31 °C with 1°C resolution point towards a near normal monsoon onset and rainfall distribution in 2011 similar to the year 2008.

Mean temperature values are calculated for each days SST data summed over the selected Nino regions and these are used in the time series for trend analysis. Similarly the distribution of number of pixels having temperatures between 25-31 °C is estimated for each day to compute the monthly averages. Fig-9 shows the time series of daily average SST values for pre monsoon months of different years over the Nino-BP region. The time series is built by analysing the daily data at weekly intervals. Fig-10 is a similar time series of mean SST values during the monsoon season (Jun-Sep). The years selected for this and subsequent plots include 2 anomalous years 2004 and 2009 with deficient rainfall and early monsoon onset and the other two, 2007 and 2008 as near normal monsoon years with 2008 being more well behaved from the view point of overall monsoon seasonal rainfall distribution over India. From Fig-9 it is clear that the basic trend of the curves are similar but there is a large variation in absolute values of mean SST from year to year. The lowest temperatures were observed in 2008 (a near perfect monsoon year) and the values up to April for the current year (2011) also shows low SSTs indicating that the monsoon during 2011 could be like 2008 unless there are some drastic systemic deviations during the monsoon months.

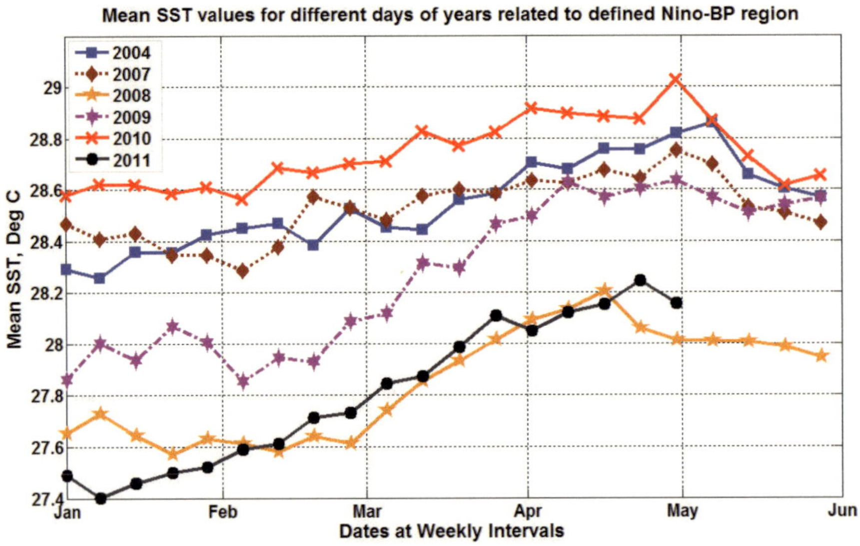

Fig. 9. Mean SST values over Nino-BP region for different days of pre-monsoon months at weekly interval for individual years (2004-11).

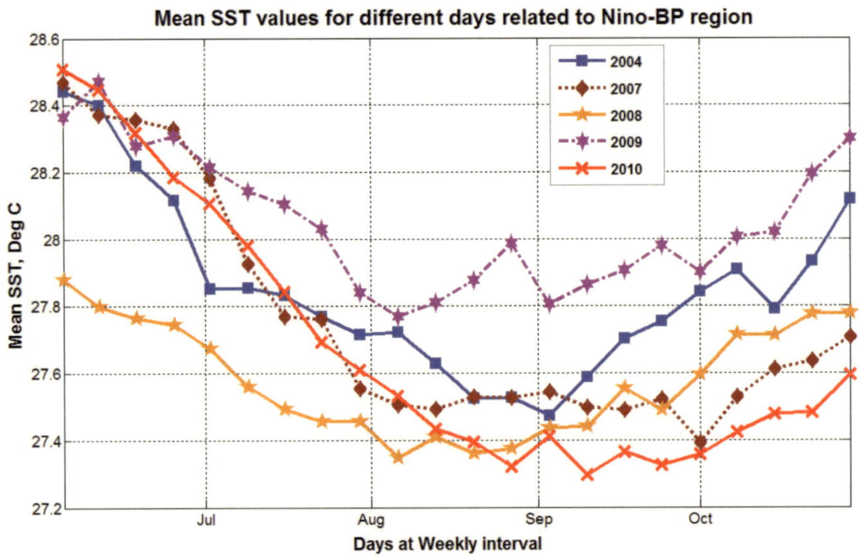

Fig. 10. Mean SST values over Nino-BP region for different days of monsoon months at weekly interval for individual years (2004-10).

For other 4 years which include 2 normal years (2007, 2010) and 2 abnormal years (2004, 2009) no definite conclusions can be drawn based on the trend and absolute values of mean SST. Fig-10 provides another clue that mean SSTs should come down to 2008 level for the monsoon to pick up. It is noted that while the mean SSTs showed gradual cooling up to end August for 2007 and 2010 the cooling trend was not enough for 2004 (12% deficient rainfall occurred compared to long period average, LPA) and 2009. In fact for 2009 mean SSTs remained high resulting in a major failure of monsoon rains (23 % deficient from LPA). Hence the mean SST over Niano-BP region can provide a better handle by monitoring it on a real time basis which may help in short-term (a week or so in advance) prediction.

In order to check if the actual pixel level temperatures can provide additional information the contours of number of pixels distributed over the temperature bins 25-31 °C for the observation days (at weekly interval) for the pre monsoon period for 4 selected years (2004, 2007, 2008, 2009) are drawn and shown in Fig-11. The pattern of variation of number of low and high temperature pixels are similar in pairs for [2007, 2008] and for [2004, 2009]. Both 2004 and 2009 years show presence of high number of pixels ≥ 28 °C. This would have implications in losing the water vapour flux transport through oceanic and pre-monsoon rains before the onset of monsoon. Sometimes this may mimic arrival of monsoon at an early date. This appears to have happened during 2004.

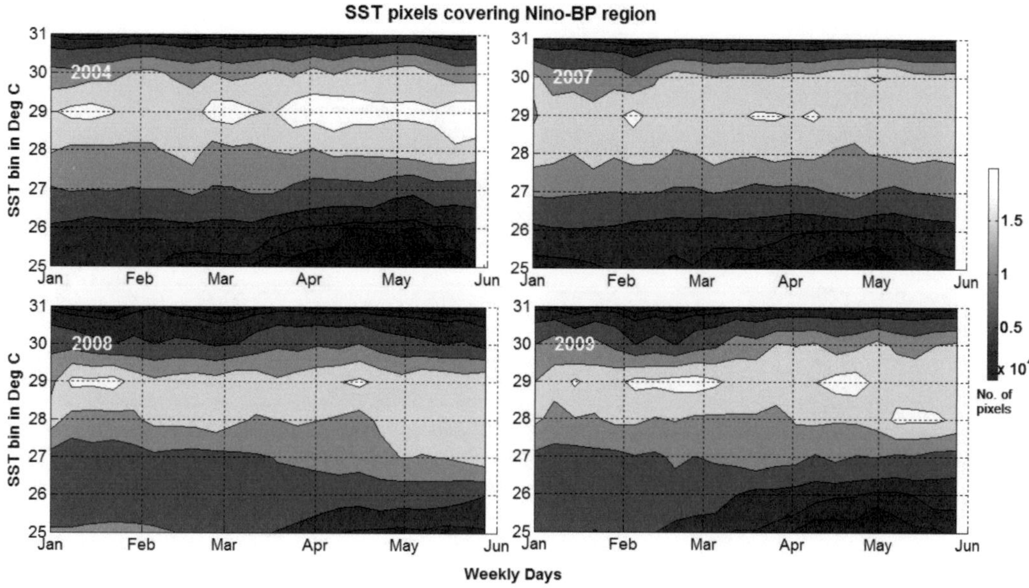

Fig. 11. Contour plots of number of pixels having different temperature values between 25-31 °C during pre-monsoon months for different years, 2004, 2007, 2008, and 2009 over Nino-BP region.

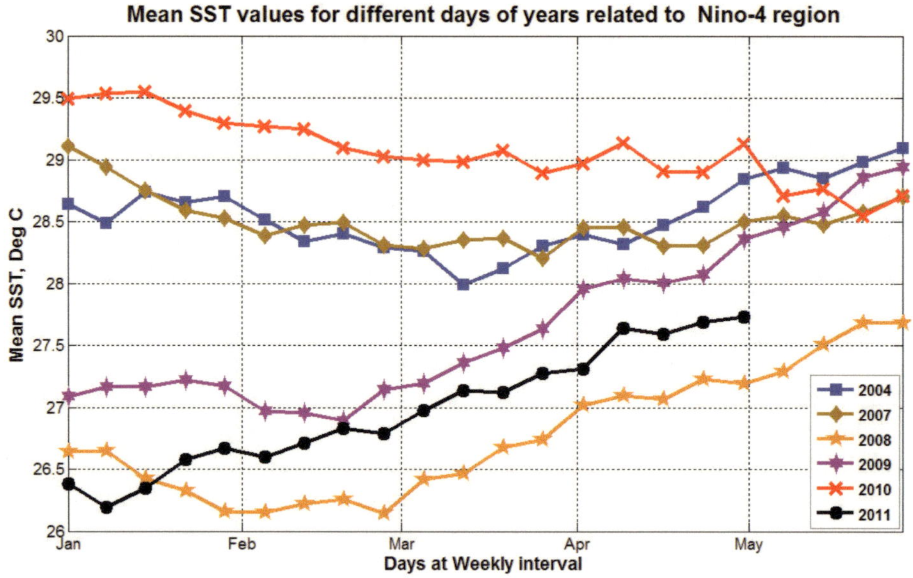

Fig. 12. Mean SST values over Nino-4 region for different days of pre-monsoon months at weekly interval for individual years (2004-11).

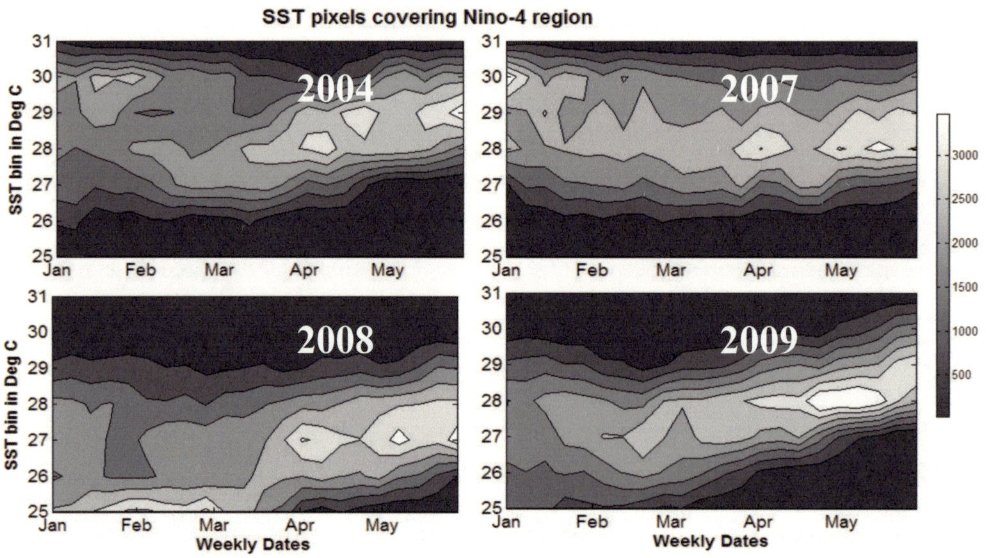

Fig. 13. Contour plots of number of pixels having different temperature values between 25-31 °C during pre-monsoon months for different years, 2004, 2007, 2008, and 2009 over Nino-4 region.

Similar analysis has been carried out for the Nino-4 region and the results presented in Fig-12 and Fig-13. The trends of mean SST over Nino-4 are similar but being a small region it could get influenced by local effects. From Fig-13 the similarities in paired years of [2007, 2008] and [2004, 2009] cannot be easily discerned as in the case of Nino-BP plots. However it would help to conduct SST analysis for both Nino-BP and Nino-4 regions as part of the monsoon forecasting and real time modelling.

For determining the characteristics of SST pixel distribution during the build up phase of the monsoon system, monthly average values are computed and shown as bar charts over Nino-BP for the years 2004, 2007, 2008 and 2009 in Fig-14. While excess number of pixels with SST≥ 28 °C is found for anomalous years 2004 and 2009 particularly in May, these were found to be only little lower during 2007. Similar analysis in Fig-15 for the Nino-4 area shows a clearer demarcation of pixel distribution comparison between the two pairs of years. During 2010 there was a strong El Nino effect from Jan-Mar and hence the prospects of monsoon looked bleak. But the situation improved subsequently with a La-Nina setting in. This change over took place at right time so that monsoon rains picked up from July onwards. A comparison of relevant parameters between 2008 and 2010 is shown in Fig-16. It can be noted that the pixel number distribution with SST in both the years are similar for the month of May which changed the prospects for a better monsoon during 2010.

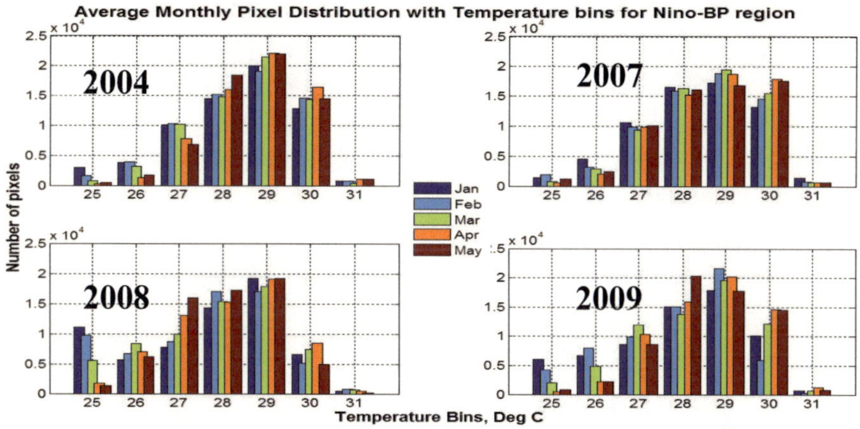

Fig. 14. Average monthly pixel (25-31 °C) number distribution for pre monsoon months of Jan-May for 2004, 2007, 2008 and 2009 over the Nino-BP region.

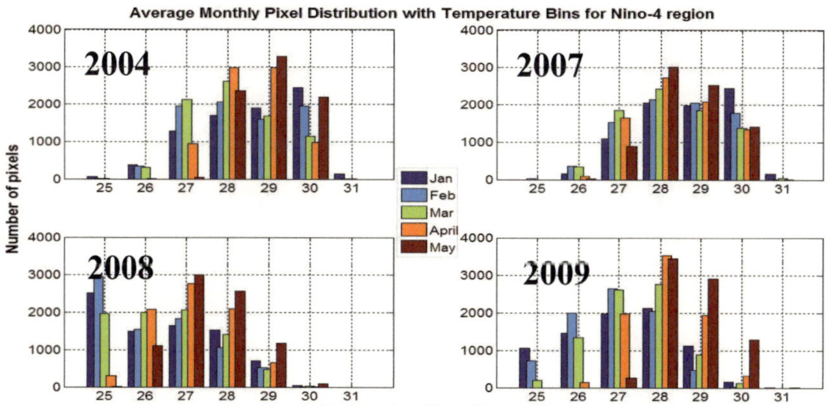

Fig. 15. Average monthly pixel (25-31 °C) distribution for pre monsoon months of Jan-May for 2004, 2007, 2008 and 2009 over the Nino-4 region.

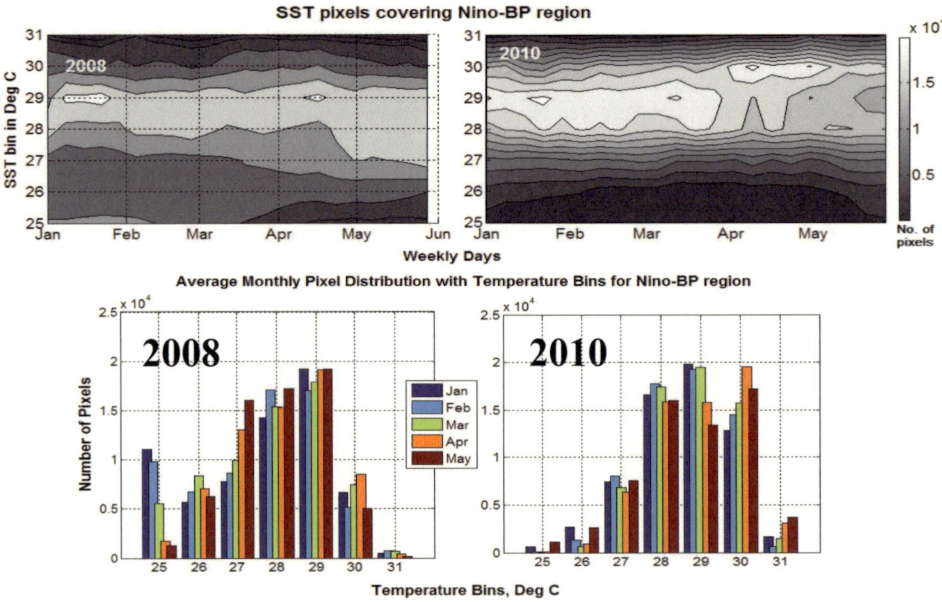

Fig. 16. Comparison of pixel number contour and monthly average pixel distribution over Nino-BP region during 2008 and 2010.

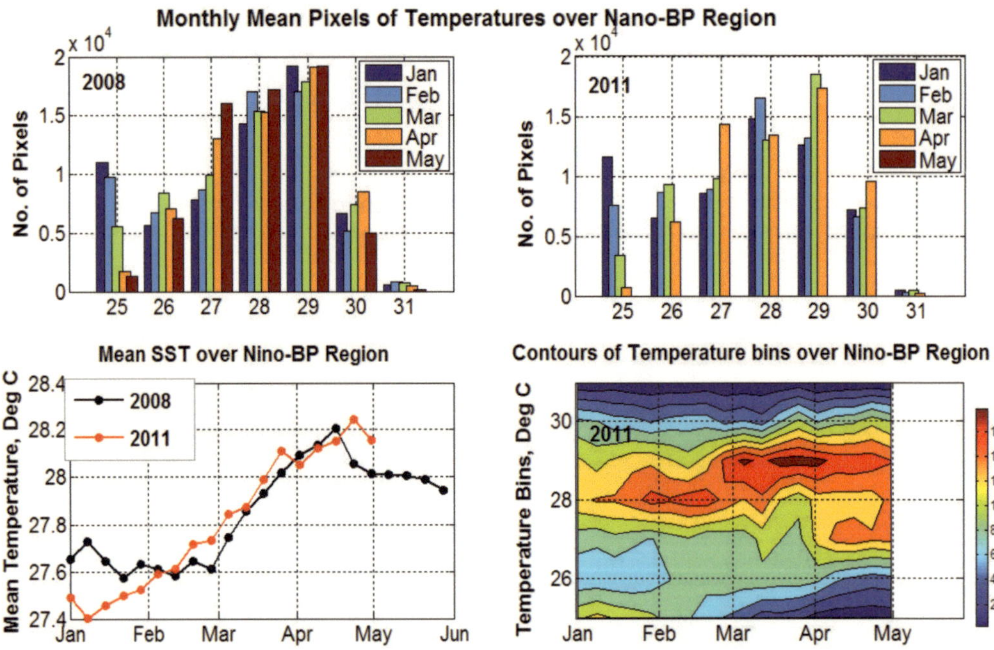

Fig. 17. (Clockwise) Comparison of monthly mean Nino-BP region pixel distribution for 2008 and up to April of 2011, time series of mean SST over Nino-BP region for 2008 and up to April, 2011 and contours of pixel numbers pertaining to temperature bins of 25-31 °C up to April of 2011.

Fig-17 shows a comparison of monsoon build up parameters of 2008 and 2011 (data used up to April 2011). It clearly shows a striking similarity in the variations of the mean monthly pixel distribution, the absolute values and the trend of mean SST over Nino-BP region between 2008 and 2011 so far (April, 2011). The contour of pixel numbers for SST bins also shows similarity to the 2008 plot up to end of April. Hence all conditions are favourable for 2011 monsoon to be a success and there are chances that it would be like the one during 2008 along with its near uniform spatial distribution.

3.4 Upper air indices of monsoon circulation

Wind and temperature data from ground to about 70 km have been collected over Thiruvananthapuram since 1971 using meteorological balloons and Russian made M-100 and Indian made RH-200 sounding rockets (Chakravarty & Datta, 1992). The rocket flights continued at regular weekly intervals up to 1990. The voluminous data has been archived and being used for various studies of troposphere-middle atmosphere coupling processes. Different types of waves like the QBO, SAO, Rossby-Gravity and Kelvin waves have been characterized using such global data sets (Fukao, 2006). Efforts have also been made to detect any upper level changes in wind pattern before the onset of the monsoon over Kerala. While there were some preliminary results on likely reversal of winds from westerlies to easterlies around 22-24 km altitudes about 4-5 days before the onset, these could not be confirmed. Taking into account that a long period data set exists and as a test year of data specifically to look for changes/reversals of upper winds in relation to monsoon activity, the Rocket Monsoon Experiment (ROMEX) was carried out during April-June, 2007 from Thiruvananthapuram under ISRO Headquarters, Bngalore. The main objective of the ROMEX campaign was to monitor the dynamical features of troposphere /stratosphere/ mesosphere from the Rocket and Balloon winds measured at frequent intervals to explore the key changes of wind patterns related to the onset features of SW monsoon over Karala coast.

The detailed results from the ROMEX campaign 2007 are available in an unpublished ISRO report. Salient campaign findings are only presented here. The long period data (1971-90) from the Thumba Equatorial Rocket Launching Station (TERLS) near Thiruvananthapuram is used to generate a statistical model of zonal winds averaged over different height ranges and then the ROMEX campaign data for 2007 is used as a test case in relation to onset date as well as seasonal rainfall. Fig-18 shows the vector wind profiles at 1 km height resolution of all the individual campaign days of balloon and rocket launches during April-June 2007. It can be noted that in particular there are 3 height ranges of interest, 11-20 km, 41-50 km and 51-60 km which show either strengthening of easterlies or reversal from westerlies to easterlies close to the onset date which was 28 May in 2007. Same data is used to get an interpolated time-height contour plot of zonal winds. The red coloured contours are for westerly winds and blue easterly. The three identified regions of interest are seen in the figure with gradual transitions of wind strength and directions.

The mean zonal winds for the identified height ranges are computed and plotted as a time series during ROMEX period. This is shown in Fig-20. It is noted that close to the onset day clear change over from westerly to easterly has taken place for the mean zonal wind in 41-50 km height range about 4-5 days in advance. The mesospheric zonal winds (mean of 51-60 km) reversed the direction just after the onset date. The easterlies in the height range (11-20 km) strengthened about 4-5 days before the onset but difficult to quantify in terms of a scale

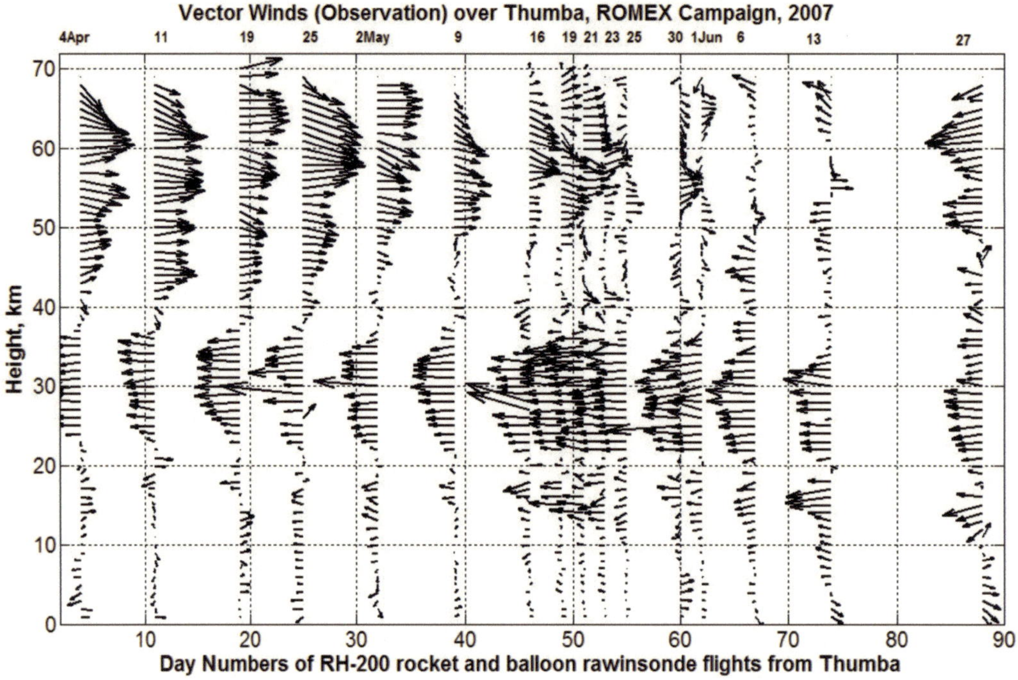

Fig. 18. Vector wind profiles of individual days of observation using RH-200 rocket and rawinsonde balloon launches from Thumba during April-June 2007 under ROMEX campaign.

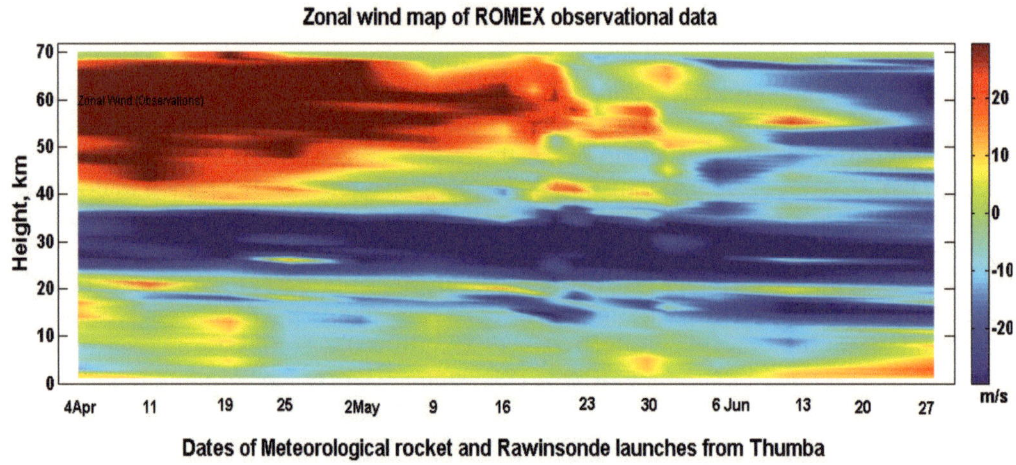

Fig. 19. Smoothed contour plot of zonal winds between 0-70 km height ranges over Thumba. Red contours show westerly winds and blue easterlies.

for such strengthening. Acquiring a value of mean zonal wind of 10 m/s in this troposphere/ lower stratosphere height range appears to be a rough figure to work with for linking with monsoon.

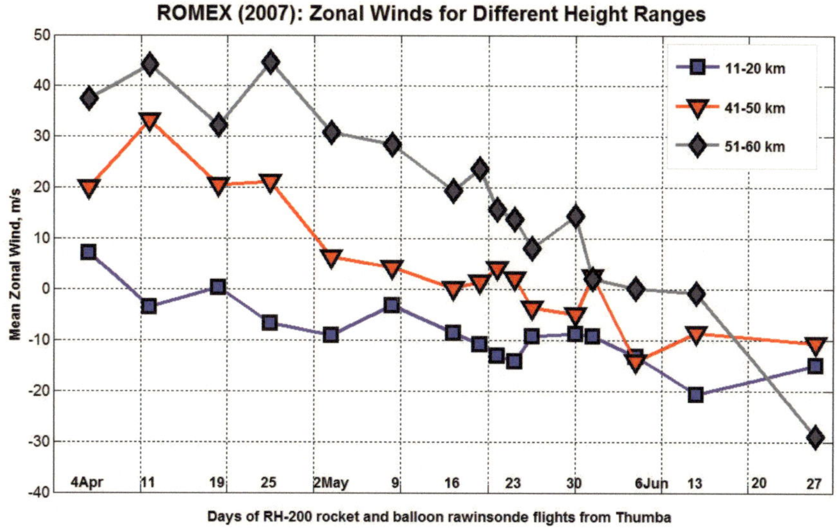

Fig. 20. Time series of mean zonal winds for height ranges, 11-20 km, 41-50 km and 51-60 km during ROMEX campaign period.

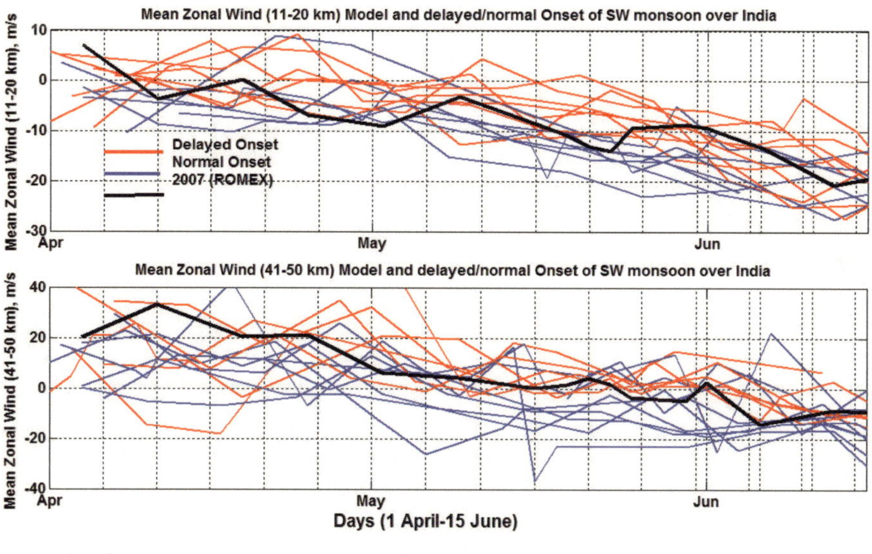

Fig. 21. Trends of mean zonal winds for 11-20 km and 41-50 km height ranges from long period (1971-90) balloon/rocket data differentiated for normal (blue) and delayed (red) monsoon and how the ROMEX data for 2007 fares as a test case (black).

Fig. 21 shows the statistical data of mean zonal winds between 11-20 km and 41-50 km distinguished in terms of normal and delayed monsoon with red and blue lines respectively. Over these climatological pattern of variation the ROMEX line for 2007 is superimposed. It is clear that the 2007 data fits closer to the blue lines which are for the normal monsoon onset days.

4. Conclusion

4.1 The rainfall during the SW monsoon period (June-September) constitutes the main source of water in India for agriculture (particularly pertaining to the 'Kharif' crops), hydroelectric power generation and drinking water requirements. There is a large inter annual and intra seasonal variation of this water resource due to variations in the monsoon genesis and progress. While the spatial distribution of monsoon rainfall is caused due to fast response parameters and local impacts, both the onset date and the season's integrated rainfall are caused by slowly varying boundary conditions and forcings like that of the sea surface temperature, snow cover etc. Hence the variation of sea surface temperature is taken up here for prognosis studies.

4.2 Based on the AQUA satellites all weather microwave sensor data a near real-time interactive computer model has been developed to extract daily minimum global SST values of 1440x720 pixels, each pixel covering 25 km x 25 km of lat-long area. The programme also selects specific oceanic region like the Nino-4 and Nino-BP to compute daily mean SST over the region and can add into previous days data to generate a real time trend. Such trends of previous years during 2003-2010 are used to study the variations and its influence on the onset dates and the seasonal rainfall. In the background of the statistics or the real-time model the data of current year is analysed up to April 2011. The progress of the absolute SST values and its trend indicate a near normal monsoon during 2011 somewhat similar in characteristics that of 2008.

4.3 There have been many studies to link the occurrence of major El Nino and La Nina events with the changes in the monsoon onset date. Such analysis is carried out in this report also and it is found that the strong El Nino/La Nina events have a negative/positive effect on monsoon. But considering the whole range of seasonal mean SOI it is found that statistically the positive SOI values have positive impact but negative SOI values have both positive and negative impacts. Thus the SOI index has only limited applicability as a predictor parameter. Hence the main purpose of this study is to make a more quantitative assessment at pixel level of the SST linked monsoon variability.

4.4 A novel sensitivity analysis is carried out by selecting a broader Pacific Ocean region called Nino-BP (defined by the author). Within this region the pixels are counted and placed in temperature bins of values 25-31 °C. The resultant matrix provides daily number of pixels distributed over these temperature bins. This pixels numbers are plotted as time-bin contours or as bar graphs. The main result from this analysis shows that larger number of pixels distributed in temperature bins ≤ 28 °C during pre monsoon or during monsoon months has a positive impact on the onset date and total seasonal rainfall. Reverse applies for larger number of pixels in temperature bins of value > 28 °C.

4.5 As collateral and useful information on the prospects of onset date, the time sequence of mean zonal wind values over TERLS between 11-20 km and 41-50 km height ranges provide the possible transition date about 4-5 days in advance by comparing its real time trend with a statistical model of long period balloon and rocket data during 1971-90.

5. Acknowledgement

AQUA/AMSR-E data are produced by Remote Sensing Systems and sponsored by the NASA Earth Science REASoN DISCOVER Project and the AMSR-E Science Team. Data are available at http://www.remss.com. Author acknowledges the help provided by Dr. K.

V. S. Namboodiri, TERLS, Vikram Sarabhai Space Centre, Thiruvananthapuram, India in coordinating the ROMEX campaign and the financial support provided by Chairman, Indian Space Research Organization (ISRO) Headquarters, Bangalore, India for the ROMEX campaign.

6. References

Ananthakrishnan, R & Soman, M. K. (1988). The onset of southwest monsoon over Kerala, 1901–1980. *J. Climatol.*, Vol.8, pp. 283–296

Chakravarty, S. C. (2009). A computer model to study the variability of grid-based Sea Surface Temperature (SST) values derived from AQUA/AMSRE satellite data and its influence on the onset of South West Monsoon near the Kerala coastal region in India. *IEEE Xplore*, pp. 1-5, ISBN: 978-1-4244-4562-2

Chakravarty, S. C.; Datta, J. & Revankar, C. P. (1992). Climatology of long-period oscillations in the equatorial middle atmosphere over Thumba, India. *Current Science*, Vol.63, No.1, pp. 33-42

Chakravarty, S. C. & Namboodiri, K. V. S. (2007). A Scientific Report on the Rocket Monsoon Experiment (ROMEX) campaign (2007). ISRO, India (unpublished)

Charney, J. G. & Shukla, J. (1981). In: *Monsoon Dynamics*, J. Lighthill, (Ed.), Cambridge University Press, Cambridge, pp. 99–110.

Chirokova, G. & P. J. Webster (2006). Interannual Variability of Indian Ocean Heat Transport. *Journal of Climate*, 19, 1013-1031

Fasullo, J. & Webster, P. J. (2002). A hydrological definition of Indian Monsoon Onset and withdrawl. *Journal of Climate*, Vol.16, pp. 3200-3211

Fukao, S. (2006). Coupling processes in the equatorial atmosphere (CPEA): A project overview. *J. Meteor. Soc. Japan*, Vol.84A, pp. 1-18

Hastenrath, S. & Greischar, L. (1993). Changing predictability of Indian monsoon rainfall anomalies? *Proc. Indian Acad. Sci. (Earth Planet. Sci.)*, Vol.102, pp. 35–47

Joseph, P. V.; Eisheid, J. & Pyle, R. J. (1994). Interannual variability of the onset of the Indian summer monsoon and its association with atmospheric features, El Nin˜o, and sea surface temperature anomalies. *J. Climate*, Vol.7, pp. 81–105, 1994

Mooley, D. A. & Parthasarathy, B. (1984). Fluctuations in all India summer monsoon rainfall during 1871–1978. *Climatic Change*, Vol.6, pp. 287–301

Munot, A. A. & Krishna Kumar, K. (2007). Long Range prediction of Indian summer monsoon rainfall. *J. Earth Sys. Sci.*, Vol.116, No.1, pp. 73-79

Nakazawa, T. (1988). Tropical super clusters within intraseasonal variations over the western Pacific. *J. Meteor. Soc. Japan*, Vol.66, pp. 823–839

Philander, S. G. H. (1990) In: *El Niño, La Niña and the Southern Oscillation*, Academic Press, San Diego, CA, pp. 1-289

Raghu Kanth, S. T. G. & Iyengar, R. N. (2003). Empirical modeling and forecasting of Indian monsoon rainfall. *Current Science*, Vol.85, pp. 1189-1201

Rajeevan, M. (2001). Prediction of Indian summer monsoon: Status, problems and prospects. *Current Science*, Vol.81, No.11, pp. 1451-1457

Rajeevan, M. D.; Pai, S., Dikshit S. K. & Kelkar, R. R. (2004). IMD's new operational models for long-range forecast of southwest monsoon rainfall over India and their verification for 2003. *Current Science*, Vol.86, No.3, pp. 422-431

Sikka, D. R. & Gadgil, S. (1980). On the maximum cloud zone and the ITCZ over Indian longitudes during the southwest monsoon. *Mon. Wea. Rev.*, Vol.108, pp. 1840–1853

Soman, M. K. & Kumar, K. K. (1993). Space–time evolution of meteorological features associated with the onset of Indian summer monsoon. *Mon. Wea. Rev.*, Vol.121, pp. 1177–1194

Waliser, D. E.; Stern, W. F., Schubert, S. D. & Lau, K. M. (2003). Dynamic predictability of intraseasonal variability associated with the Asian summer monsoon. *Q. J. R. Meteorol. Soc.*, Vol.129, pp. 2897-2925

4

The Analysis of Influence of River Floods on Biotic Components of Floodplain Ecosystems with the Help of MATLAB Simulation

Vladimir Petrovich Bolotnov
Yugra State University
Russia

1. Introduction

The Ob River occupies a central place in Western Siberia. Its basin comprises all spatial and dynamic variability typical for Western Siberian ecosystems. The river floodplains are the most dynamic parts and in the same time host most of the human activities. However, at present spatial planning of economic activities in the floodplain areas cannot be based on water regime and geomorphologic processes, because relevant inventory of relief and hydrological monitoring data are hardly accessible. Moreover, for nature conservation, in terms of planning, area selection and management, and data of biodiversity of floodplain ecosystems are missing.

This research intends to fill these gaps in knowledge. In addition factual relations between ecosystem productivity of different floodplain units and hydrological regime need to be studied. There to a hydro-ecological monitoring scheme for analyses of the Ob-Irtysh floodplain of the region Middle Ob will be set up.

The research will be based on the already developed hydro-ecological zone maps and hydrological data of hydro-meteorological stations (river stages dynamics) representative for different river floodplain sections.

The monitoring results of a period of more 50 years stage observations flood hydrographs have been plotted and frequencies and duration of floods and relations with geomorphologic characteristics of floodplain relief and flood depths been calculated. These data may need to be evaluated more thoroughly and thereafter compared with ecosystem productivity data, which will be gathered within the scope of this project. The bird population is considered as the most sensitive element of the ecosystem.

Birds are an important component of ecosystems. They function as the consumers of the first and second orders in the trophic chain of an ecosystem. The main factor determining the annual dynamics of the bird population in the West Siberia is migration. In autumn the majority of bird population leaves for south, in spring they come back, and the time of return coincides with the period of spring high water in the Ob. This period also coincides with the breeding stage. The floodplain of the Ob attracts birds in the first place. It is related to the warming action of the waters that the river brings from south to north and to the more productive and diverse habitat conditions than in the interfluve territory. The Ob valley serves as a kind of air channel, along which the majority of birds moves. The years when the water-content parameters are close to the mean annual values are especially favorable, while those with low or extremely high water-content parameters are unfavorable (Adam A. M. & Bolotnov, 1982-2010). Thus, from the point of view of the monitoring of the state of the floodplain ecosystem the birds serve as a good indicator of its state in terms of hydro-thermal conditions. In addition to that, they occupy an important place in the nature management of the region, since a significant part of the waterbird population is a major hunting resource actively used by the local people and hunters from other regions.

2. A Model of the population dynamics of birds in the river floodplain

In the early 1980s, various large-scale projects of the change of the Ob flow as a result of hydroplant reservoirs construction (Katun and Krapivinski hydroplants) were developed as well as the projects to divert some of the waters to south, regional projects to change the irrigation of territory in terms of farming and fishing ameliorations, realization of which resulted in the local changes of the flooding conditions in the floodplain of the middle Ob. At the same time a scheme of interaction of the birds and water regime of the Ob was formed (Adam A. M. & Bolotnov, 1982-2001, Ravkin,2004, Vartapetov,2004). Accumulation of the empirical data allowed the experts to pass on to the building of a model of the bird population dynamics in the middle course of the Ob (Adam A. M. & Bolotnov, 2000-2001). It was represented as the structural scheme of the model, mathematical description (system of equations and graphs of the relations between the components of ecosystem based on real data) and complemented with the results of the modeling of a real object, which allowed us to improve its structure.

2.1 The physiographic and ecological description region research

The simulation model is built for the central region of the Ob floodplain in Tomsk oblast with the area of 4142 km2 located within the administrative boundaries of Kolpashevo raion. Flowing through the territory of Tomsk region from the south-east to the north-west, the Ob River crosses the sub zone of the south and partially of the northern taiga. The length of the area is equal to 1169 km, which is almost 1/3 of the whole Ob River length (3676 km). The further rivet goes from the south to the north the higher watering it shows due to river inflows. The main phase of the water regime is snow-rain flood, which can be observed during spring-summer period from April till August. The is 70% of annual outflow drains during the period of spring high water. The Ob River valleys are characterized by vast floodplain, cut across with numerous channels, floodplain rivers, lakes. It's width changes from 6km in the south (Kozhevnikovo hydrometric station) to 20 km in the north (Moltchanovo, Alexandrovskoye hydrometric stations) The course of the river is badly curved and crossed with little islands in many zones.

It causes the river banks' erosion which was assisted by small depths and low speeds of a flow. Inclination of the water surface is insignificant - 0,044 ‰. Average speed of a flow to a lowest water level is 0,5…0,7 м/с, and in a period of high water is 2,0…2,5 м/с. The average annual outflow varies from 60 km3 (Pobeda hydrometric station) to 195 km3 (Alexandrovskoye hydrometric station).

Floods wave through the river valley. As a result the maximal levels are reached non-simultaneously in river ranges but move in time one relatively another. Combining in one draft the schedules of flood waving in different ranges (Fig.3) we can find an obvious conception of the river regime in this very period in different ranges and of meadow high and duration.

Spring level increase normally starts in the second part of April (early and late periods are the beginning or the end of April), even while freezing over. In general water level flow of the Ob river we observe one wave with intensive increase and very slow reduce. In the area of Tom river inflow we can observe crested water flow or two-three weaked waves of flood, appeared as a result of split of multy-peaked flood in the upper reaches of the Ob river. Duration of the floodplain can last from 120 days while "friendly" springs till 150 days. An average duration of a low meadow flood can consists of 8-12 days by Kruglikovo hydrometric station, 63 days by Kolpashevo hydrometric station and 68 days by Alexandrovskoye hydrometric station. The longest period of middle Ob meadow flood lasts for 2-3,5 months. Although in the north from Alexandrovskoye water point given water horizons can be observed for 2-2,5 months later than around Kruglicovo hydrometric station in a period of long springs. The end of floodplain normally comes in July or August. An average height of water level increase above pre-flood period is equal to 5vm (before Tom river inflow), than 7-8 and than the highest 9-11 (Alexandrovskoye hydrometric station). Duration of level increase period is about 30-35 days with average insensitivity of increase as of 30-35cm per 24 hours.

Analysis of yearly water point level shows that the whole meadow of the Ob river is filled with water when floodplain reaches the maximal level 10-1% of provision. That's why we rarely see the common flood, it happens once per 30-50 years or even more seldom. At the same time the low meadow of the Ob river from Kolpashevo hydrometric station to the northern boundary goes under water every year. So the low part of the meadow is more adopted for floodplain impact and low water floods or floods for short periods can be born badly. This situation is quiet rare as the Ob river (in the lower area of the Ket river inflow) exists in a natural regime and high side inflow, huge water cumulative basin, which forms water reserves while autumn-winter season. These reserves provide obligatory spring floodplain. When analyzing the flood the meadow area is usually divided into high, middle and low areas. This dividing is equal to levels which are higher than 25 % of provision and average multy-year frequency of flooding once per 4 years, close to 50 % of provision and flooding once per 2 years, and lower than 75 % of provision, with every year flooding. Often this division happens not objectively - by vegetation which is a vivid indicator of flooding. However the usage of counting characteristics of provision lets apply fixed marks of the flood level and refer them to meadow relief and find not only the fact of flooding and also give quantity characteristics of its duration, height of filling and starting and finishing date. It is very important for the low meadow areas which are flooded every year but also have differences in parameters. Dividing of the low meadow territory within the boundaries of 100–95 % of provision permits basically perform the part from the whole annually flooded territory.

For this purpose we used the long-term observations (1977-2000) conducted in spring and summer, when the influence of spring high waters and other ecological factors on the spatial-temporal structure of the bird population was studied in detail. The average bird population in the floodplain varies from 1000 (willow forests) to 47 ind/km2 (river). The highest population density is recorded in the villages on the river banks, which varies from 1500 in the first half of summer to 4000 ind/km2 in the second half. The value of the parameters decreases as the complexity of habitats diminishes, the relief lowers, and the moisture level grows (from forests and shrubs to the meadows of high ridges, meadows of depressions, lakes and watercourses). In the second half of summer almost in all habitats the bird abundance increases 1.5 times. In the forest habitats the yellow-breasted bunting, coal tit, and long-tailed tit dominate in abundance, and in the shrub habitats, the reed bunting. The yellow-breasted and reed buntings dominate in meadows, too. In the over-wet and wet meadows and lakes the Pallas's grasshopper warbler and garganey are abundant. The sand martin dominates on the Ob and outlets. In the villages the Eurasian tree sparrow and barn swallow dominate. In total about 128 bird species live in the area, which can be divided into 6 ecological groups by their habitats: forest-shrub birds, 59 species; birds of dry meadows, 9 species (the common quail, skylark); birds of wet meadows, 12 species (the corn crake, great snipe, common snipe); water-bog birds on the over-wet and flooded meadows, 8 species (the Eurasian bittern, mallard); birds of the waterbodies, 21 species (the common teal, common pochard, tufted duck); birds associated with villages, 11 species (the barn swallow, Eurasian tree and house sparrows) (Vartapetov, 1984, Yudkin, 1987). The group of birds of wet meadows is the most dynamic by the value of the year-to-year changes.

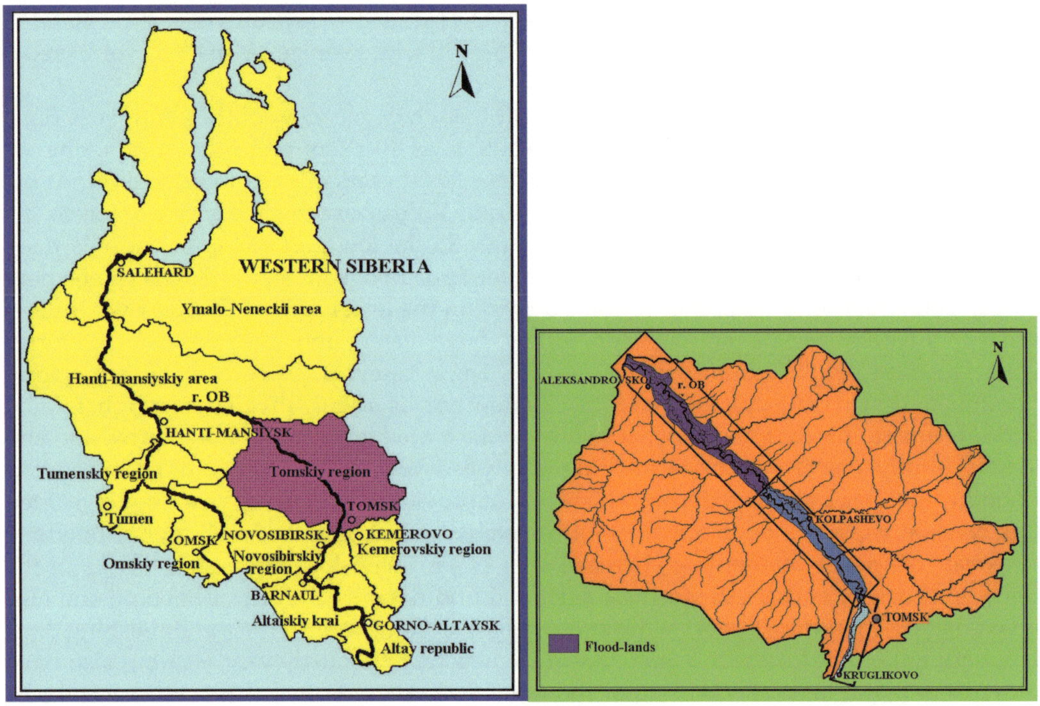

Fig. 1. Maps-schemes of regione research.

2.2 Foundations of the modeling

The model of dynamics of the bird population is built on the principles of system dynamics suggested by Jay Forrester (Forrester, 1978). It is based on the idea of phase coordinates of the system characterizing the system state in a given moment. If the external influence on the system is known, the knowledge of the phase coordinates in a moment of time helps to determine the system state in the following moments. After Forrester we use the term "stock" to mark this parameter and "flow" to characterize its changes. The basic cells building the system are the chains of feedback and feedforward. The flow is the reason of the stock changes. The data on the stocks are the inputs for the flow equations, which regulate the flows. The variables of the flows depend only on information on stocks. One stock influences another through the flows. Two main loops that influence the bird population density value are represented in Figure 1. The upper loop determines the flow of density increase (FDI), the lower, the flow of density decrease (FDD). NFDI and NFDD are normal flow of density increase and normal flow of density decrease corresponding to the mean annual conditions.

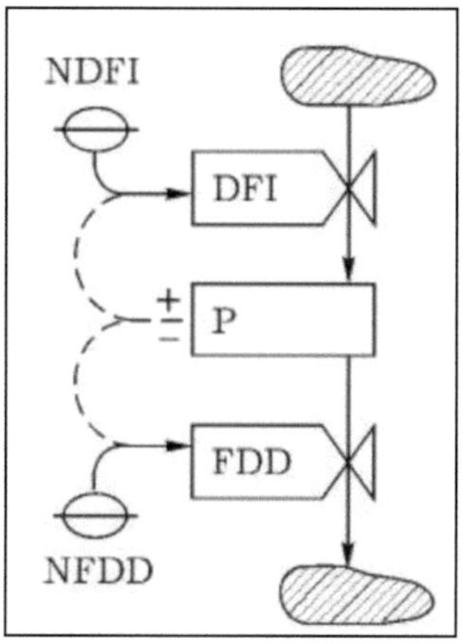

Fig. 2. Basic loops of feedback and feedforward in the model structure.

The model reflects the interaction of the biological component of the floodplain ecosystem (birds) with the external natural conditions, i.e., we consider the system "biocomponent-environment" based on the principles of self-regulation. The environment includes the species territory, vegetation, climate factor, influence of high water. The high water is a leading factor for the given territory. AF (anthropogenic factor) is the abbreviation used in the model; it means the sum of anthropogenic impact and environmental changes (AF + EC). This is supposed to underline the leading position of this factor in the system dynamics, since the anthropogenic factor can change environment by 50% and more through change of the conditions of the floodplain flooding (farming and fishing amelioration), birds shooting in the spring hunting period, factor of trouble during hay-making, fishing, recreation, etc. The use of the system "component of ecosystem-environment-anthropogenic factor" is typical of the models of this kind. In the given system the block AF has an expressed social function and is determined by the economical and social laws of the society. Analysis of the organization of this block at the given stage is not significant, since the model is of prognostic character with respect to the real changes of the water regime. The effect of the social factor was specified through limiting or changing the effect of the natural factors. The orientation of the model concept for the purpose of the region management would require creating a social block. Now the approaches to the forming of the social block (AF) are being formed based on the ecological- economical criteria of the nature management, which are given in (Adam, Mamin, 2000, Adam,et al., 2000).

2.3 Structure of the model

Figure 2 shows the concept of the simulation model reflecting the relation between the dynamics of the bird population density and abiotic, biotic, and anthropogenic factors of the natural-territorial complex of the floodplain of the middle Ob. It reflects the basic

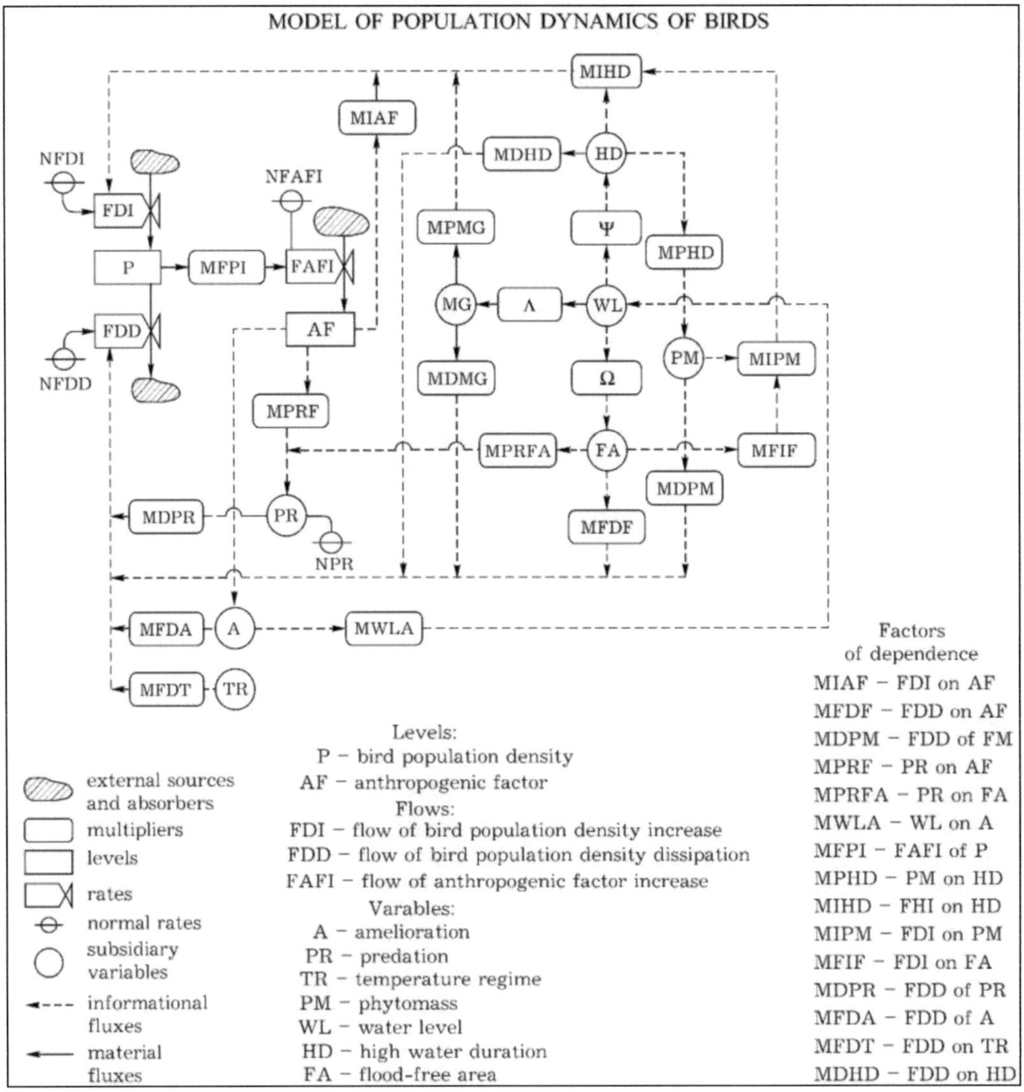

Fig. 3. Structure of the model of the dynamics of the bird population density in the floodplain of the middle Ob.

interrelations between the variables (factors) included in the model. The following parameters are chosen as the stocks forming the system structure: bird population density (P) and anthropogenic factors (AF). The marks of irregular shape ("cloud-like")—inflows or outflows—are positioned outside the system. Any closed loop is a feedback loop. The stock introduced to the system (AF) reflects the rational human activity that should lead to a positive effect, therefore, AF provokes the growth of bird population. The share of the human interference with nature that results in negative consequences (poaching, nest devastation, change in the natural habitats) leads to a decrease in the bird population. These phenomena are marked with the "predation" variable (PR). There is a feedback between the stocks (P) and (AF), too. Its idea is that with high bird population density the number of birds affected by human activity grows. The feedback is realized with the multiplier (MFPI), which increases the flow of the AF increase (FAFI) or leaves it unchanged depending on the density population value. The change of the stocks of the spring high waters by human activity is expressed with the multiplier of dependence of the stock on the anthropogenic factor (MSAF).

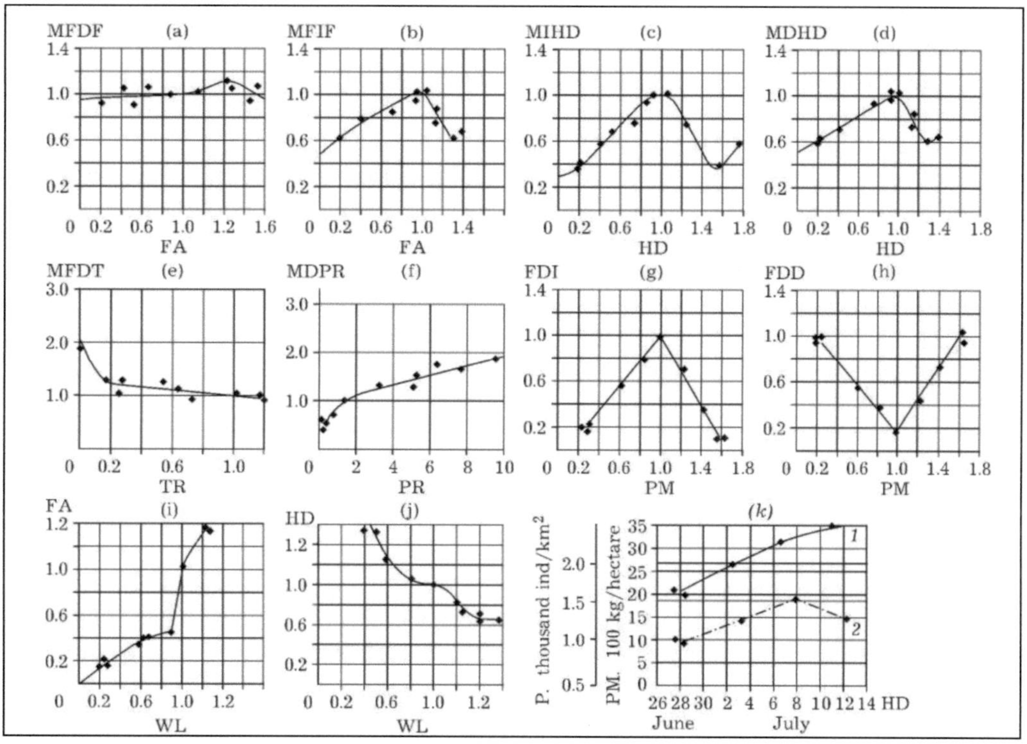

Fig. 4. Empiric graphs of the basic multipliers of the model.

From 1971 to 1989 on the territory of Kolpashevo raion of Tomsk oblast the amelioration was conducted. Our studies show that the amelioration greatly influences the bird population. It allowed us to single it out as the (A) variable. The impact of amelioration on the flow of the bird population decrease is described with the multiplier of the dependence of the flow of the population decrease on amelioration (MFDA).

The spatial-temporal structure and bird population density in the floodplain are determined by the yearly spring high waters. Their levels, time and duration influence the bird distribution over the types of habitats depending on their height situation and on the species composition of the ornitocomplexes. The hydrological regime in the model is set by the following variables: water level (WL), high water duration (HD), and flood-free area (FA). The low high waters cause a decrease in the bird population density due to the free distribution of the meadow and shrub communities over the territory of the floodplain, migration of the water-birds, whereas the high flood increases the bird population density. In the model migration is marked with the (MG) variable, which is a function of WL.

Dependence of migration on the water level is realized through the multiplier of dependence of MG on WL (MMGL). Dependences of FDI and FDD on MG are realized through the multipliers MIMG and MDMG respectively. The area of the flood-free territory determines such vital conditions as the presence of territory for nesting, trophic resources and death by predating. With high flood the birds concentrate on the flood-free area (FA), and the waterbirds inflow. The share of the chicks dying of predation increases, and the reproduction success is lowered by the overpopulating. Thus, there are dependencies of FDI and FDD on FA. In the model they are realized through the multiplier of dependence of FDI on FA (MFIF) and multiplier of dependence of FDD on FA (MFDF) (Figure 3 shows only some graphs of dependencies).

The FDI and FDD are influenced by the high water duration (HD), which is a function of the water level (WL). Its value modifies the FDI and FDD through the multipliers of dependence of FDI and FDD on HD (MIHD, MDHD) (see Fig. 3c,d).

A sharp drop in temperature (frosts) in the nesting period leads to the decrease in bird population due to the death of chicks and clutches. To consider the impact of temperature we introduced the variable of temperature regime (TR) into the model, which influenced the FDD through the multiplier of dependence of FDD on temperature (MFDT) (Fig. 3e).

One of the factors limiting the bird population is predation, which is especially dramatic during the nesting period. Under predation we mean an immediate effect on the birds of the preying animals and an indirect human influence that promotes it (depriving the nests their defense devices during hay-making, disclosing the nests and hatches by troubling, etc.). In the model predation is represented with the (PR) variable, which influences the FDD through the multiplier of dependence of FDD on PR (MDPR) (Fig. 3f). Predation depends to a certain degree on the flood-free area (FA), and, as was mentioned above, increases as the areas suitable for nesting decrease. This relation is expressed with the multiplier of dependence of PR on FA (MPRFA).

The model structure includes an auxiliary variable, phytomass of meadows (PM), which expresses the height of meadow vegetation and occupied area (Shepeleva, 1986). If its values are low or high, the bird population decreases. The parameter of phytomass of meadows (PM) influences the FDD through the multiplier of dependence of FDD on phytomass (MDPM), and on FDI, through the multiplier of dependence of FDI on phytomass (MIPM). It is known that the meadow productivity in the floodplain is influences by the duration of the flooding of the floodplain during high water [10]. In the model it is expressed through the multiplier of dependence of the phytomass increase on the high water duration (MPHD) (Fig. 3k).

Migrations conditioned by the character of spring high waters are typical of the birds inhabiting the floodplain. The larger is the number of birds claiming a nesting area, the greater is the influence of the spring high waters.

Duration and high level of the high waters result in an increase in waterbird population accompanied by the general tendency of decrease in the bird population density. Very low high waters decrease a share of water and near-water birds and cause migration of the dry-meadow species from the interfluve part into the floodplain. The optimal state of the bird population is observed in the years with high but short high waters. In the model the bird migration is represented as the variable (MG), and dependencies are expressed through the multipliers of FDI and FDD on migration (MIMG and MDMG).

2.4 Mathematic description of the basic processes

To describe the analytical structure of the model expressing the quantitative relations between the outside and auxiliary state variables we used the method of finite-difference approximation. The outside variables of the model PR, PM, TR, MG, WL are defined as the functions of time t. The population density of birds in any moment of time is defined as the density in the antecedent moment of time plus the density added due to *FDI* and minus the density decreasing due to *FDD* in the embraced period.

$$P^t = P^{t-1} + (TPP^{t-1,t} - TDP^{t-1,t}) \bullet \Delta t, \quad (1)$$

where P^t is population density of birds in the given moment of time, ind./km²; P^{t-1}, population density of birds in the
antecedent moment of time, ind./km²; $TPP^{t-1,t}$, flow of density increase on the time interval Δt = {t−1, t}, ind./km²; $TDP^{t-1,t}$, flow of density decrease on the interval Δt = {t−1, t}, ind./km²; Δt, time interval or time step.

The flow of density increase is a component of the loop of positive feedback. The basic flow of increase depends on the density (P) and normal flow of density increase (NFDI). However, the real flow of population density increase depends also on the conditions in the other parts of the system (anthropogenic factor, hydro-logical regime, etc.). The influence of the other parts of the system is introduced by the multipliers, which modify the basic flow of the increase in the density population of birds. Under normal conditions, which are considered a starting point in comparison, the multipliers should not change the basic flow of density increase and are equal to 1. Then they can acquire the values more or less than 1. The equation of FDI *is* as follows:

$$FDI^{t,t+1} = P^t \bullet NDFI \bullet MIAF \bullet MIFA \bullet MIHD \bullet MIMG \bullet MIPM, \quad (2)$$

where F $FDI^{t,t+1}$, is the flow of the density increase on the following interval, ind./km²; P^t, population density in the given moment, ind./km²; NFDI, normal flow of the density increase, 1/t; MIAF, the multiplier of dependence of the flow of increase on anthropogenic factors; MIFA, the multiplier of dependence of the flow of increase on the flood-free area; MIHD, the multiplier of dependence of the flow of increase on the high-water duration; MIMG, the multiplier of dependence of the flow of increase on migrations; MIPM, the multiplier of dependence of the flow increase on the phytomass.

The flow of the density decrease is a part of the reversed feedback. The basic flow of decrease equals the population density *P*, multiplied by the normal flow of the density decrease NFDD. The real flow of the decrease depends on the conditions in the other parts of the system. Amelioration, predation, hydrological and temperature regimes, and phytomass of meadows influence the FDD with the multipliers. The equation of FDD is as follows:

$$FDD^{t,t+1} = P^t \bullet NFDD \bullet MFDA \bullet MDHD \bullet MFDT \bullet MDPR \bullet MDPM \bullet MFDA \bullet MDMG, \quad (3)$$

where $FDD^{t,t+1}$ is the flow of the density decrease on the following interval, ind./km²; MFDA, the multiplier of dependence of the flow of decrease on the flood-free area; MDHD, the multiplier of dependence of the flow of decrease on the high-water duration; MFDT, the multiplier of dependence of the flow of decrease on temperature; MDPR, the multiplier of dependence of the flow of decrease on predation; MDPM, the multiplier of dependence of the flow of decrease on phytomass; MFD A, the multiplier of dependence of the flow of decrease on amelioration; MDMG, the multiplier of dependence of the flow of decrease on migration.

Anthropogenic factor in the model is included in the loop of the positive feedback with the level P. It is supposed that the variable AF is a monotonously increasing function of time. Thus, in the present moment of time it is determined by its value in the previous moment of time plus increase of FAFI (flow of the anthropogenic factor increase):

$$AF^{t} = AF^{t\text{-}1} + FAFI^{t\text{-}1,t} \bullet \Delta t, \tag{4}$$

where AF^{t}, $AF^{t\text{-}1}$ are the value of the anthropogenic factors in the present and previous moments of time; $FAFI^{t\text{-}1,t}$, the flow of the anthropogenic factor increase on the previous interval 1/t.

The flow of anthropogenic factor increase FAFI equals the basic flow or, in this case, normal flow of anthropogenic factor increase multiplied by the multiplier of dependence of FAFI on population density (MFPI). This multiplier in normal conditions is equal to 1 and begins to work in extreme situation, when the population density of birds drops sharply:

$$FAFI^{t,t\text{-}1} = NFAFI^{t\text{-}1} \bullet MFPI^{t}, \tag{5}$$

where $FAFI^{t,t\text{-}1}$ is the flow of the anthropogenic factor increase on the following interval *1/t;* NFAFI, the normal value of the anthropogenic factor *1/t;* $MFPI^{t}$, the value of the multiplier MFPI in the present moment of time.

Let us consider the mathematical description of the auxiliary variables: variable WL is the function of time and is given a priori: WL = F(t), variable TR is also a predictable function of time TR = $\Phi(t)$.

In the model the variable PR is determined by its value in normal conditions and state of two multipliers in the given moment of time, i.e.

$$PR^{t} = NPR \bullet MPRFA^{t} \bullet MPRAF^{t}, \tag{6}$$

where PR^{t} and NPR are the parameters of predation in the present moment of time and corresponding to the normal
conditions; $MPRFA^{t}$, $MPRAF^{t}$, the multipliers of dependence of predation on the flood-free area and anthropogenic factor.

The duration of the high-water and the flood-free area depend only on the water level:

$$HD = \Psi(WL), FA = \Omega(WL), MG = \Lambda(WL), \tag{7}$$

The variable A in the model is represented by the relative value Sa/S, where Sa is the area of the ameliorated lands, S, the area of Kolpashevskii raion.

The parameter of phytomass in the present moment of time is determined by its normal value multiplied by the multiplier of dependence of the meadow phytomass on the high-water duration (MPHD):

$$PM^{t} = NPM \bullet MPHD^{t}, \tag{8}$$

where PM^{t} is phytomass in the given moment of time t, centner/hectare; NPM, normal phytomass, centner/hectare;

$MPHD^t$, the multiplier of dependence of the phytomass on the high-water duration in the given moment of time.

The equation of the initial conditions is written in the following form: t_0 is the initial reference point; P_0, initial density of bird population, ind./km^2.

The values of FDI, FDD and FAFI necessary for the first calculation of the model are as follows:

$$FDI^{to,to+1} = Po^t \bullet NFDI \bullet MIFA \bullet MIHD \bullet MIAF \bullet MIPM, \quad (9)$$

$$FDD^{to,to+1} = Po \bullet NFDD \bullet MFDA \bullet MDHD \bullet MFDT \bullet MDPR \bullet MDPM \bullet MFDA, \quad (10)$$

$$FAFI^{to,to+1} = NFAFI \bullet MFPI^t. \quad (11)$$

In the system the following types of equations are used: the equation of stocks, of flows, auxiliary (describing the auxiliary variables), and of initial conditions.

When considering an interval of time, first, the equations of stocks are solved (it is believed that the equations of the initial conditions are solved before). Then obtained results are used in the equation of the flows. The auxiliary equations are introduced for ease and are solved immediately after solving the equations of stocks.

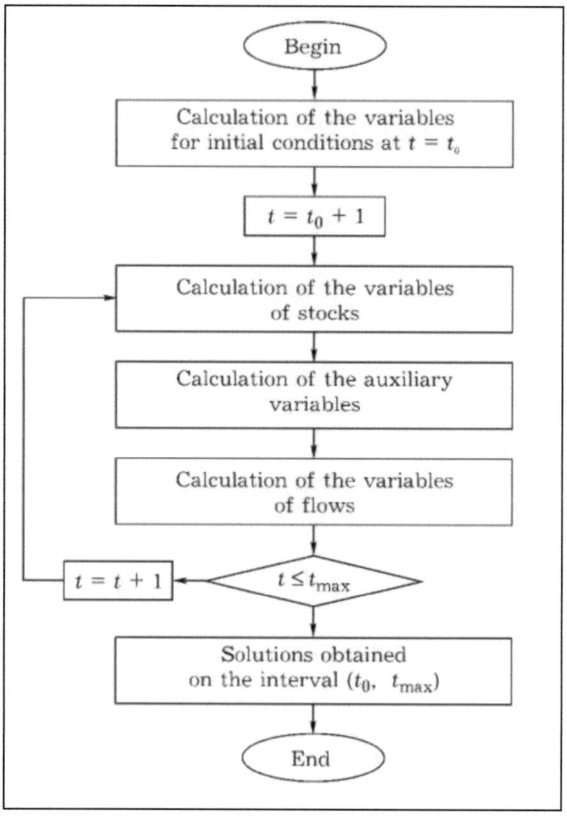

Fig. 5. Logical scheme of calculation of the system of equations.

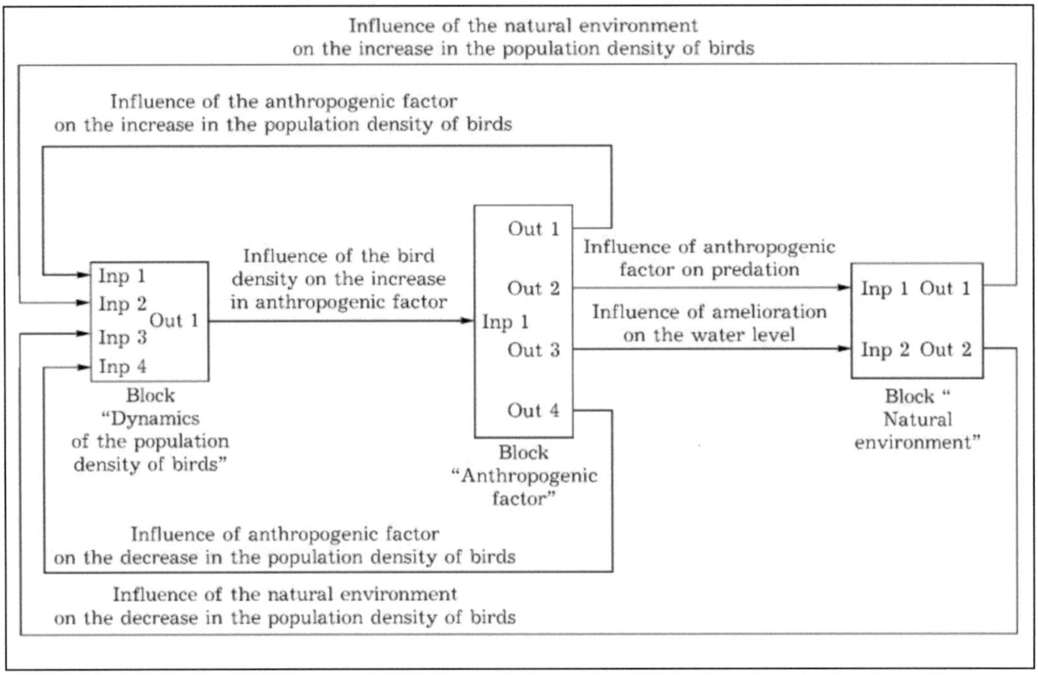

Fig. 6. Basic model of the dynamics of the bird population in the floodplain of the Ob realized with the help of MATLAB 5.2.1.

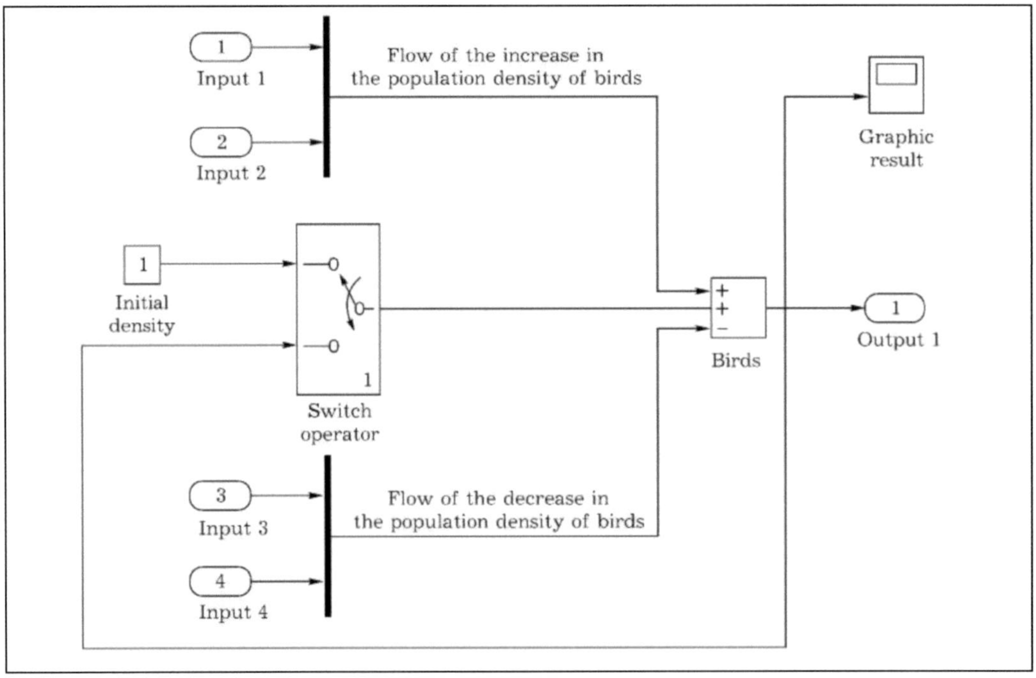

Fig. 7. Block "Dynamics of the bird population".

The general scheme of the equations is as follows:

$$P^{to} = Po; \tag{12}$$

$$FDI^{to,to+1} = Po \bullet NDFI \bullet MIAF \bullet MIFA \bullet MIHD \bullet MIMG \bullet MIPM; \tag{13}$$

$$FDD^{to,to+1} = Po \bullet NFDD \bullet MFDA \bullet MDHD \bullet MFDT \bullet MDPR \bullet MDPM \bullet MFDA; \tag{14}$$

$$FAFI^{to,to+1} = NFAFI \bullet MFPI^{t}; \tag{15}$$

$$AF^{to} = AFo; \tag{16}$$

$$P^{t} = P^{t-1} + (FDI^{t-1,t} - FDD^{t-1,t}) \bullet \Delta t; \tag{17}$$

$$FDI^{t,t+1} = P^{t} \bullet NFDI \bullet MIAF \bullet MIFA \bullet MIHD \bullet MIPM; \tag{18}$$

$$FDD^{t,t+1} = P^{t} \bullet NFDD \bullet MFDA \bullet MDHD \bullet MFDT \bullet MDPR \bullet MDPM \bullet MFDA \bullet MFMG; \tag{19}$$

$$AF^{t} = AF^{t-1} + FAFI^{t-1,t} \bullet \Delta t, \tag{20}$$

$$FAFI^{t,t+1} = NFAFI \bullet MFPI^{t}. \tag{21}$$

$$WL = F(t); \tag{22}$$

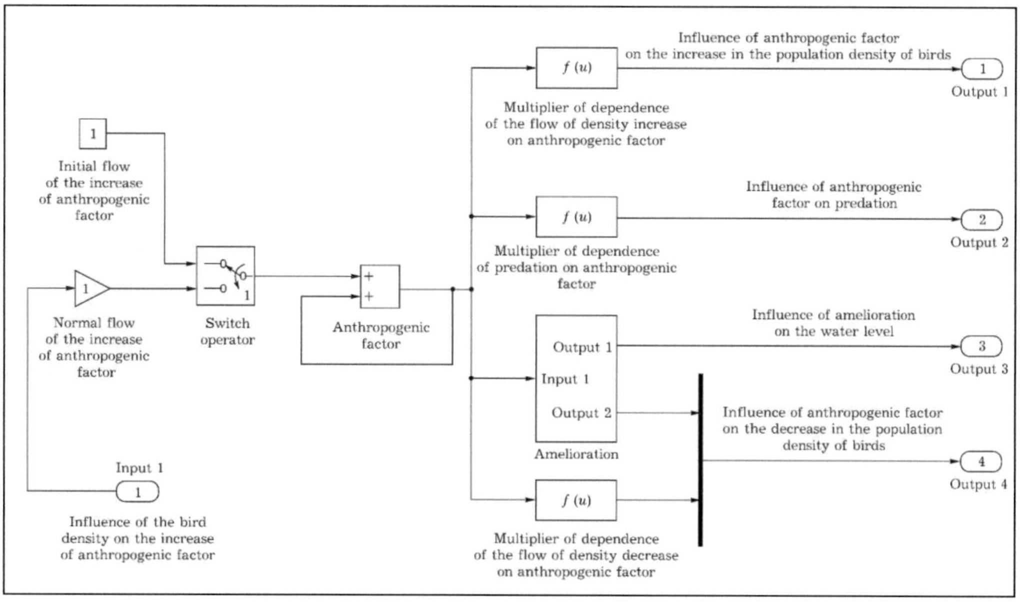

Fig. 8. Block "Anthropogenic factor".

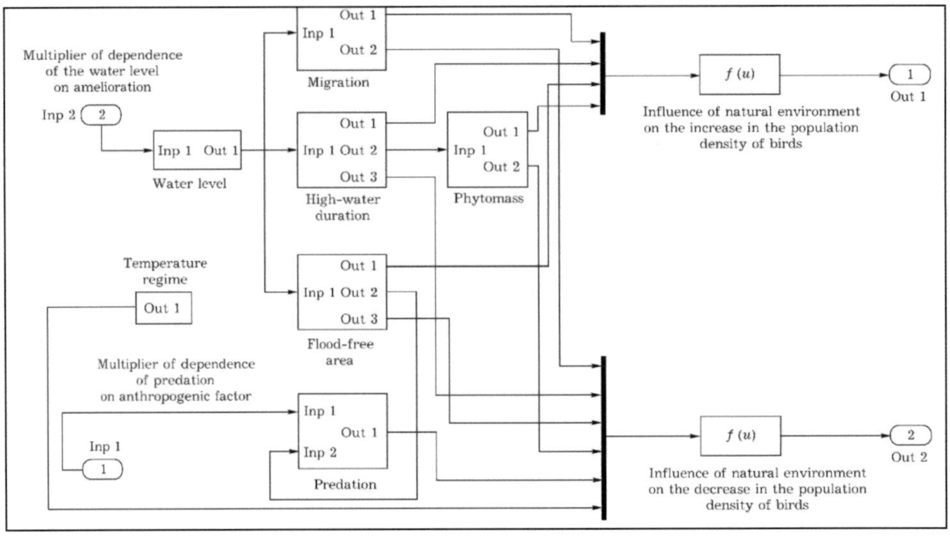

Fig. 9. Block "Natural envaronment".

$$HD = \Psi(WL); \tag{23}$$

$$FA = \Omega(WL); \tag{24}$$

$$TR = \Phi(t); \tag{25}$$

$$MG = \Lambda(WL); \tag{26}$$

$$PR^t = NPR \bullet MPRA^t \bullet MPRAF^t\ ; \tag{27}$$

$$A = \mathrm{f}(t); \tag{28}$$

$$PM^t = NPM \bullet MPHD^t\ . \tag{29}$$

the scheme (Fig. 4). The value of any multiplier is chosen automatically from the composed tables of multipliers for each year. The model is also realized with the help of MATLAB 5.2.1 software (D'yakonov et al., 2001, Gul'tyaev, 1999). This software was chosen because in includes the system of visual modeling SIMULINK. SIMULINK allows one to combine two basic approaches to the model creation, analytical and imitational, to consider nonlinear problems with continuous and discrete time. There is a library of blocks in SIMULINK, which are the means for developing and building the models (S-models). It is possible to create new elements and group them into blocks and to create hierarchic models. The S-models with hierarchic structure of unlimited nesting are possible to create. The results can be presented in both graphic and digital forms. The process of creating the S-models with SIMULINK consists in the constructing a scheme from the blocks preserved in the library SIMULINK. To make an S-model the Drag-and-Drop technology is used, which facilitates the work.

The Figs. 2-5 show an S-model with hierarchic structure and three basic blocks with a link between them: "Dynamics of the population density of birds", "Anthropogenic factor", and "Natural environment", each of them is a model of a lower level.

The quantitative presentation of the stock, flow and auxiliary variables is based on the experimental data on the real system. When determining the constants and variables, the conditions of 1977 were taken as the reference points, i.e., the state of the system is described as related to this year. The dynamics of the population density of birds is followed for 1977-2000, with spring-summer period considered within each year conditions. The step of modeling is accepted as equal to one year. All variables of the model are characterized with relative values.

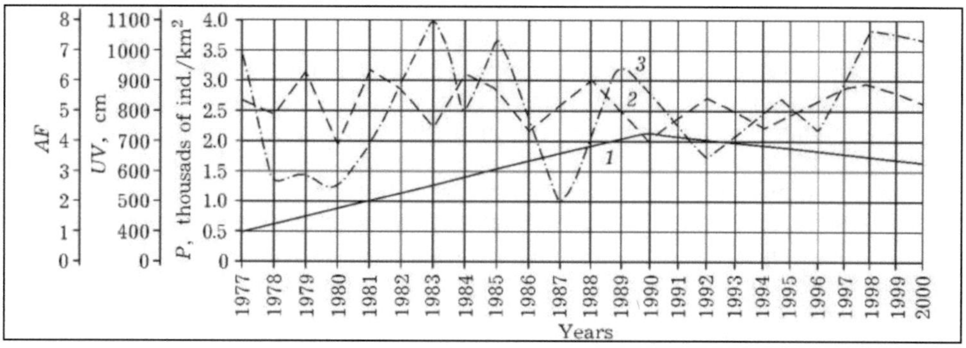

Fig. 10. Ratio of basic values characterizing the state of an ornithocomplex, as anthropogenic factor changes: 1, AF; 2, WL; 3, P.

2.4 The results of the modeling

The results obtained upon modeling represented on Fig. 6 confirmed the supposition that hydrological regime is the basic factor regulating the bird population. Analysis of the obtained data shows that the highest density of birds in the flood-plain of the middle Ob is determined by the high-waters (50% of provision), the lowest values of the density is determined by low high-waters (less than 75% of provision), while high high-waters give more than 25% of provision. The development of amelioration reduced the times of the flood-plain flooding, the canal cutting resulted in the increase in the number of swimming and near-water groups of birds in the first half of summer, and fast drying up of the flood-plain attracted birds of forbs meadows. However, the factor of disturbance, nest destruction, due to machinery working, resulted in a decrease in the population density of birds in 1990-2000 and change in the structure of the bird community on the whole.

3. Conclusion

The partial change in hydrological regime and industrial use of the flood-plain lands with moderate amelioration does not affect the dynamics of birds. If the area of amelioration grows to 50% of the total area of the flood-plain, the existing ecosystem will be destroyed in the lowest high-waters (75% of provision and less) and will not be able to restore for 4 years. It is necessary to control the scale of amelioration and not to allow the system to begin irrevocable destruction.

The built model is of theoretical and applied character. The structure of the model can be used as basic for biotic components of the flood-plain ecosystem when predicting the basic tendencies of their behavior and monitoring. It is built for the component which plays an indication role. Introduction of certain changes into the parameters of water regime can help in determining the upper and lower limits. When they are passed, the flood-plain ecosystem begins to change in general.

For conservation of ecosystem values in the Ob river floodplain the following aspects should considered:

- Preferably land use types with low impact should be developed: (eco)-tourism, recreation, trade, small scale agriculture (diary, pastures)
- Preservation an equally balanced land use between natural and semi-natural ecosystems, given the ecological potentials
- Hay-making is most suitable land use for wet meadows
- Land reclamation development should focus on high floodplain parts
- Development of health-improving recreation.

The conservation of natural resources is achieved by combination of two units. The first unit provides annual observation of high water regime of Middle Ob flood-land in comparison with long-term data. Second unit is human activity management, which includes the preparation of recommendations for the main resource users: administrators, farmers, hunters and fisherman. It is expected that by the management measures to be developed within this scheme the effective land use may increase with up to 60%. The concept hydro-ecological monitoring of the Middle Ob River floodplain has been developed on a platform for the organization of scientifically based, regionally adapted, and ecologically regulated nature management.

Author to express one's thanks of professor Tomsky State University, PhD A.M. Adam for data presentation and cause in hard expedites.

4. References

Adam A. M. & Bolotnov, V. P., (1982). *Analysis of Influence of the Spring High Water over the Structure of the Bird Population in the Floodplain of the Middle Ob for the Purpose of Nature Protection*. Deposited in VINITI No. 1040-82 [in Russian].

Adam A. M., Bolotnov V. P., and Sekisova S. E., (2001), *inProblems of Geography of Siberia* .TGU, Tomsk, , Issue 24, pp. 211-218 [in Russian].

Adam A. M. and Mamin R. G., *Natural Resources and Ecological Safety of West Siberia* (POLTEKS, Moscow, 2000) [in Russian].

Adam A. M., Novoselov A. L., and Chenurnykh N. V. (2000), *Ecological Problems of the Regions of Russia* (VINITI, Moscow,) [in Russian

Bolotnov V. P. , Sekisova,S. E., and Adam A. M., (2001). "Environment of Siberia, the Far East, and the Arctic," in *Selected Paper Presented at the International Conference ESFA 2001, Tomsk, Russia* (International Research Center of Environmental Physics and Ecology, Russian Academy of Science, 2001), pp. 348-361.

Gul'tyaev A. K., (1999) MATLAB 5.2.1. Imitation Modeling inWindows: Practical Manual (KORONA print, Sankt-Petersburg) [in Russian].

D'yakonov V. P. ,Abramenkova I. V., and Kruglov V. V., (2001). MATLAB 5.2.1 with Bump Packs (Knowledge, Moscow) [in Russian].

Forrester J., (1978).*World Dynamics* (Nauka, Moscow) [Russian translation].

Ravkin, Yu. S., (1984). *Spatial Organization of the Bird Population in the Forest Zone (West and Central Siberia)* (Nauka, Siberian Branch, Novosibirsk,) [in Russian].

Shepeleva L. F. (1986), Ekologiya, No. 2, 3.

Vartapetov D. G., (1984). *Birds of the Taiga Interfluves of the West Siberia* (Nauka, Siberian Branch, Novosibirsk,) [in Russian].

Yudkin V. A., Ravkin Yu. S., Blinov V. N., et al., (1987). *Spatial-Temporal Dynamics of the Fauna (Birds and Small Mammals)* (Nauka, Siberian Branch, Novosibirsk,) [in Russian].

5

Data Reduction for Water Quality Modelling, Vaal Basin

Bloodless Dzwairo[1], George M. Ochieng'[1], Maupi E. Letsoalo[1] and Fredrick A.O. Otieno[2]
[1]*Tshwane University of Technology*
[2]*Durban University of Technology*
South Africa

1. Introduction

Constructing models, comparing their predictions with observations, and trying to improve them, constitutes the core of the scientific approach to understanding complex systems like large river basins (Even et al., 2007). These processes require manipulation of huge historical data sets, which might be available in different formats and from various stakeholders. The challenge is then to first pre-process the data to similar lengths, with minimal loss of integrity, before manipulating it as per initial objectives. In the Upper and Middle Vaal Water Management Areas (WMAs) of the Vaal River, bounded by Vaal dam outlet and Bloemhof dam inlet, the overall objective of on-going research is to model surface raw water quality variability in order to predict cost of treatment to potable water standard. This paper reports on part of the overall research. Its objective was to show how a huge and non-consistent water quality data set could be downsized to manageable aspects with minimal loss of integrity. Within that scope, challenges were also highlighted.

One of the more important forms of knowledge extraction is the identification of the more relevant inputs. When identified, they may be treated as a reduced input for further manipulation. In water quality data analysis, data collection, cleaning and pre-processing are often the most time-consuming phases. All inputs and targets have to be transferred directly from instrumentation or from other media, tagged and arranged in a matrix of vectors with the same lengths (Alfassi et al., 2005). If vectors have outliers and/or missing values these have to be identified for correction or to be discarded. More complex mathematical correlations are sometimes employed to identify redundant, co-linear inputs, or inputs with little information content (Alfassi et al., 2005).

Sources and sinks of variables in hydrodynamics, also known as forcing functions, are the cause of change in water quality (Martin et al., 1998). To capture intermediate scale processes that are spotty in spatial extent, extensive sampling and averaging of the calibration data over sufficient spatial scales is done to capture that condition over time. Although many water constituents are non-conservative in nature, a few conservative ones that approach ideal behaviour under limited conditions, could be used for modelling and calibration.

The study area is a major focus of modelling and pollution tracing in the Vaal basin, South Africa, (Dzwairo et al., 2010b, Cloot and Roux, 1997, DWAF, 2007, Gouws and Coetzee, 1997, Naicker et al., 2003, Pieterse et al., 1987, Stevn and Toerien, 1976, Dzwairo et al., 2010a, Dzwairo and Otieno, 2010, Herold et al., 2006).
Data sets spanning many years have been collected by various stakeholders including the Department of Water Affairs (DWA) and Water Boards which treat bulk water for potable use. For management of the basin as a whole these data sets come handy but the major challenge is collating them into uniform and useable data, while noting that the different stakeholders monitor selected parts of the basin for their own specific purposes. Some sampling points might be dropped off or new points picked up as emerging pollution threats require tracing and monitoring in order to mitigate effects. Still a useable data set has to be constructed to monitor pollution and other threats, in addition to informing and alerting decision makers regarding environmental and human health issues. This paper shows how inconsistent and scattered data sets from 13 monitoring points were pre-treated and downsized to SO_4^{2-} inter-relationships. SO_4^{2-} is a very important parameter in surface water quality variability in this region because of the existence of gold and coal mining activities. Threats from acid mine drainage are real.

2. Study area

The study area as indicated in Fig. 1 shows spatial relationships of the sampling points located on VR and its tributaries as follows: B1-B10 on Blesbokspruit River (BR); K10-K10, K6-K25 and K9-K19 on Klip River (KR); K12-N8 on Natalspruit River (NR); K1-R2 on Withokspruit River, which is a tributary of Rietspruit River (RR); K3-R3 on another tributary of RR; K2-R1 and K4-R4 on RR; S1-S1 and S4-S2 on Suikerbosrant River (SR); and V7-VRB37 and V9-VRB24 on Vaal River (VR).

3. Methods and materials

Water quality data from 13 surface raw water quality monitoring points covering the period 1 January 2003 to 30 November 2009 was manipulated to remove limits of detection as well as gaps in sampling periods. An example of raw data is presented in Table 1 for sampling points Y and Z and for only Chl-α, COD, EC and DOC. The extracted data sample covered 5 July 2004 to 26 July 2004.
Using the list of variables in Table 2, comparisons among points entailed obtaining or converting the raw data to match sampling periods among the points. Although there are several interpolation techniques, cubic interpolation was chosen for the time-series data set because the method is shape-preserving. Interpolation created date-interpolated daily data using Matlab R2009b.

3.1 Manipulating data falling below or above detectable limits

Data that was above limit (e.g. $500 < x$) was assumed to be one magnitude higher than the given value, whereas that which was reported as below detectable limit (e.g. $x < 1.1$) was multiplied by 0.75 to give absolute values that could be manipulated as normal data (Ochse, 2007).

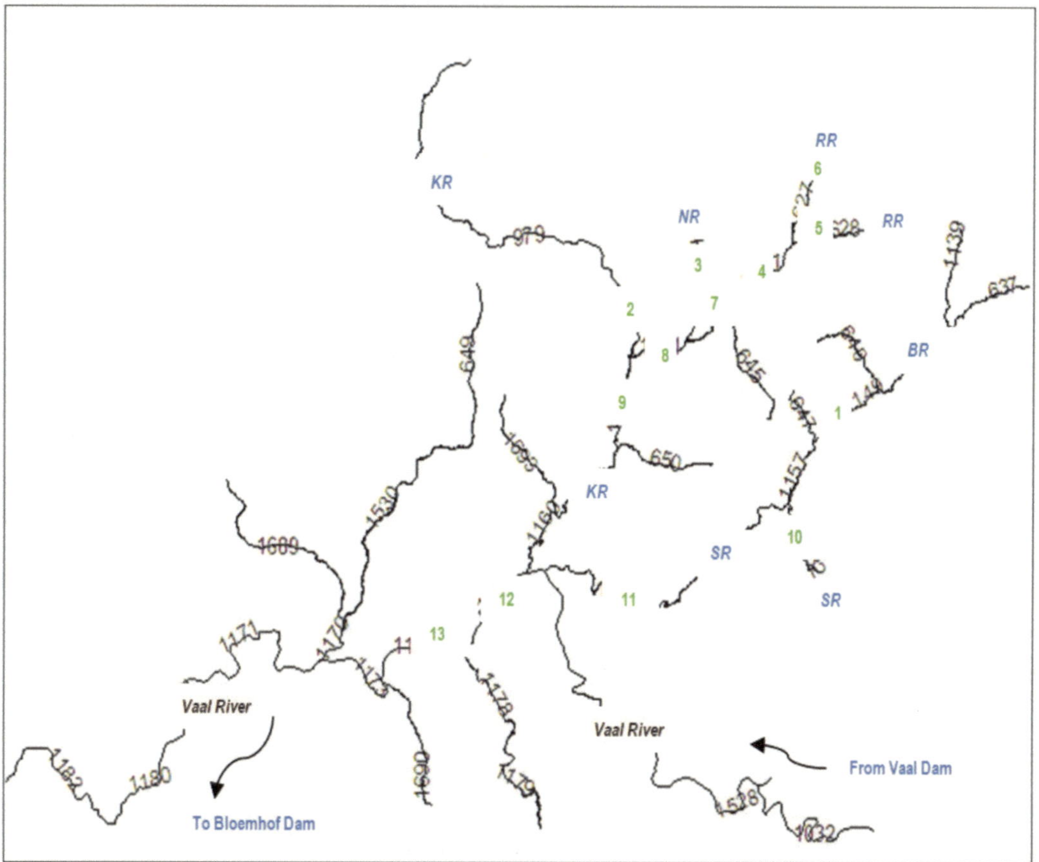

B1-B10	K10-K10	K12-N8	K1-R2	K2-R1	K3-R3	K4-R4	K6-K25	K9-K19	S1-S1	S4-S2	V7-VRB37	V9-VRB24
1	2	3	4	5	6	7	8	9	10	11	12	13

Fig. 1. Monitoring points in study area bounded, by the two dams.

Date	Chl-α	COD	EC	DOC	Chl-α	COD	EC	DOC
Sampling point	Y				Z			
5-Jul-04					17.00	19.00	105.00	4.90
7-Jul-04	8.10	20.00	80.00	8.30				
12-Jul-04					5.60	19.00	99.00	6.10
19-Jul-04					8.30	21.00	96.00	
21-Jul-04	74.00	27.00	88.00	8.70				
26-Jul-04					6.90	24.00	97.00	5.50

Table 1. Raw data for monitoring points Y and Z.

Parameter	Unit	Description	Abbreviation
so42_	mg/L	sulphate	SO_4^{2-}
cn_	mg/L	cyanide	CN^-
ec	mS/m	conductivity	EC
do	mg/L	dissolved oxygen	DO
fc	CFU/100mL	faecal coliforms	Fc
Hg	µg/L	mercury	Hg
Cl_	mg/L	chloride	Cl^-
f_	mg/L	fluoride	F^-
no2_	mg/L	nitrite	NO_2^-
no3_	mg/L	nitrate	NO_3^-
Low_Hg	µg/L	low mercury	Hg
Mn	mg/L	manganese	Mn
pH	-	-	-
po43_	mg/L	phosphate	PO_4^{3-}
s	mg/L	sulphur	S
ss	mg/L	suspended solids	SS
Temp	^oC	temperature	-
T_Silica	mg/L	total silica	-
Turb	NTU	turbidity	-
nh4_	mg/L	ammonium	NH_4^+
Chla	µg/L	chlorophyll -α	Chl-α
cod	mg/L	chemical oxygen demand	COD
doc	mg/L	dissolved organic carbon	DOC
Mo	mg/L	molybdenum	Mo
Si	mg/L	silicone	Si
p	mg/L	phosphorus	P
Fe	mg/L	iron	Fe

Table 2. Parameters under consideration.

3.2 Matlab codes for cubic interpolation

3.2.1 Cubic interpolation

Data interpolation is an application based on underlying geometric algorithms. Data may be uniform, that is, sampling occurs over uniform intervals or it may be scattered, that is, sampling occurs over irregular intervals. When the sample data is scattered, the interpolation techniques use a triangulation-based approach as a basis for computing interpolated values. Table 3 provides a Matlab code for date-interpolating a single column. To interpolate many columns, the single-column code was adjusted as in Table 4.

3.2.2 Challenges during interpolation

An empty cell at any position of the matrix, for example a missing date or value, returned an error similar to the one in Table 5.

```
% Load the data with lots of missing dates. Note that in this example
% missing dates are not represented by NaN but are left out completely

>>[data,textdata] = xlsread('book.xls');

% Convert the text date to date numbers (you may have to change the date
% format depending on how your dates appear in Excel)

>>dates = datenum(textdata,'mm/dd/yyyy');

% Plot the data

>>plot(dates,data,'LineStyle','none','Marker','o')

% Show the x axis as a date

>>datetick('x')

% Create a new date series starting at the first date in dates and
% ending at the last but with every date in-between

>>newDates = dates(1):dates(end);

% Interpolate to find the missing data

>>newData = interp1(dates,data,newDates,'cubic');

% Convert the date numbers to strings and then to cell arrays

>>stringDates = cellstr(datestr(newDates));

% Combine the dates and the data

>>outputData = [stringDates, num2cell(newData')];

% Write the data to Excel
>>xlswrite('outbook.xls',outputData);
```

Table 3. Coding for interpolating a single column.

```
>>newDates = dates(1):dates(end);

%Run the tic toc (3 instructions below at once by copying and pasting, it should give elapsed time as eg 0.305720 seconds)

>>tic
newColumnData = interp1(dates,columnData,newDates,'cubic');
toc

Elapsed time is 0.305720 seconds.

%In a new figure, plot both the new data and the existing data

figure

>>plot(newDates,newColumnData,dates,columnData,'LineStyle','none','Marker','o')

%Change date format to years

>>datetick('x')

%Convert the date numbers to strings and then to cell arrays

>> stringDates = cellstr(datestr(newDates));

%Combine the dates and the data

>>outputData = [stringDates, num2cell(newColumnData)];

Write the data back to Excel
```

Table 4. Code for interpolating many columns.

```
>tic
newColumnData = interp1(dates,columnData,newDates,'cubic');
toc

Warning: NaN found in Y, interpolation at undefined values will result in undefined values.
In interp1 at 178

Warning: All data points with NaN in their value will be ignored.
In polyfun\private\chckxy at 103
In pchip at 59
In interp1 at 283

Elapsed time is 0.042557 seconds.
```

Table 5. NaN.

Another common error was that of a misplaced decimal point or full stop during data capture (Table 6). Matlab would not be able to manipulate this entry for interpolation because it was not a value. A duplicated or non-formatted date would also present an error that would require debugging before a complete interpolated data set could be obtained. These, among other similar errors, required manual debugging through a whole data set, each a 2526 x28 matrix. With a perfect matrix, an interpolation took a fraction of a second.

Measured parameter	Measured parameter
72.00	0.29
3.75.0	0.31
70.00	0.29

Table 6. A highlighted error arising from data capture.

The 13 sampling points' data was interpolated to the same lengths from 1 January 2003 to 30 November 2009, for the 27 parameters, and then combined into one file for processing using Stata, in order to reduce the matrix. Analysis used case-wise correlation, factor analysis, multivariate linear regression and one-way ANOVA.

4. Results

Initial inspection indicated that the data exhibited gross temporal inconsistency. Sampling dates did not match, in addition to missing values. Table 7 shows the interpolated data for points Z and Y for 5 to 21 July 2004.

Date	Chl-α	COD	EC	DOC	*Chl-α*	*COD*	*EC*	*DOC*
Sampling point		Y				Z		
5-Jul-04					*17.00*	*19.00*	*105.00*	*4.90*
6-Jul-04					*16.26*	*19.00*	*104.74*	*4.97*
7-Jul-04	8.10	20.00	80.00	8.30	*14.58*	*19.00*	*104.04*	*5.14*
8-Jul-04	8.80	20.13	80.12	8.32	*12.36*	*19.00*	*103.06*	*5.37*
9-Jul-04	10.80	20.35	80.44	8.35	*9.97*	*19.00*	*101.92*	*5.63*
10-Jul-04	13.93	20.66	80.94	8.37	*7.80*	*19.00*	*100.77*	*5.86*
11-Jul-04	18.01	21.04	81.59	8.39	*6.21*	*19.00*	*99.75*	*6.03*
12-Jul-04	22.87	21.50	82.33	8.41	*5.60*	*19.00*	*99.00*	*6.10*
13-Jul-04	28.35	22.01	83.15	8.44	*5.75*	*19.07*	*98.41*	*6.09*
14-Jul-04	34.28	22.56	84.00	8.46	*6.14*	*19.26*	*97.82*	*6.06*
15-Jul-04	40.48	23.16	84.85	8.48	*6.66*	*19.54*	*97.26*	*6.01*
16-Jul-04	46.79	23.78	85.67	8.51	*7.24*	*19.88*	*96.76*	*5.96*
17-Jul-04	53.04	24.43	86.41	8.54	*7.76*	*20.25*	*96.36*	*5.90*
18-Jul-04	59.05	25.08	87.06	8.58	*8.15*	*20.64*	*96.10*	*5.85*
19-Jul-04	64.66	25.73	87.56	8.61	*8.30*	*21.00*	*96.00*	*5.80*
20-Jul-04	69.70	26.38	87.88	8.65	*8.22*	*21.39*	*96.03*	*5.75*
21-Jul-04	74.00	27.00	88.00	8.70	*8.02*	*21.86*	*96.12*	*5.70*

Table 7. Date-interpolated data for monitoring point Y and Z.

A full length raw data set for Z (2003 to 2009), shown in Fig. 2, was interpolated and graphed in Fig. 3, for only 4 out of the 27 variables, that is, Chl-α, COD, EC and DOC, to reduce congestion and enhance clarity to the cubic interpolation concept.

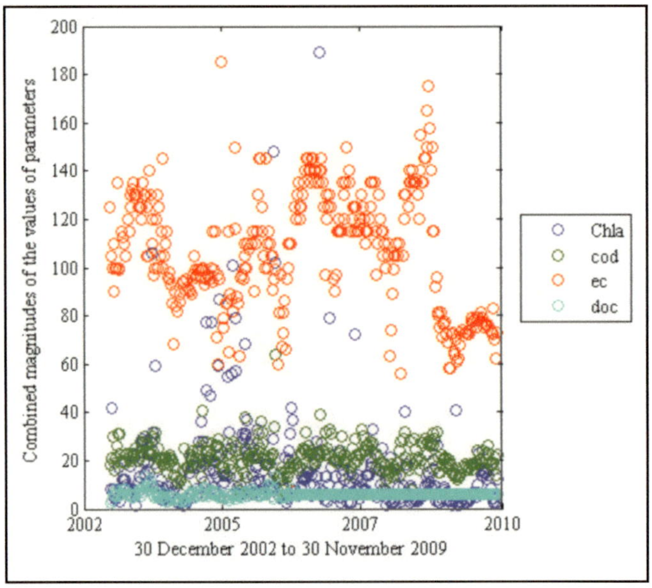

Fig. 2. Monitoring point (Z)'s raw input data.

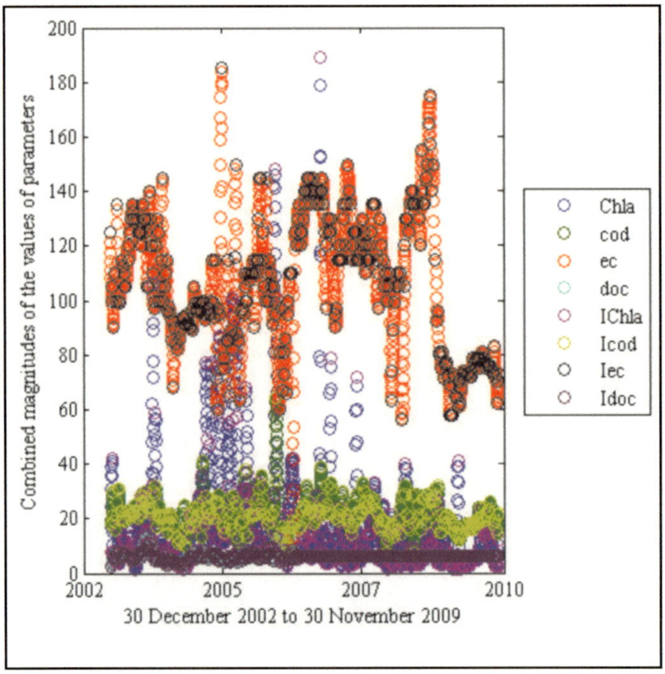

Fig. 3. Monitoring point (Z)'s cubic-interpolated data.

Whereas Fig. 2 showed a legend with 4 data sets, Fig. 3's legend included the interpolated data, colour-coded for clarity. IChla, Icod, Iec and Idoc (IChl-α, ICOD, IEC and IDOC) represented the interpolations of the 4 variables used. Daily interpolation was chosen for this study because after interpolation, any other data interval, for example monthly or yearly variation, could be computed without repeating the time-consuming interpolation process.

4.1 Case-wise correlation analysis

Although case-wise correlation analysis indicated that SO_4^{2-} had a significant linear relationship with all variables except DO, it was strongly positively correlated with EC (0.8720), Cl^- (0.7273), S (0.9053) and Mn (0.4779). It was strongly negatively correlated with pH (-0.5380). Table 8 provides detailed output.

4.2 Factor analysis

The major aim of factor analysis is to orderly simplify a large number of interrelated measures to a few representative constructs or factors (Ho, 2006). The 27 variables were subjected to this technique for that reason, to reduce the data set. The data was collapsed into 3 latent constructs (Table 9 and Table 10).

Their Eigen values were noted to be 5.82041, 2.62148 and 2.12070. Factors 1 and 3 were cross-loaded thus Table 11 was constructed because DOC appeared to be conceptually relevant to Factor 3 (physical parameters) while cod remained relevant to Factor 1 (conductivity related). Factor 2 incorporated unique variables which were not cross-loaded into any of the other factors but for which no good common description could readily be assigned. Variables which could not be placed into any of the 3 factors were also deleted from Table 11, effectively reducing the variables, (see Ho, 2006).

	cn_	ec	do	fc	Hg	Cl_	f_
cn_	1.0000						
ec	0.0908*	1.0000					
do	-0.0106	0.0112*	1.0000				
fc	0.0014	0.0217*	0.0141*	1.0000			
Hg	-0.0523*	-0.1087*	0.0110	-0.0594*	1.0000		
Cl_	0.0783*	0.8699*	0.0039	0.0062	-0.0192*	1.0000	
f_	-0.0053	0.1819*	-0.0404*	0.0239*	-0.1666*	0.0259*	1.0000
no2_	-0.0708*	-0.1365*	0.1629*	0.0809*	0.1839*	-0.0458*	-0.0787*
no3_	-0.0628*	0.1223*	0.1033*	0.0658*	0.1916*	0.0876*	0.0115*
so42_	0.0961*	0.8720*	-0.0064	0.0288*	-0.2013*	0.7273*	0.2798*
Low_Hg	-0.0009	0.2998*	0.0450*	-0.0260*	-0.2516*	0.1762*	0.3496*
Mn	0.0147*	0.3936*	-0.0102	0.0668*	-0.1783*	0.1815*	0.2316*
pH	0.0290*	-0.4242*	0.0481*	-0.0856*	0.1456*	-0.1382*	-0.3480*
po43_	-0.0367*	-0.0858*	0.0283*	0.0418*	0.1250*	-0.0193*	-0.0683*
s	0.0807*	0.8861*	-0.0176*	0.0226*	-0.1974*	0.7435*	0.2593*
ss	-0.0302*	-0.2024*	-0.0336*	0.0138	0.0350*	-0.1852*	-0.0387*
Temp	-0.0120*	-0.0369*	-0.0424*	0.0201*	-0.0948*	-0.0544*	0.0481*
T_Silica	-0.0343*	0.1377*	-0.0693*	0.0422*	-0.1797*	-0.0889*	0.2674*
Turb	-0.0434*	-0.2525*	-0.0862*	0.0284*	-0.0893*	-0.2899*	0.0213*
nh4_	0.0267*	0.3493*	-0.0444*	0.2118*	-0.0952*	0.2378*	0.1670*
Chla	0.0039	0.0918*	0.1341*	-0.0320*	0.0218	0.1432*	0.0204*
cod	-0.0546*	-0.2345*	-0.0950*	0.0367*	-0.2205*	-0.1833*	-0.1091*
doc	-0.0661*	-0.4022*	-0.0080	-0.0702*	0.0607*	-0.2446*	-0.1826*
Mo	-0.0172*	-0.0089	0.0123*	0.0099	-0.0743*	0.0042	0.1316*
Si	-0.0335*	0.1380*	-0.0697*	0.0420*	-0.1789*	-0.0880*	0.2640*
p	-0.0621*	-0.1345*	0.0126*	0.0885*	0.1870*	-0.0679*	-0.0701*

Fe	-0.0026	0.2262*	-0.0275*	-0.0253*	-0.1989*	0.0694*	0.1825*

	no2_	no3_	so42_	Low_Hg	Mn	pH	po43_
no2_	1.0000						
no3_	0.2349*	1.0000					
so42_	-0.1744*	0.0673*	1.0000				
Low_Hg	0.0043	-0.0671*	0.3492*	1.0000			
Mn	-0.1449*	0.1893*	0.4779*	0.3674*	1.0000		
pH	0.2318*	-0.3675*	-0.5380*	-0.2211*	-0.6252*	1.0000	
po43_	0.1689*	0.1384*	-0.1203*	-0.0227*	-0.0982*	0.1494*	1.0000
s	-0.1950*	0.1345*	0.9053*	0.3696*	0.4557*	-0.5663*	-0.1342*
ss	0.1240*	-0.0633*	-0.1845*	-0.0333*	-0.1029*	0.1072*	0.0077
Temp	0.0630*	-0.0771*	-0.0238*	0.0534*	0.0040	-0.0540*	-0.0178*
T_Silica	-0.0896*	0.2473*	0.3091*	0.0611*	0.4608*	-0.5813*	-0.0378*
Turb	-0.0204*	-0.1152*	-0.1688*	0.0356*	-0.0306*	-0.0228*	-0.0251*
nh4_	-0.0580*	0.2917*	0.4024*	0.1017*	0.4185*	-0.5250*	-0.0108
Chla	-0.0342*	-0.1310*	0.0877*	0.1332*	-0.1281*	0.2824*	-0.0399*
cod	0.0019	-0.0659*	-0.2149*	-0.0550*	-0.1509*	0.1585*	0.0490*
doc	0.1798*	-0.1293*	-0.4339*	-0.0791*	-0.3741*	0.5086*	0.1084*
Mo	0.3506*	0.0616*	-0.0121*	0.2235*	-0.0400*	0.0553*	0.0226*
Si	-0.0888*	0.2485*	0.3090*	0.0569*	0.4613*	-0.5798*	-0.0380*
p	0.2196*	0.2139*	-0.1467*	-0.0735*	-0.1026*	0.1271*	0.3997*
Fe	-0.0672*	0.0155*	0.3688*	0.2579*	0.3347*	-0.3531*	-0.0490*

	s	ss	Temp	T_Silica	Turb	nh4_	Chla
s	1.0000						
ss	-0.1908*	1.0000					
Temp	-0.0181*	0.1191*	1.0000				
T_Silica	0.2816*	-0.0421*	0.0921*	1.0000			
Turb	-0.1748*	0.4495*	0.1172*	0.1098*	1.0000		
nh4_	0.3914*	-0.0889*	-0.0171*	0.4106*	-0.0744*	1.0000	
Chla	0.0871*	-0.0764*	0.1166*	-0.2724*	-0.0942*	-0.0613*	1.0000
cod	-0.2205*	0.0726*	0.0453*	-0.0157*	0.1842*	-0.1168*	0.2257*
doc	-0.4562*	0.2118*	0.0307*	-0.2426*	0.2224*	-0.3000*	0.1317*
Mo	-0.0146*	0.1181*	0.0840*	-0.0464*	-0.0400*	-0.0398*	-0.0106
Si	0.2797*	-0.0429*	0.0911*	0.9992*	0.1082*	0.4096*	-0.2750*
p	-0.1633*	0.0182*	0.0381*	0.0554*	-0.0311*	-0.0118*	-0.0532*
Fe	0.2761*	-0.0276*	0.0350*	0.3531*	0.1083*	0.3579*	-0.0873*

	cod	doc	Mo	Si	p	Fe
cod	1.0000					
doc	0.5436*	1.0000				
Mo	0.0334*	0.0810*	1.0000			
Si	-0.0168*	-0.2441*	-0.0451*	1.0000		
p	0.0381*	0.1008*	0.0430*	0.0570*	1.0000	
Fe	-0.0369*	-0.1302*	-0.0176*	0.3519*	-0.0767*	1.0000

Table 8. Case-wise correlation analysis from CN to Fe.

Factor	Eigenvalue	Difference	Proportion	Cumulative
Factor1	5.82041	3.19894	0.5510	0.5510
Factor2	2.62148	0.50078	0.2482	0.7992
Factor3	2.12070	1.29933	0.2008	1.0000

Table 9. Factor analysis/correlation.

Variable	Factor1	Factor2	Factor3	Uniqueness
cn_				0.9977
ec	0.6603			0.4260
do				0.9881
fc				0.9666
Hg	-0.4816			0.7544
Cl_	0.7176			0.1997
f_				0.9921
no2_		0.5019		0.7768
no3_		0.8243		0.3693
so42_	0.8206			0.2361
Low_Hg	0.6888			0.6217
Mn		0.7274		0.5483
pH		-0.4832		0.6090
po43_				0.9908
s	0.8318			0.2598
ss			0.8475	0.3456
Temp			0.3315	0.8679
T_Silica		0.6666		0.2333
Turb			0.8739	0.2462
nh4_		0.7095		0.5037
Chla				0.8587
cod	0.6745		0.4000	0.5787
doc	0.7211		0.3964	0.4579
Mo	0.4133			0.8677
Si		0.6684		0.2326
p				0.9023
Fe			0.6249	0.6065

(blanks represent abs(loading)<.33)

Table 10. Rotated factor loadings (pattern matrix) and unique variances.

EC and Cl^-, together with FC, Hg, F^-, NO_3^-, Low_Hg, Mn, pH, S, SS, Temp, T_Silica, Turb, NH_4^+, COD, Si, P and Fe, were good predictors for SO_4^{2-} concentration, and the fitted model explains 82% of the total variation (Table 12).

4.3 One-way ANOVA

Table 13 gives the means and standard deviations for each of the sampling points over the entire sampling period.

Comparison of SO_4^{2-} by sample_ID (Table 14) showed that K6-K25, K9-K19, V7-VRB37 and V9-VRB24; K10-K10 and K3-R3; and K2-R1 and K4-R4, were statistically similar. The mean values of $SO_4^{2-}$of the remaining sampling points were significantly different.

Variable	Factor1	Factor2	Factor3	Uniqueness
ec	0.6603			0.4260
Hg	-0.4816			0.7544
Cl_	0.7176			0.1997
no2_		0.5019		0.7768
no3_		0.8243		0.3693
so42_	0.8206			0.2361
Low_Hg	0.6888			0.6217
Mn		0.7274		0.5483
pH		-0.4832		0.6090
s	0.8318			0.2598
ss			0.8475	0.3456
Temp			0.3315	0.8679
T_Silica		0.6666		0.2333
Turb			0.8739	0.2462
nh4_		0.7095		0.5037
cod	0.6745			0.5787
doc			0.3964	0.4579
Mo	0.4133			0.8677
Si		0.6684		0.2326
Fe			0.6249	0.6065

(blanks represent abs(loading)<.33)

Table 11. "Clean" factors.

Source	SS	df	MS		
				Number of obs =	7578
				F(26, 7551) =	1330.85
Model	122818707	26	4723796.43	Prob > F =	0.0000
Residual	26802038.4	7551	3549.46873	R-squared =	0.8209
				Adj R-squared =	0.8203
Total	149620746	7577	19746.7	Root MSE =	59.577

so42_	Coef.	Std. Err.	t	P>|t|	[95% Conf.	Interval]
cn_	-22.32404	18.52691	-1.20	0.228	-58.64195	13.99386
ec	.3736444	.0227941	16.39	0.000	.3289616	.4183271
do	.0131522	.0926716	0.14	0.887	-.1685098	.1948143
fc	.0000566	.0000189	2.99	0.003	.0000195	.0000938
Hg	-89.09861	11.70687	-7.61	0.000	-112.0473	-66.14989
Cl_	.7573463	.042237	17.93	0.000	.67455	.8401425
f_	32.3612	8.280861	3.91	0.000	16.12841	48.59399
no2_	-10.90126	13.10631	-0.83	0.406	-36.59327	14.79075
no3_	3.180277	1.003154	3.17	0.002	1.213816	5.146738
Low_Hg	-4.527516	.8473181	-5.34	0.000	-6.188495	-2.866536
Mn	51.43273	4.405735	11.67	0.000	42.79626	60.06919
pH	-7.478322	2.569807	-2.91	0.004	-12.51586	-2.440786
po43_	.8106866	.7992836	1.01	0.310	-.7561315	2.377505
s	1.743953	.0246683	70.70	0.000	1.695596	1.79231

ss	.072502	.0324992	2.23	0.026	.0087946	.1362095
Temp	2.217133	.3666414	6.05	0.000	1.498414	2.935852
T_Silica	9.155261	3.393863	2.70	0.007	2.502346	15.80818
Turb	-.3478313	.0465679	-7.47	0.000	-.4391174	-.2565452
nh4_	-4.445574	.9591881	-4.63	0.000	-6.32585	-2.565299
Chla	.0047781	.0346057	0.14	0.890	-.0630587	.0726149
cod	.326694	.0819311	3.99	0.000	.1660862	.4873018
doc	.0588864	.4554843	0.13	0.897	-.8339896	.9517625
Mo	302.1217	183.4853	1.65	0.100	-57.56057	661.804
Si	-25.85465	7.243482	-3.57	0.000	-40.05389	-11.65541
p	8.823756	2.506464	3.52	0.000	3.910389	13.73712
Fe	40.61979	13.49268	3.01	0.003	14.17039	67.0692
_cons	104.0456	25.89705	4.02	0.000	53.28019	154.811

Table 12. Regression.

	Summary of so42_		
Sample_ID	Mean	Std. Dev.	Freq.
B1-B10	405.26118	140.67122	2526
K1-R2	66.18701	115.52301	2526
K10-K10	120.27818	58.483346	2526
K12-N8	303.80768	116.03529	2526
K2-R1	1128.8242	815.12126	2526
K3-R3	121.64965	170.8744	2526
K4-R4	1123.08	607.58752	2526
K6-K25	172.05588	44.633777	2526
K9-K19	163.85514	45.159634	2526
S1-S1	21.228942	11.581847	2526
S4-S2	346.77498	144.27252	2526
V7-VRB37	159.3354	44.584895	2526
V9-VRB24	154.30907	45.776534	2526
Total	329.7421	462.44325	32838

Analysis of Variance

Source	SS	df	MS	F	Prob > F
Between groups	4.1391e+09	12	344925487	3926.94	0.0000
Within groups	2.8832e+09	32825	87835.795		
Total	7.0223e+09	32837	213853.757		

Bartlett's test for equal variances: chi2(12) = 7.4e+04 Prob>chi2 = 0.000

Table 13. One way ANOVA.

(Sidak)

Row Mean- Col Mean	B1-B10	K1-R2	K10-K10	K12-N8	K2-R1	K3-R3
K1-R2	-339.074					
	0.000					
K10-K10	-284.983	54.0912				
	0.000	0.000				
K12-N8	-101.453	237.621	183.529			
	0.000	0.000	0.000			
K2-R1	723.563	1062.64	1008.55	825.017		
	0.000	0.000	0.000	0.000		
K3-R3	-283.612	55.4626	1.37148	-182.158	-1007.17	
	0.000	0.000	1.000	0.000	0.000	
K4-R4	717.819	1056.89	1002.8	819.272	-5.7442	1001.43
	0.000	0.000	0.000	0.000	1.000	0.000
K6-K25	-233.205	105.869	51.7777	-131.752	-956.768	50.4062
	0.000	0.000	0.000	0.000	0.000	0.000
K9-K19	-241.406	97.6681	43.577	-139.953	-964.969	42.2055
	0.000	0.000	0.000	0.000	0.000	0.000
S1-S1	-384.032	-44.9581	-99.0492	-282.579	-1107.6	-100.421
	0.000	0.000	0.000	0.000	0.000	0.000
S4-S2	-58.4862	280.588	226.497	42.9673	-782.049	225.125
	0.000	0.000	0.000	0.000	0.000	0.000
V7-VRB37	-245.926	93.1484	39.0572	-144.472	-969.489	37.6857
	0.000	0.000	0.000	0.000	0.000	0.000
V9-VRB24	-250.952	88.1221	34.0309	-149.499	-974.515	32.6594
	0.000	0.000	0.004	0.000	0.000	0.007

Row Mean- Col Mean	K4-R4	K6-K25	K9-K19	S1-S1	S4-S2	V7-VRB37
K6-K25	-951.024					
	0.000					
K9-K19	-959.225	-8.20074				
	0.000	1.000				
S1-S1	-1101.85	-150.827	-142.626			
	0.000	0.000	0.000			
S4-S2	-776.305	174.719	182.92	325.546		
	0.000	0.000	0.000	0.000		
V7-VRB37	-963.745	-12.7205	-4.51974	138.106	-187.44	
	0.000	1.000	1.000	0.000	0.000	
V9-VRB24	-968.771	-17.7468	-9.54607	133.08	-192.466	-5.02633
	0.000	0.929	1.000	0.000	0.000	1.000

Table 14. Comparison of SO_4^{2-} by Sample_ID.

5. Discussions and conclusions

Case-wise correlation, focussing on SO_4^{2-} , indicated that the variable 'DO' was not significant. Among the other significant variables, it was noted that SO_4^{2-} was highly significantly correlated to EC, Cl^- and S.

Factor analysis yielded some underlying correlations to support the case-wise correlation analysis. In addition to grouping the variables into 3 factors, the variables which were highly correlated to SO_4^{2-} from case-wise correlation, were loaded together with SO_4^{2-} in Factor 1. This was expected because factor analysis is also based on the assumption that all variables are correlated to some degree. Factor 3 was made up of largely physical parameters while Factor 1 contained variables that had something to do with conductivity of a water sample. Factor 2 did not exhibit any cross-loading with the other 2 factors, yet it was still very difficult to assign a common description to it. Variables CN, DO, FC, F^-, PO_4^{3-}, Chl-α and P could be safely deleted as they were not loaded into any of the 3 factors.

Multivariate linear regression indicated that out of the 26 variables that could predict SO_4^{2-}, only 20 were significant, accounting for 82% of the total variation of SO_4^{2-}.

While correlation and regression provided linear relationships, factor analysis, on the other hand, could be used for data reduction. Even though sometimes it is difficult to find a common name to assign to a factor, still, based on these statistical approaches, individual factors or elements within a factor could be further analysed as necessary, with minimal loss of data integrity.

From one-way ANOVA, SO_4^{2-} mean concentration values indicated that monitoring point K2-R1 (1128.82±815 mg/L) was within the vicinity of the source of SO_4^{2-}. Attenuation of the variable was noted as its mean value decreased along the Rietspruit River at K4-R4 and then Klip River at K6-K25 and K9-K19, before Klip River discharged into the Vaal River. From monitoring point B1-B10 (also close to a source of SO_4^{2-}), another established route was through S4-S2, before Suikerbosrant River discharged into the Vaal River upstream of the Klip River. Surface raw water containing high levels of SO_4^{2-} was not draining via K1-R2 and S1-S. Based on SO_4^{2-} mean concentration values only and for management purposes, K1-R2 and S1-S could be left out of the monitoring programme, saving on financial resources. Comparison of SO_4^{2-} by sample_ID showed that K6-K25, K9-K19, V7-VRB37 and V9-VRB24; K10-K10 and K3-R3; and K2-R1 and K4-R4, were significantly similar.

The major challenge was pre-processing of the non-consistent water quality data over the 7 years. Non-consistent data was as a result of missing data, largely where some of the stakeholders dropped or established some water quality variables and monitoring points over the years as monitoring prioritizations changed because of new and emerging pollution threats. The challenge of insufficient and inconsistent data for water quality modelling remains a limitation in the formulation of good and practically useable models. However, interpolations and correlations, including factor analysis and regression, could help build better data sets, especially for pollution trending in river basin management. This could be used to support large-scale public decisions.

6. Acknowledgement

The financial assistance of the South African Department of Science Technology (DST) is hereby acknowledged. Opinions expressed and conclusions arrived at, are those of the authors and are not necessarily to be attributed to the DST. The authors would also like to thank Tshwane University of Technology for hosting and co-funding this research. DWA, the Water Research Commission, Rand Water Board (co-funding), Midvaal Water Company and Sedibeng Water, are also sincerely acknowledged, especially for providing very valuable and vital data.

7. References

Alfassi, Z. B., Boger, Z. & Ronen, Y. (2005). *Statistical treatment of analytical data,* Oxford, Blackwell Science Ltd, 0-632-05367-4, CRC Press, Australia.

Cloot, A. & Roux, G. L. (1997). Modelling algal blooms in the middle Vaal River: a site specific approach. *Water Research,* 31, 2, 271-279, 0043-1354.

DWAF (2007). Integrated water quality management plan for the Vaal River system. Pretoria, South Africa.

Dzwairo, B. & Otieno, F. A. O. (2010). Integrating quality and cost of surface raw water: Upper and Middle Vaal Water Management Areas South Africa. *Water Science and Technology: Water Supply* 10, 2, 201–207, 1606-9749.

Dzwairo, B., Otieno, F. A. O. & Ochieng', G. M. (2010a). Making a case for systems thinking approach to integrated water resources management (IWRM). *International Journal of Water Resources and Environmental Engineering,* 1, 5, 107-113 2141-6613.

Dzwairo, B., Otieno, F. A. O., Ochieng', G. M. & Letsoalo, M. A. (2010b). Downsizing water quality data for river basin management - Focussing on Sulphate: Vaal River, South Africa. *Proceedings of the 11th WaterNet/WARFSA/GWP-SA Symposium: 'IWRM for National and Regional Integration: Where Science, Policy and Practice Meet. Elephant Hills Hotel, Victoria Falls, Zimbabwe. 27 October - 29 October, 2010.*

Even, S., Billen, G., Bacq, N., Théry, S., Ruelland, D., Garnier, J., Cugier, P., Poulin, M., Blanc, S., Lamy, F. & Paffoni, C. (2007). New tools for modelling water quality of hydrosystems: An application in the Seine River basin in the frame of the Water Framework Directive. *Science of The Total Environment,* 375, 1-3, 274-291.

Gouws, K. & Coetzee, P. P. (1997). Determination and partitioning of heavy metals in sediments of the Vaal Dam System by sequential extraction. *Water SA,* 23, 3, 217-226, 0378-4738.

Herold, C. E., Le Roux, P. J., Nyabeze, W. R. & Gerber, A. (2006). WQ2000 Salinity Model: enhancement, technology transfer and implementation of user support for the Vaal system. Umfula Wempilo Consulting. Pretoria, South Africa.

Ho, R. (2006). *Handbook of univariate and multivariate data analysis and interpretation with SPSS.,* Florida, Chapman and Hall/CRC: Tailor and Francis Group, 1584886021.

Martin, J. L., Mccutcheon, S. C. & Martin, M. L. (1998). *Hydrodynamics and Transport for Water Quality Modeling* Taylor & Francis, Inc, 978-0873716123.

Naicker, K., Cukrowska, E. & Mccarthy, T. S. (2003). Acid mine drainage arising from gold mining activity in Johannesburg, South Africa and environs. *Environmental Pollution,* 122, 1, 29-40, 0269-7491.

Ochse, E. (2007). *Seasonal rainfall influences on main pollutants in the Vaal River barrage reservoir: a temporal-spatial perspective.* Magister Artium MA, University of Johannesburg.

Pieterse, A., Roos, J., Roos, K. & Pienaar, C. (1987). Preliminary observations on cross-channel and vertical heterogeneity in environmental and algological parameters in the Vaal River at Balkfontein, South Africa. *Water SA,* 12, 4, 173-184, 0378-4738 .

Stevn, D. J. & Toerien, D. F. (1976). Eutrophication levels of some South African impoundments. IV. Vaal dam. *Water SA,* 2, 2, 53-57.

6

Modelling Reliability Based Optimization Design for Water Distribution Networks

Mohamed Abdel Moneim
*Holding Company for Water and Wastewater,
Arab Republic of Egypt*

1. Introduction

There is a growing concern on the capacity of water utilities via governmental regulatory agencies regarding potential optimization and reliability for water distribution network. Generally, water distribution networks comprise about 60% of the total budget for a complete framework of a water supply system. According to this fact, achieving an optimum solution for water distribution networks as models' outcome of reliability-based optimization design has become the great concern to save considerable amount of allocated budget. During the last decade many authors were interested in studying optimization and reliability for water distribution networks that include solving non-linear hard problem of the network hydraulic equations. The optimization and reliability models of water distribution networks have number of varieties in studying aspects that include efficiency, accuracy, different sizes/scales of networks, and the consumed run time to define the optimum solution. During the current decade, considerable amount of attention has been given to reliability of water distribution networks in conjunction with the optimization to achieve maximum benefits with the minimum cost. This concern has been extended to cover the risk management for water distribution networks as a way to embark on facing the shortage of water resources all over the world or improving asset management programs. The main objective of this chapter is to develop standalone model divided into four sub-models using MATLAB environment programming language. The developed model and its corresponding sub-models would acquaint an optimum solution for a given water distribution network that achieve both least cost design and reliability based optimization design in the mean time. The main model is called RELOPT and can be used as a tool to implement: modeling reliability-based optimization design, deterioration analysis of water pipe networks, risk analysis and assessment, and decision support system. RELOPT is integrated with four sub-models those are: optimization search engine model that is based on a new technique driven from Genetic Algorithms approach is called Linear Adaptive Genetic Algorithm (LAGA); pre-estimation optimization model that is based on Average Gradient Method (AGM) to accelerate the process of the optimization search engine; reliability model that is based on load resistance concept for calculating system reliability. Through this chapter the number of subjects will be discussed those are: background of water distribution systems, definition of problem in statement, main objectives, history of optimization and techniques, history of reliability and techniques, proposed optimization technique, the advantage of the new optimization technique, proposed reliability evaluation technique, proposed risk assessment technique, resultant decision support system, applications of the proposed model using existing cases studies, and conclusion including outcomes and recommendations. Developing the main model and it's sub-models in using MATLAB power with some snapshots will be discussed.

2. Chapter objectives

The objectives of this chapter have one common target that is to define the reliability-based optimization design for a water distribution network using modelling technique of MATLAB programming language. The following tasks have to be achieved:

1. Acquainting optimum least-cost design for water distribution networks using new efficient and time consumed method.
2. Define risk components for water distribution networks.
3. Define the most critical components of water distribution networks that affect the level of serviceability under different cases of operation (i.e. define level of service under risk).
4. Analysis, evaluation and treating reliability for water distribution networks.
5. Define the reliability of water distribution network over a given period of time.
6. Define the optimum solution of water distribution network that achieve the optimum lease-cost design and certain accepted reliability in one time (reliability-based optimization).
7. Develop stand alone reliability-based optimization model comprising all the above mentioned objectives

3. Previous studies

Solving the hydraulic equations for water distribution networks is a constrained non-linear hard programming problem (CNLHP) due to the nature of the non-linearity of the decision variables such as pipe diameters. For a given water distribution network, huge number of solutions could be selected through a range of the decision variables to select the best solution which arise the problem to be combinatorial optimization problems (Gupta and Kapoor 1994). Hamdy A. (1997) stated that some mathematical models may be so complex that is impossible to solve them by any of the available optimization algorithm and such cases heuristics are used instead of mathematical models to search for a good solution near the best or the optimum one. The advantage of heuristics over an exact optimization algorithm is that it is usually much faster to execute. Dorigo and Thomas (2004) stated that recently, many researchers have focused their attention on a new class of algorithms called meta-heuristics. A meta-heuristic is a set of algorithmic concepts that can be used to define heuristic methods applicable to a wide set of different problems. The use of meta-heuristics has significantly increased the ability of finding very high quality solutions to hard, practically relevant combinatorial optimization problems in reasonable time. Intelligent algorithms models are becoming essential tool to solve such non-linear hard problems for water distribution networks. Number of intelligent algorithms had been developed based on the meta-heuristic concept such as Simulating Annealing (SA), Tabu Search (TS), Guided Local Search (GLS), Greedy Randomized Adaptive Search Procedure (GRASP), Iterated Local Search (ILS), Evolutionary Computation (EC), Scatter Search, and Ant Colony Optimization (ACO).

4. Model components

Getting the reliability-based optimization design for water distribution networks requires searching among a number of available population set of solutions, thus; RELOPT model consists of the following components (Moneim AM, 2009):

1. Hydraulic solver EPANET: consists of the dynamic libraries that are required to be called by MATLAB program for hydraulic analysis.
2. Pre-estimation model (AGM): this sub-model provides the lower and upper bounds that are required for OPTWNET to start optimization search process.
3. Optimization model (OPTWNET): defines the optimum solution using LAGA.
4. LAGA automatic search engine module.
5. Reliability model (RELWNET): this model is connected with three sub-models those are: minimum cut-sets model; Generic Expectation Function model; and reliability calculation model. The model passes the final calculated reliability to the main model RELOPT.

4.1 Main model

The main model is the main driver for RELOPT and contains all links to call or retrieve sub-models or any external. Figure 1 represents the RELOPT model organization chart. The main model is coded in MATALB language and is designed to send and receive variables, input data, and outputs from different sub-models parties. The Main Model is playing a managing role between the different models by receiving and passing inputs and outputs between the models EPANET, AGM, OPTWNET, and RELWNET. Once a new water network had registered within EPANET environment, the input file name should be provided within the Main Model. During the run; EPANET is returning back an output file name to the Main Model. The Main Model is calling the pre-estimator AGM and receiving back the outputs which are the upper and lower bounds for LAGA search engine. The Main Model is passing the outputs from AGM to LAGA and receiving the outputs from LAGA which are the water network pipe diameters (decision variables). The Main Model is passing the water network data to the reliability model REWNET and receiving the calculated reliability measure of the current network in hand.

4.2 Pre-estimation model

The pre-estimation model is playing very important role in this application as it defines the upper and lower bounds for the optimization search process that is carried out by LAGA. Generally, defining the upper and lower bounds for optimization process decreases the search space which speeds up the optimization search and hence reduces the consumed run time. The pre-estimation model utilizes the Average Gradient Method (AGM) which depends on defining the critical node of minimum residual pressure within the network. The pre-estimator model AGM passes the upper and lower bounds to the optimization model OPTWNET to start searching of optimum solution among population of feasible solutions.

4.3 Optimization model

The optimization model OPTWNET uses LAGA and genetic optimization search engine. Figure 2 represents the OPTWNET model organization chart. The model RELWNET is running using the upper and lower bounds received from the pre-estimation model and passes out the pipe diameter decision variables to the main model. The number of generation used by LAGA is limited to 5 and the population size is limited to 10. Experiments have shown that these limits are enough for LAGA to define the global optimization solution for a water network. OPTWNET passes the resulting optimized decision variables to the main model which passes by its role to the reliability model RELWNET.

4.4 Reliability model

The reliability model RELWNET uses load-resistance principal to calculate the system reliability for water distribution networks (Moneim et al., 2010). Figure 3 represents RELWNET model organization chart. The RELWNET is dealing with the optimized decision variables obtained by OPTWNET. RELWNET is linked to sub-model Minimum Cut Set (MCS) to define the failure components. Following up the definition of failure components, Generic Expectation Function (GEF) sub-model is called by RELWNET to calculate the reliability of the network and passing the calculated reliability to the OPTWNET. OPTWNET is now assign penalty factor to each network passed on three constraints those are; pressure, velocity and reliability. The LAGA optimization search engine arranges the solutions by descending order through the model OPTWNET according to fittest solution. The optimum solution is passed back to the Main Model and final hydraulic check is carried out by EPANET.

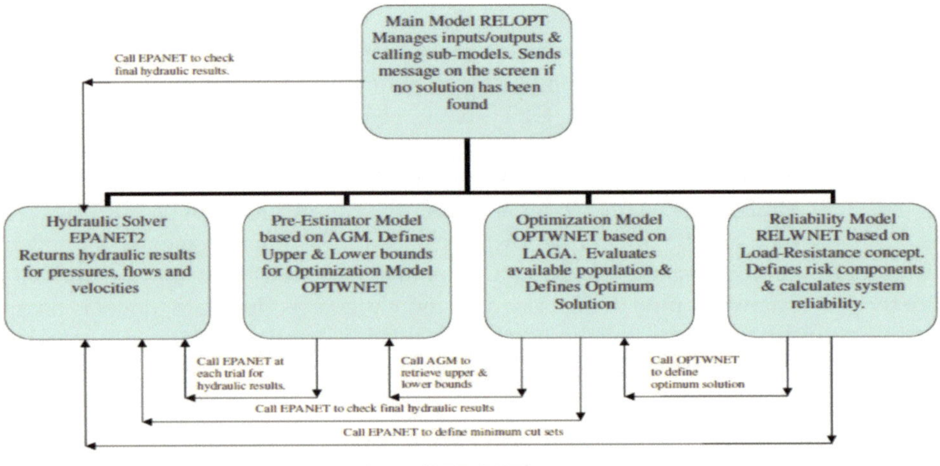

Fig. 1. Main Model Organization Chart (RELOPT).

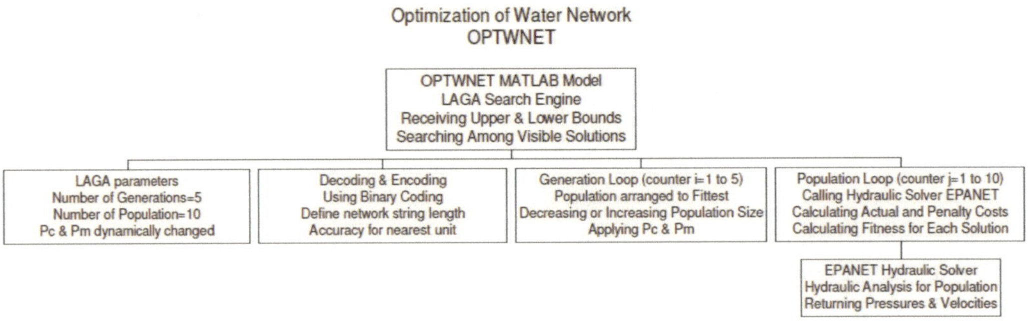

Fig. 2. OPTWNET Organization Chart.

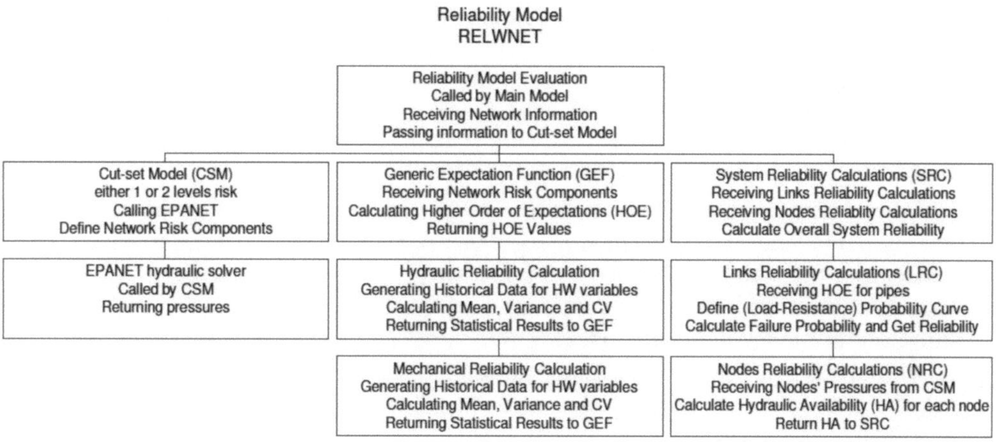

Fig. 3. RELWNET Organization Chart.

5. Optimization technique

Heuristics from Nature approach has been presented by (Colorni et al. 1992a, 1992b) presented methods that depend on as a non-derivative optimization method. The authors stated that Heuristics derived from Nature algorithms considered as a border between Operation Research (OR) and Artificial Intelligence (AI). These algorithms take inspiration from physics, biology, social, and use a certain amount of repeated trials for the Non-Programming Hard Combinatorial Optimization Problem (NPHCOP). Heuristics are obtained by one of the following application methods:

1. Using certain amount of repeated trials;
2. Employing one or more "agents" such as neurons, particles, chromosomes, ants, genetic algorithms, and so on;
3. Operating (in case of multiple agents) with a mechanism of competition-cooperation;
4. Embedding procedures of self-modifications of the heuristics parameters or of the problem representation.

5.1 Genetic Algorithms (GA)

Genetic Algorithms is one of the methods derived from Heuristics from Nature approach. GA is numerical optimization algorithms inspired by both natural selection and natural genetics. David A Coley (1999) demonstrated that GA is a general method capable of being applied to an extremely wide range of problems. David illustrates that GA has proved capabilities to solve many large complex problems where other methods experienced difficulties. Amongst many practical problems and areas which GA has been successfully applied are image processing; prediction of three dimensional protein structures; medicine; analysis of time series; solid-state physics; robotics; water distribution networks; training and designing artificial intelligence systems such as neural networks and control. David summarizes the main components of typical GA as follows:

1. A number or population of guesses of solutions to the problems;
2. A way or a method to evaluate how good or bad the individual solutions within the population;
3. A method for mixing fragments of the better solution to form new better solutions;

4. A mutation operator to avoid permanent loss of diversity within the solutions.

David defined three main operators for the typical GA states below:

1. Selection: selection is used to apply pressure upon the population in a manner similar to that natural selection found in biological systems. Poorer performing individuals are disappearing out and the better is surviving. Better individuals are then having greater chance of performing new fitter genes;
2. Crossover: this operator allows solutions to exchange information in a way similar to that used by natural organism undergoing sexual reproduction. Information can be totally changed (100 %); fixed point crossover (constant percentage crossover) or variable point crossover (non-constant percentage crossover);
3. Mutation: mutation is used to randomly change (flip) the value of single bits within individual strings. The importance of mutation operator securing evolving of string that includes the global optimum as the mutation allows the population to "leapfrog" over the global optimum.

5.2 Linear Adaptive Genetic Algorithm (LAGA)

Attia and Horacek (2001) developed Linear Adaptive Genetic Algorithm (LAGA) to solve unconstrained optimization problems. The method is depending on applying modification to the internal Genetic Algorithm parameters like cross over and mutation probabilities based on generation index. The LAGA method is then becoming dynamically process and case sensitive with respect to the optimum solution.

The cross over probability rate P_c and mutation probability rate P_m are concluded in GA operation to provide faster convergence when compared to constant probability rates. P_c is set up to its highest value at the start of the optimization process and decreases linearly as the generation number is progressing.

$$P_c=\frac{0.5}{M\;1}(g\;1)+1 \qquad (1)$$

Where: g= number of the current generation,

M= total number of generation.

Unlike the crossover probability is the mutation probability which is not needed at the beginning of the optimization search as the population is very distinct. As the generation is progressing the solution starts to come slightly closer to the optimum, the mutation probability is then come to the view picture and starts from 0.005 and increased linearly up to 0.5.

$$P_m=\frac{0.005}{M\;1}(g\;1) \qquad (2)$$

5.3 Application of LAGA to water networks optimization

LAGA approach has been employed for the first time in this research to solve the problem of water distribution network optimization. LAGA proved faster convergence and time consuming for optimization problems (Attia and Horacek, 2001) and it is prospective to solve water distribution network optimization problem. The first problem when applying LAGA for water distribution network optimization is that LAGA was adopted to solve direct unconstrained optimization problems. Hence, it is simple to define the population range and substitute directly in the objective function to evaluate the corresponding selected input variables. LAGA has been adopted to select the population for network solution (string of pipe diameters) and linked to hydraulic solver EPANET to evaluate each network solution according to predefined cost function. The second problem is that the search space for given pipe diameter limit was very large and that slowed down the convergence process. This problem had been eliminated by applying pre-estimation for the upper and lower bounds of diameter population as being explained in the forthcoming section 3.14. Figure 3.5 illustrates the flow chart for LAGA optimization technique. As being introduced in this chapter, the problem of water distribution networks need evaluation of each selected network solution by linking to hydraulic solver such as EPANET. This process is affecting the consumed run time for specific problem and as a result the expected run time to get the final solution will be much longer. The following advantages of LAGA technique are helping to reduce and accelerate the run time:

1. LAGA uses dynamic concept for the main parameters of GA process that allow changing the values of both cross over and mutation probability at the start of each generation. This mechanism is accelerating the searching process to allocate an optimum solution in shorter time than the traditional Genetic Algorithm;
2. LAGA reduces the population size as the optimization process tends to catch on the optimum solution. Conversely, LAGA increases the population size as the optimization process could not catch up an optimized solution. This mechanism adds another time consuming facility in case an optimum solution has been identified.

6. Multiple optimization agents

It has been noticed during the first run of LAGA for water network optimization that the search process for the optimum solution was not fast convergence and that because the difference between the upper and lower limits of the population search space was quite large. The lower and upper limits of the search space should conclude the available minimum and maximum commercial pipe diameter. This fact cause the search process to take time and the convergence is slow down. To eliminate unnecessary effort and time during the search process, pre-estimation optimization agent has been applied. The lower and upper bounds of the population search space can be defined. Moreover, it will be more efficient to apply the pre-estimation optimization process not only for the overall search space but also for each pipe within the network. The pre-estimation optimization process had accelerated the search process and reduced the required run time. New model had been developed to predict the lower and upper bounds of the search space and linked to LAGA main optimization model. That could be known as Meta-Model Development (MMD). The new model is called Average Gradient Method (AGM) for water networks optimization.

6.1 Average gradient method for water networks optimization

The average Gradient Method for water networks optimization is mainly depending on defining the most critical node within the water distribution networks and the critical path to the source node is then calculated. The method was driven from the principal that if the pressure at most critical node in the water network has been controlled to be greater than or equal to the minimum residual pressure, the resulting pipe diameter could be good estimation to start the optimization search process by LAGA. The following steps summarize the AGM:

1. Define the required minimum pressure and let us refer it as (Pm);
2. Calculate the total required demands of the entire water network nodes and let us refer it as (Qt);
3. Assuming flow velocity of 1 m/s, the corresponding pipe diameter (D) to convey the total required demand is then can be calculated;
4. Set all pipe diameters within the entire network to be equal to (D);
5. Calculate the corresponding pipe network cost and let us refer it as (Fo);
6. Solve the water network hydraulically using the hydraulic solver EPANET;
7. Define the most critical node within the entire network. The critical node is that node which has pressure less than the minimum residual pressure provided by the analyzer before the analysis starts;
8. Calculate the shortest path that lead from the defined critical node to the source node and let us refer it as (LS);
9. Calculate the head at the critical node = Pm + Node Elevation;
10. Calculate the difference between the source head and the critical node head = Head at source - Head at critical node = Hm;
11. Calculate the average gradient (Gv) = Hm/LS
12. Apply Hazen William formula for each pipe within the entire network using the calculated average gradient

$$Q=0.278*C*D^{2.63}*G_v^{0.54} \tag{3}$$

Where Q = resulting pipe flow for the current hydraulic analysis (m3/s)
C= Hazen William friction factor
D= required pipe diameter to be calculated
Gv= average network gradient

1. The corresponding pipe diameter for each pipe within the network is then can be calculated;
2. Calculate the pipe network total cost (Fn);
3. Calculate the difference between (Fn) and (Fo). If the difference is greater than certain defined limit (say 1000 unit cost). Repeat steps from 6 up to 14. If the difference between (Fn) and (Fo) is less than or equal to the defined limit. Stop the process. The resulting pipe diameters are considered the lower bound for the search space population. The upper bound then is equal to 1.2 of the lower bound.

6.2 Formulation of LAGA optimization technique

Hydraulics of water distribution network is a complex task due to the non linear formulation of the pipe network flow functions. Consequently, applying optimization technique to search amongst available solutions to the assign the local or global optimum solution is not a simple or direct substitution task. GA search engine has the ability to pick up a certain number of available network solutions and throw the solutions into the population basket to evaluate each solution using the hydraulic solver EPANET and that is called the first generation for GA process. The evaluation process is based on how much the violation of each network solution about the pre-defined minimum pressure (desirable limits of serviceability). As long as the a certain solution is near to the desirable limits of serviceability the penalty factor is intended to be close to zero and vice versa, as long as the network solution is violated about the desirable limits of serviceability the penalty factor is intended to a value greater than zero. The objective function for water distribution networks is usually used as the cost function comprising the pipe lengths and diameters. The cost function can take the following general form:

$$MIN(F)=\sum_{i=1}^{n} C_i * D_i * l_i + F_p + F_v \tag{4}$$

Where F = total cost of the current network and MIN is referring to minimization.
F_p =penalty cost due to pressure violation.
F_v = penalty cost due to velocity violation
C= unit cost for each pipe diameter category
D= pipe diameter
l= pipe length
i=pipe number
n=denotes to total pipe number within the network

6.3 Adaptation of penalty cost for pressure violation

The penalty cost can be applied according to the three cases those are:
Case of minimum allocated pressure P_{min} is greater than minimum desirable pressure R_p and the difference does not exceed 10%:
The penalty cost F_p is determined according to the following equation:

$$F_p = \frac{F}{R_p}(R_p - P_{min}) \tag{5}$$

If the minimum allocated pressure of the current solution is greater than the desirable minimum pressure the resulting penalty cost will have negative value which will decrease the total corresponding cost function. Conversely, if the minim allocated pressure of the current solution is less than the desirable minimum pressure, the resulting penalty cost will have positive value which will increase the corresponding cost function.

1. Case of minimum allocated pressure P_{min} is less than minimum desirable pressure R_p and the difference does not exceed 10%:

$$F_p = \frac{F}{R_p}(R_p - P_{min}) * 1000 \tag{6}$$

2. Case of more than 10% difference between the actual minimum pressure and the minimum desirable pressure and the solution is invisible:

$$F_p = \frac{F}{R_p}| R_p - P_{min} | * 1000 \tag{7}$$

3. Case number 2 and 3 will eliminate the solutions that violate about the optimum solution even if it is a feasible solution. The factor 1000 (this factor can be increased to any other value) will increase the cost value to an imaginary amount which secures disappearing of any violated solutions that exceed 10 % of the desirable minimum pressure.

6.4 Adaptation of penalty cost for velocity violation

The penalty cost can be applied according to the three cases those are:

1. Case of 10% difference between the actual maximum velocity and the maximum desirable velocity:

The penalty cost F_v is determined according to the following equation:

$$F_v = \frac{-1*F}{Vr} | V_a - V_r | \quad (8)$$

Where V_r = desirable maximum velocity.

V_a = Actual maximum velocity of the current solution.

If the actual maximum velocity of the current solution is greater or less than the desirable maximum velocity within a limit of 10% of the resulting penalty cost will have negative value which will decrease the total corresponding cost function.

2. Case of more than 10% difference between the actual maximum velocity and the maximum desirable velocity and the solution is visible:

$$F_p = \frac{-1*F}{Vr} | V_r - V_a | *1000 \quad (9)$$

Case number 2 will eliminate the solutions that violate about the optimum solution even if it is a visible solution. High velocities might cause pipe corrosion and high power loss. The factor (1000) will increase the cost value to an imaginary amount which securing disappearing of any violation solutions that exceed 10 % of the desirable maximum velocity.

7. Reliability calculation using load-resistance analysis

The load-resistance analysis shall be applied to calculate the reliability of water distribution networks. It has been stated by (Y.K. Tung and Mays, 1985) that the resistance or strength of any component is defined as the ability of the component to accomplish its required mission with satisfactory state without a failure when subjected to an external stress. Stress is the loading of the component which may be a mechanical load, an environmental exposure, a flow rate, temperature fluctuation, etc. the stress loading tends to cause failure of the component. When the strength of the component is less than the stress imposed on it, the failure occurs. This type of analysis can be applied to the reliability analysis for components of water distribution systems. Equation 10 is a real translation to this concept stated very recently by (Yeou and Ben, 2005). The safety margin SM is a performance index that reflects the reliability performance of the network. Knowing the probability distribution for the (SM) will help in computing the area under the probability curve that securing positive value of SM . The Safety Margin SM is solely the reliability of the system RS and can take the following form:

$$RS = P(Y > X) = P(Y \quad X > 0) \quad (10)$$

Where Y is the resistance of the system and X is its loading. Accordingly, the reliability of a hydraulic system is defined as the probability of the resistance Y to exceed the loading X. The resistance of a hydraulic system is essentially means the flow carrying capacity of the system and the loading is essentially the magnitude of the actual flows through the system that satisfy the required demands. Due to uncertainties of hydraulic behavior, the load and the resistance should be dealt as random variables and their probability distribution are essentially needed to develop a reliability model. The system Reliability RS can be calculated after the probability of system failure can be calculated. MATLAB built-in probability functions can be used to generate any number of historical data for both the load that is carried by a pipe and the resistance that is can be calculated using Hazen-William equation.

7.1 Defining risk components using cut-set method

It has been mentioned by (Moneim et al., 2010) that the cut-set method is powerful for defining the failure/risk components for complex systems such as water distribution networks. The cut set is defined as the set of system components which when failed causes the failure of the whole system. The cut set method utilize the minimum cut set that can be defined as the set which when failed cause the failure of the whole system but when any one component of the set has not failed, it does not cause failure of the system failure. The minimum cut set implies that all of its components must be in failure mode to cause failure of the whole system. Therefore component of a minimum cut set are effectively connected in parallel and each cutest is connected in series. The following form expresses calculation of reliability for a system:

$$PF=\sum_{k=1}^{S} P(C_k) \tag{11}$$

Where PF = Probability of failure of the whole system

$P(C_k)$ = Probability of failure for the minimum cut set number k

S = total number of the minimum cut set.

It is easier to define the failure components and calculate the failure probability of each one, then the overall system failure cab be calculated simply according to the following sections.

7.2 Combining hydraulic and mechanical reliability

It has been stated by (Moneim et al., 2010) that hydraulic and mechanical failures are considered two independent events that might occur within water distribution networks. Hence, hydraulic and mechanical failures are two events statistically independent as the probability of any one of them is unaffected by the occurrence of the other. According to the multiplication law for independent events, the probability that two independent events will both occur is simply the product of their probabilities and that can be mathematically expressed according to the following equation:

$$P(A \cap B)=P(A).P(B) \tag{12}$$

By defining the minimum cut-sets of a water distribution network, the overall failure probability for pipes and junctions within the water distribution network (PF) can be calculated. (Moneim et al., 2010) have developed the reliability model RELWENT which has been applied to calculate the reliability of water distribution networks. The overall system reliability can be expressed using the following equation:

$$RS=1-P=1-\sum_{i}^{M}(1-HA)*PF \tag{13}$$

Where: RS = Overall system reliability

P = Overall system failure

HA = Hydraulic availability at junction nodes
PF = Combined hydraulic and mechanical failure probability for pipes.
In case the hydraulic availability at junction nodes has been found equal 1 (i.e 100% meets the required residual pressures), the term HA should be excluded from equation (13).

8. Application example

A simple 2-loop network represented in Figure 4 consists of 7 nodes, one reservoir and 8 pipes have been obtained from the literature (Alperovits & Shamir, 1977). All pipes are equally length 1000 m and the Hazen-Williams coefficient of friction is assumed to be 130 for all pipes. The minimum required residual pressure for all demand nodes is 30m. The unit cost for pipe diameters is represented in Table 1 while Table 2 provides the data of nodes' demands and elevations.

Diameter (In.)	1	2	3	4	6	8	10	12	14	16	18	20	22	24
Unit Cost	2	5	8	11	16	23	32	50	60	90	130	170	300	550

Table 1. Unit Cost per meter length of pipe.

Node Number	1	2	3	4	5	6	7
Demand (m3/hr)	-1120	100	100	120	270	330	200
Elevation (m)	210	150	160	155	150	165	160

Table 2. Node number, demands and elevation.

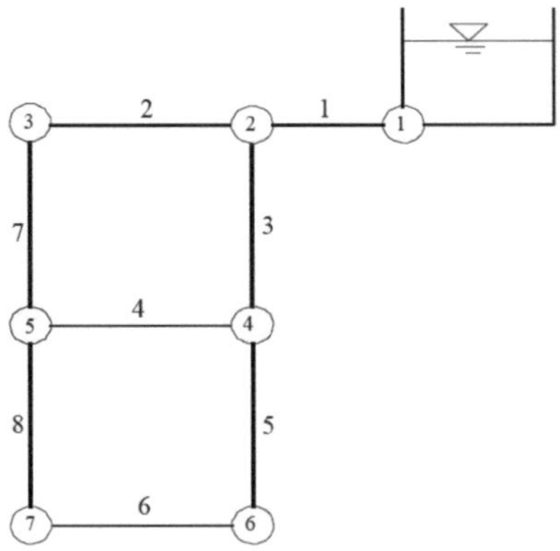

Fig. 4. Example 2-Loop Water Network.

8.1 Solution steps

The following steps are applied for the example application:

1. Open EPANET model interface, draw and create the input file format.

2. Units are to be set to SI units.
3. Nodes should have consecutive numbers from 1 to the total number of nodes including the source node.
4. Pipes should have consecutive numbers from 1 to the total number of pipes.
5. Base demands and elevations should be given for all nodes.
6. Pipe lengths and friction factor should be given for all pipes.
7. No need to give any diameters for pipes at all.
8. Head for the source nodes should be given.
9. Create *.inp for the network and export by EPANET.
10. Open MATLAB environment and feed in the name of the *.inp input file in the main model.
11. An option input parameter for optimization and reliability in the same run needs to be fed in. Parameter of 1 is to be set if the reliability and optimization are required in the same run. 0 for optimization run only.
12. Save the main model and run.

8.2 Solution criteria

The model has been run to obtain the optimum design for the 2-loops example network Figure 1. The genetic parameters for LAGA search engine have the following criteria:

1. The number of generation for optimization = 2
2. The number of population for optimization = 10
3. The number of generation for reliability-based optimization =2
4. The number of population for reliability-based optimization =6
5. Limit of lower bound for decision variables (i.e. pipe diameter) = 90% of the resulted diameters obtained from the pre-estimator AGM model.
6. Limit of upper bound for decision variables (i.e. pipe diameter) = 110% of the resulted diameters obtained from the pre-estimator AGM model.
7. Minimum required system reliability RS =0.8
8. Minimum required node reliability RN = 0.85
9. Minimum required residual pressure at all nodes = 30.0m

8.3 Results interpretation

The 2-loop water network example has been run for both optimization and reliability and the results are discussed in the following sections.

8.3.1 Optimization results using 2 generations

The results for optimization have obtained after 13.60 seconds using LAPTOP of 1.7 MHZ, and 2 G RAM. The cost of the optimum design is found 388,500 using the unit prices interpolation driven from Table 1. The cost of the network according to the restricted list in Table 1 is found 447,000 with a minimum residual pressure (29.6 m). Although the obtained residual pressure is considered invisible, the run illustrates how much effective for the optimization model OPTWNET to consume run time. The search engine LAGA has improved the pre-estimated optimum cost by AGM model from 492,000 to 447,000. The obtained optimum pipe diameters are: 20 14 12 10 1 12 14 8 that stand for pipe IDs: 1 2 7 8 6 5 3 4. Hydraulic results of this optimization process are illustrated in Appendix A.

8.3.2 Optimization results using minimum 100 generations

The results for optimization have obtained after 135.34 seconds (2.25 minutes) using of the same previous configuration. The cost of the optimum design is found 427,000 using the unite cost of the commercial diameters illustrated in Table 1. The minimum obtained residual pressure is (30.13 m). The optimum pipe diameters for this run are: 18, 14, 14, 10, 1, 14, 14, and 8 those stand for the pipe IDs: 1, 2, 7, 8, 6, 5, 3 and 4.

8.3.3 Reliability results

The results for reliability-based optimization have obtained after 34.3 seconds using LAPTOP of the same configuration stated above. The cost of the optimum solution based reliability is found 1,288,000 (i.e. 300% increased comparing to optimization-based cost only) with system reliability 0.951 and nodal reliability 0.9668 while the original system and nodal reliability are 0.8708 and 0.93 respectively. The results for the obtained reliability versus residual pressure and cost are illustrated respectively through Fig. 5 and Fig. 6.

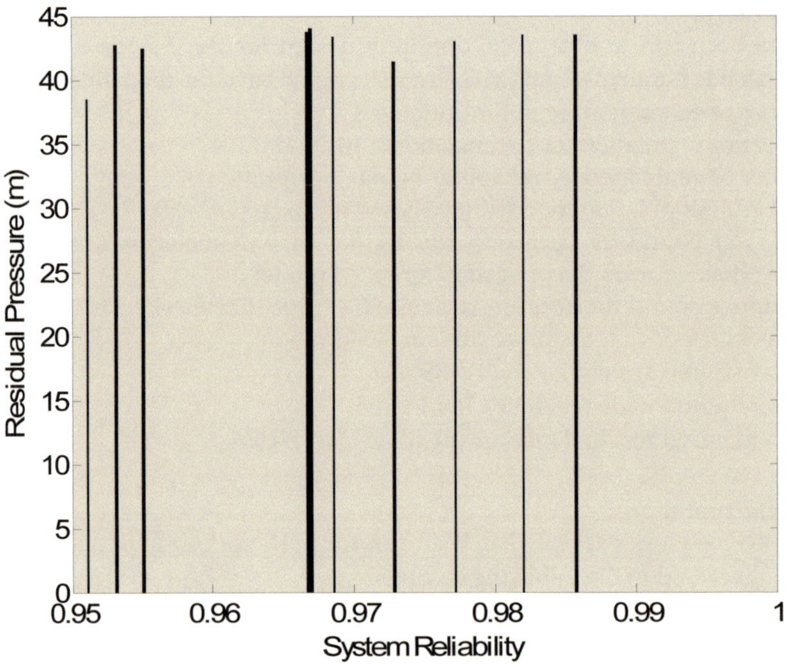

Fig. 5. Reliability versus Residual Pressure for 2-loop Network.

8.3.4 Getting reliability for the optimum solution

The water network of 2-loops has been run to get the reliability of the optimum design obtained in previous section. The reliability of the obtained optimum solution has found 0.8708 and the nodal reliability for the network nodes are 0.9912 0.9609 0.9456 0.8708 0.9609 0.9039. The condition of getting optimum design-based cost doesn't mean that network is reliable. According to this fact, specific reliability level should be defined before applying reliability-based optimization model for a water distribution network.

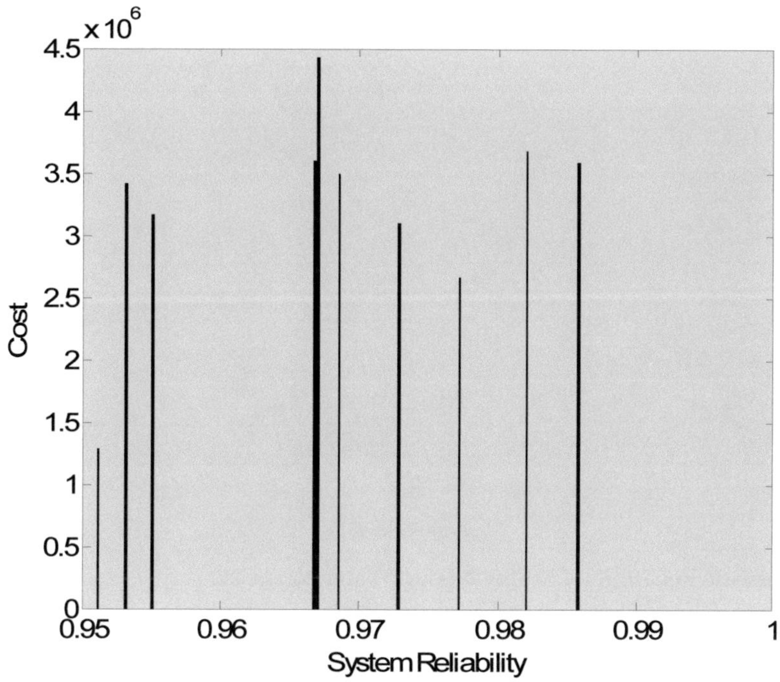

Fig. 6. Reliability versus Cost for 2-Loop Water Network.

8.3.5 Characteristic reliability-cost relationship

To verify the relationship between the reliability and the cost of the water distribution network, several runs have implemented under different reliability constraints starting from 0.5 up to 0.95. The following cost equation has been obtained by applying curve fitting to the data of Table 1:

$$C=\sum_{i=1}^{N} 6.85 * e^{0.1312D} * L \quad (14)$$

Where: D_i = Pipe diameter in inches for pipe and L_i is the pipe length in meters.

The results indicated that relationship between the cost and the reliability is directly proportional which is logically expected. The point of issue is that a characteristic equation can express the relationship between the cost and reliability and accordingly the cost can be calculated for a given value of reliability. This can help when specific allocated budget needs to be adopted for a given water network. Fig. 7 illustrates the relationship between the cost and system reliability for the 2 loop water network.

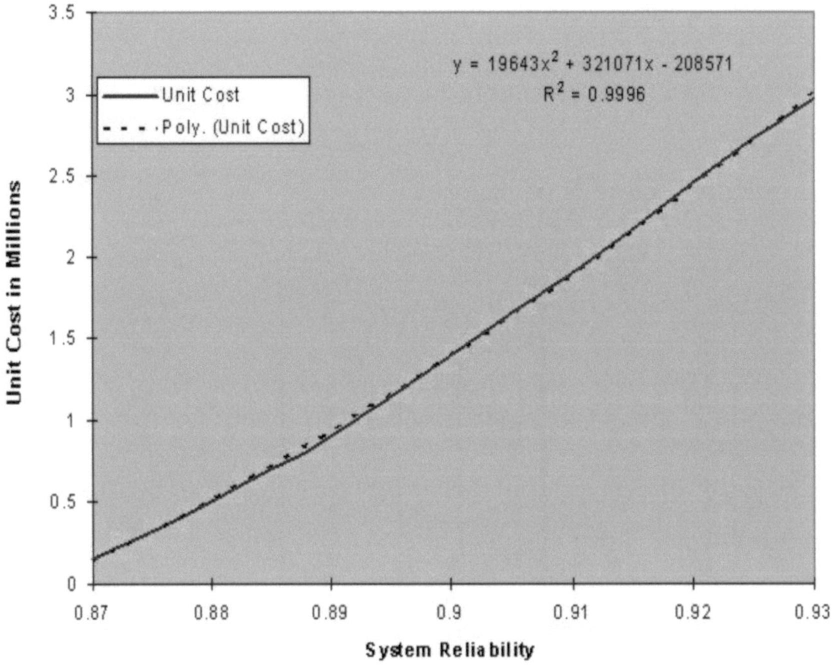

Fig. 7. Characteristic Reliability-Cost for 2-Loop Water Network.

9. Conclusion

In this chapter new model for reliability-based optimization has been developed using MATLAB programming language to define an optimum and reliable design for water distribution networks. The results indicated that the model RELOPT provides acceptable level of confidence when has applied to reliability-based optimization problems. RELOPT consist of four models those are: Pre-estimation mode called Average Gradient Model (AGM); hydraulic solver EPANET; optimization model OPTWNET based on new genetic algorithm concept called Linear Adaptive Genetic Algorithm (LAGA); and Reliability model RELWNET based on load resistance concept for reliability evaluation. The minimum cut sets method has been adopted to define the risk components for complex systems such as water distribution networks. Generic Expectation Functions (GEF) has been adopted to define the probability distribution for the difference between the load and resistance and hence the failure probability has been calculated to calculate the system reliability. It has been illustrated through that achieving reliability-based optimization represents the optimum solution for water distribution networks when considered as constraint during the optimization search process. Optimization of design-based cost is normally securing the function of the water distribution networks during normal operation while reliability-based optimization is normally securing the function of the water distribution network under risk. Giving that the risk has been occurred is an important approach to apply during the design of water distribution networks especially for large scale networks. Optimization cost for water networks could save nations' budget while designing a new network but shall not securing strategic decisions under certain risks or failures. On another point of view, while certain failure has occurred, budget may exceed normal levels to overcome such risks. Reliability-based optimization helps decision makers to adopt pre optimum strategic maintenance/operation programs or emergency scenarios to overcome lots of problems caused by network failures. Increasing the current construction budget for optimization based cost design of a water network to accommodate its reliability, will save more investment in future giving that certain risks have occurred.

10. Acknowledgment

The author is so grateful to his professors Dr. Ahmed Moawad who has supported me along my researches development with his value time and advices. The author also submit his greetings to his professors Dr. Anas Al Molla, Dr. Ayman Al Salawy, Dr. Abdel Badee Salem and Dr. Amgad El-Ansary who have given their value advices and encouraging through my research and life of experience. Great thanks to everybody who has helped me with an advice, time, word and/or technical data which with no doubt has a positive effect to improve my work.

11. References

Alperovits E. and Shamir, U., (1977). Design of optimal water distribution systems. Water Resources Research, Vol. 13(6), pp. 885-900.

Attia A. and Horacek P., (2001). Adaptation of genetic algorithms for optimization problem solving. 7th Intern. Mendel conference on soft computing pp. 36-41, Brno, Cizek Republic.

Colorni, A., M. Dorigo and V. Manniezzo (1992a). Distributed optimization by ant colonies. In: Proceedings of the First European Conference on Artificial Life (ECAL-91) (F.J. Varela and P. Bourgine, Ed.). The MIT Press. Cambridge MA. pp. 134–142.

Colorni, A., M. Dorigo and V. Manniezzo (1992b). An investigation of some properties of an ant algorithm". In: Parallel problem solving from nature, Vol 2. (R. M¨anner and B. Manderick, Ed.). North-Holland. Amsterdam, pp. 509–520.

David A Coley, 1999. An Introduction to Genetic Algorithms for Scientists and Engineers. World Scientific Publishing Company.

Dorigo, M., and Thomas, S., (2004). Ant colony optimization. MIT Press, Cambridge, Massachusetts, London, England.

Gupta, I., Gupta, A., and Khanna, P. (1999). Genetic algorithm for optimization of water distribution systems. Environmental Modelling & software Vol.-4, pp. 437-446.

Hamdy, A. T., 1997. Operation research an introduction. Sixth Edition, Prentice-Hall International, Upper Saddle River, New Jersey.

Moneim A.M., Moawad A.K., Molla A., and Selawy A. (2010). RELWANET: Reliability Evaluation Model for Water Distribution Networks. Australian Journal of Water Resources, Volume 14 No. 1.

Su, Y. C., Mays, L. W., Duan, N. and Lansey, K. E. (1987). Reliability-based optimizationmodel for water distribution system. Journal of Hydraulic Engineering, ASCE, 114(12), 1539-1556.

Y. K. Tung, (1985). Evaluation of water distribution network reliability. Hydraulics and Hydrology in the Small Computer Age, Proceedings of the Specialty Conference, American Society of Civil Engineers, Hydraulics Division, Vol.1, Lake Buena Vista, Florida, August 12-17, 1985.

7

Integrated Cyber-Physical Simulation of Intelligent Water Distribution Networks

Jing Lin, Sahra Sedigh and Ann Miller
Department of Electrical and Computer Engineering, Missouri University of Science and Technology
USA

1. Introduction

In *cyber-physical systems (CPSs)*, embedded computing systems and communication capability are used to streamline and fortify the operation of a physical system. Intelligent critical infrastructure systems are among the most important CPSs and also prime examples of pervasive computing systems, as they exploit computing to provide "anytime, anywhere" transparent services. While the added intelligence offers the promise of increased utilization, its impact must be assessed, as unrestricted cyber control can actually lower the reliability of existing infrastructure systems.

As a practical example, *water distribution networks (WDNs)* are an emerging CPS domain. Physical components, e.g., valves, pipes, and reservoirs, are coupled with the hardware and software that support intelligent water allocation. An example is depicted in Fig. 1. The primary goal of WDNs is to provide a dependable source of potable water to the public. Information such as demand patterns, water quantity (flow and pressure head), and water quality (contaminants and minerals) is critical in achieving this goal, and beneficial in guiding maintenance efforts and identifying vulnerable areas requiring fortification and/or monitoring. Sensors dispersed in the physical infrastructure collect this information, which is fed to algorithms (often distributed) running on the cyber infrastructure. These algorithms provide decision support to hardware controllers that are used to manage the allocation (quantity) and chemical composition (quality) of the water. As WDNs become larger and more complex, their reliability comes into question.

Modeling and simulation can be used to analyze CPS performability, as direct observation of critical infrastructure is often infeasible. Accurate representation of a CPS encompasses three aspects: computing, communication, and the physical infrastructure. Fundamental differences exist between the attributes of cyber and physical components, significantly complicating representation of their behavior with a single comprehensive model or simulation tool. Specialized simulation tools exist for the engineering domains represented in critical infrastructure, including power, water, and transportation. These tools have been created with the objective of accurately reflecting the operation of the physical system, at high spatial and temporal resolution. As is the case with specialized models of physical systems, intelligent control is not reflected in these tools. Despite the existence of simulation tools for cyber aspects such as computing and communication, differences in temporal resolution and

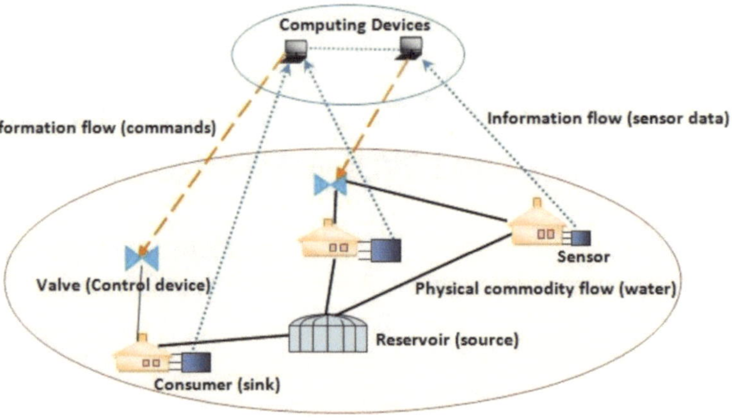

Fig. 1. An intelligent water distribution network.

data representation and the lack of well-defined interfaces pose considerable challenges to linking these simulation tools in a fashion that accurately represents the CPS as a whole.

In the first part of this chapter, we articulate the available simulation tools and the challenges present in integrated simulation of CPS, where the goal is to accurately reflect the operation and interaction of the cyber and physical networks that comprise the system. A solution is presented for the CPS domain of intelligent WDNs. The proposed solution utilizes EPANET to simulate the physical infrastructure of the water distribution network and Matlab to simulate the cyberinfrastructure providing decision support. Communication between the two simulators replicates the interactions between cyber and physical components of WDNs, and facilitates the observation of physical manifestations of intelligent control decisions. This communication between the simulators takes place without user intervention, as all information relevant to each simulator has been identified and extracted from the output of the other. Information flows from the physical simulator to the cyber simulator, replicating the operation of sensors in the physical infrastructure. The cyber simulator processes this data in Matlab, and provides decision support for water allocation, in the form of setting for control elements in the physical infrastructure. This information is provided to the physical simulator, which applies these settings. This process repeats for the duration of the simulation, as it would in the actual operation of a CPS.

The second part of this chapter addresses computation in the CPSs, specifically, the role of cyberinfrastructure in CPSs. We present an agent-based framework for intelligent environmental decision support. Due to the flexibility of software agents as autonomous and intelligent decision-making components, the agent-based computing paradigm is proposed for surmounting the challenges posed by a) fundamental differences in the operation of cyber and physical components, and b) significant interdependency among the cyber and physical components. The environmental management domain used as a model problem is water distribution, where the goal is allocation of water to different consuming entities, subject to the constraints of the physical infrastructure. In the cyber-physical approach to this problem, which is implemented by intelligent WDNs, the cyberinfrastructure uses data from the physical infrastructure to provide decision support for water allocation. We adopt *game theory* as the algorithmic technique used for agent-based decision support in an intelligent

WDN. In this initial effort, our focus is on providing decision support for the quantity of water allocated to each consuming entity. Game theory is a natural choice for complex resource allocation problems such as water distribution, where hydraulic and physical constraints, ethical concerns, and economic considerations should be represented. The investigation of game theory as the computational algorithm for water quantity allocation is assisted by Matlab, due to its powerful computational capability and ability to support advanced techniques, such as distributed decision support algorithms. EPANET provides the data used by the distributed computing algorithm to decide on water quantities.

In the third part of the chapter, we study the combination of game theory and the integrated cyber-physical simulator, and investigate how different configuration of actuators based on the game theory strategy can influence the malfunction of the purely physical WDN in the EPANET. When the faults are injected into the physical infrastructure (represented by EPANET) by setting certain combination of the actuators, we observe the effect on the operation of the WDN. This effort sheds light on how the advanced algorithm in cyber network can affect the purely water network through the integrated simulator and the limitation of using EPANET to simulate the possible failures on the WDN. Furthermore, the effort can validate the functionality that the game theory has in maintaining the equilibrium, and how the equilibrium is reached in the EPANET reflected by the change of values in node demand and flow level. The insight gained can be used to develop mitigation techniques that harden the WDN against failures, ensuring a return on the considerable investment made in adding cyberinfrastructure support to critical infrastructures.

Based on the completed work in the three parts, we conclude our contribution and present our plan of research in the future.

2. Related work

As public safety concerns and prohibitive cost necessitate the use of modeling and simulation for validation of intelligent environmental decision support systems (EDSSs), the utilization of EDSSs in managing critical infrastructure has been investigated in numerous studies. A general introduction to integrated decision support systems for environment planning is provided in Kainuma et al. (1990). Applications of EDSSs include prevention of soil salinization Xiao & Yimit (2008), regional environment risk management in municipal areas Wang & Cheng (2010), and environmental degradation monitoring Simoes et al. (2003). Examples particularly relevant to this book chapter are Xiao & Yimit (2008), which presents an integrated EDSS for water resource utilization and groundwater control; and Serment et al. (2006), which defines the major functionalities for an EDSS dedicated to the hydraulic management of the Camargue ecosystem. Discussion on available models and tools, such as GIS, and database management systems, is presented in Rennolls et al. (2004), which also presents an application of biogeochemical modeling for sustainability management of European forests.

Resource management algorithms have also been proposed for intelligent regulation. For instance, hedging rules have been utilized to minimize the impact of drought by effectively reducing the ongoing water supply to balance the target storage requirement Tu et al. (2003). Applications of game theory include optimization of rate control in video coding Ahmad & Luo (2006), allocation of power in frequency-selective unlicensed bands Xu et al. (2008), and power control in communications MacKenzie & Wicker (2001). Most relevant to this book chapter is the use of game theory in analyzing water resources for optimal allocation Yu-Peng et al. (2006). Unlike our work, where the focus is to enable environmental management, specifically water allocation, through the use of CPSs; the focus of Yu-Peng et al. (2006) is on incorporating social and economic factors to provide a solution that maximizes the overall value of water resources while satisfying both administrative resources allocation mandates and consumer requirements.

This book chapter presents an EDSS, with the broader goal of applying the insights gained to similar CPSs. Many CPSs, especially critical infrastructure systems, can be viewed as commodity transport networks. WDNs are an example, as are smart grids and intelligent transportation systems. The commodity transported varies from one domain to another, but the systems share the goal of allocating limited resources under physical constraints, and leverage the intelligent decision support provided by cyber infrastructure in achieving this goal.

As an emerging research area, the body of literature specifically related to CPSs is limited. A considerable fraction of related work examines critical infrastructure systems. The focus of the majority of studies related to CPSs, e.g., Haimes & Jiang (2001); Pederson (2006); Rinaldi (2004); Svendsen & Wolthusen (2007) is on interdependencies among different components of critical infrastructure. A relatively comprehensive summary of modeling and simulation techniques for critical infrastructure systems, an important category of CPSs, is provided in Rinaldi (2004). Related challenges are enumerated in Pederson (2006), where system complexity is identified as the main impediment to accurate characterization of CPSs. Other challenges include the low probability of occurrence of critical events, differences in the time scales associated with these events, and the difficulty of gathering data needed for accurate modeling. Our work is one of few studies in the emerging field of CPSs to go beyond qualitative characterization of the system to quantitative analysis.

Several challenges to the development of a generic framework for the design, modeling, and simulation of CPSs are articulated in Kim & Mosse (2008). Features described as desirable for such a framework include the integration of existing simulation tools, software reusability, and graphical representation of the modeling and simulation environment. The work presented in this book chapter meets all these criteria.

The study most closely related to the work presented in this book chapter is Al-Hammouri et al. (2007), where a method is proposed for integration of the ns-2 network simulator with the Modelica framework, a modeling language for large-scale physical systems. The paper highlights the challenge of two-way synchronization of the simulators. The key difference between this study and our work is that we link to a specialized simulator capable of accurately representing the operation of the physical infrastructure, in this case a WDN, at high resolution. The WDN simulator, and other related simulation tools are described in the next section of this book chapter.

3. Simulation tools and integration challenges

Our approach to simulation of a CPS is based on the use of existing simulation tools for the cyber and physical networks, respectively. This choice is due to the powerful capabilities of specialized tools in representing their domain (cyber or physical), which allows the focus of our work to shift to accurate representation of the interactions between the cyber and physical networks.

3.1 Simulation tools for the physical infrastructure of WDNs

Several tools are available for simulation of the physical water distribution infrastructure. Examples include EPANET, which can capture both quantity and quality of water throughout a distribution network United States Environmental Protection Agency (2011a); RiverWeb, which is focused on river basin processes National Center for Supercomputing Applications (2011); Water Quality Analysis Simulation Program (WASP), which provides watershed, water quality, and hydrodynamic models United States Environmental Protection Agency (2011d). Also considered for our study was Waterspot, which simulates water treatment plants Dutch Ministry of Economics (2011); the Ground Water and Rainmaker Simulators United States Environmental Protection Agency (2011c), which is mainly a teaching tool; and the General Algebraic Modeling System (GAMS), which provides a high-level modeling system for the mathematical programming and optimization National Institute of Standards and Technology (2011).

Among these simulators, EPANET provides the most detailed representation, as it can capture the layout of a WDN and track the flow of water in each pipe, the pressure at each node, the depth of the water in each tank, and the concentration of a chemical substance throughout the network during a simulation period United States Environmental Protection Agency (2011a). The simulator is provided at no charge by the Environmental Protection Agency. The extensive capabilities, ease of use, and lack of licensing fees motivated the choice of EPANET as the simulator for the physical infrastructure of WDN in our study.

The most recent release, EPANET 2.0, was the version used. Objects in EPANET can be classified as nodes, links, map labels, time patterns, curves and controls. Each node can in turn be a junction, reservoir, or tank, and each link can be a pipe, pump, or valve. The topology depicted in Fig. 2 is a very simple WDN as visualized by EPANET. It is composed of one reservoir, one tank, one pump, one valve, five junctions, and several pipes that connect these elements. A reservoir is a node that represents an infinite external source or sink of water United States Environmental Protection Agency (2011b), and is used to model an entity such as a lake, river, or groundwater aquifer. A tank is a node with storage capacity, where the volume of stored water can vary with time during a simulation. A junction is a point in the network where links join together and where water enters or leaves the network. When a junction has negative demand, it indicates that water is entering the network at that point.

Pumps and valves are two primary actuators that can be turned on and off at preset times, or in response to certain conditions in the network. Fluids possess energy, and the total energy per unit weight associated with a fluid is denoted as "head." On many occasions, energy needs to be added to a hydraulic system to overcome elevation differences, or losses arising from friction or other factors. A pump is a device to which mechanical energy is applied and transferred to the water as total head, so it can add more energy to the fluid. The flow through a pump is unidirectional. If the system requires more head than the pump can produce, the pump is shut down. Therefore, pumps can be turned on and off at preset times, when tank levels fall below or above certain set-points, or when the pressure at a certain node falls below or above specified thresholds.

A valve is an element that can be opened or closed to different extents, to vary its resistance to flow, thereby controlling the movement of water through a pipe. The status of each valve can be specified for all or part of the simulation by using control statements. Pipes are links that convey water from one point in the network to another. The direction of water flow is from

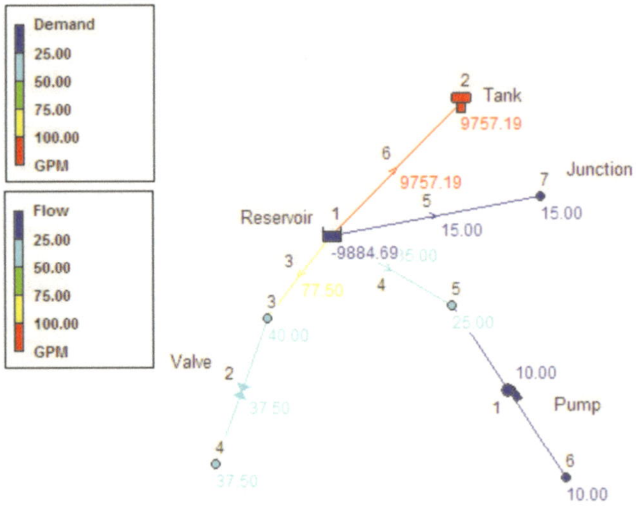

Fig. 2. A simple topology in EPANET

the end at higher hydraulic head to that at lower head, due to the effect of gravity. A negative label for a flow indicates that its direction opposes that of the pipe.

In the WDN depicted in Fig. 2, the reservoir is providing water to the tank and a number of different junctions. This topology can serve as a simple and abstract representation of a lake that provides water to consuming entities spread throughout a city. The reservoir in this figure always contributes water into the network, so its demand value is negative. The value of the demand indicates the amount of water contributed, in this case 9884.69 gallons per minute (GPM). The tank consumes the highest amount of water. Each junction is also labeled with its demand value, and each pipe with its flow speed. The entire graph is color-coded to simplify the categorization of demand or flow. The demand values of pumps and valves vary in accordance with the nodes they control.

A more complex topology is depicted in Fig. 3, which shows a screen capture at hour 8:00 of a 24-hour simulation period. This figure also depicts node groupings, circled in green, that can facilitate study of a subset of the nodes in the topology.

After simulating the system for the specified duration, EPANET can provide a report in graph, table, or text form. Among the various reports available, the full report provides the most comprehensive data, including the initial and updated values of all properties of the nodes and links within each simulation time step (one hour by default). The water flow, pressure at each node, depth of water in tanks and reservoirs, and concentration of chemical substances can be tracked from the recorded data. Figs. 4 and 5 present snapshots of the link and node information, respectively, of the full report.

3.2 Simulation tools for the cyber infrastructure of WDNs

Matlab R2010b was used to represent computational aspects of the CPS, due to its powerful mathematical tools and capability of supporting a diverse range of I/O formats, which is critical to successful interfacing to simulators for the physical and communication aspects. This version of Matlab provides support for parallel computing, which is essential for

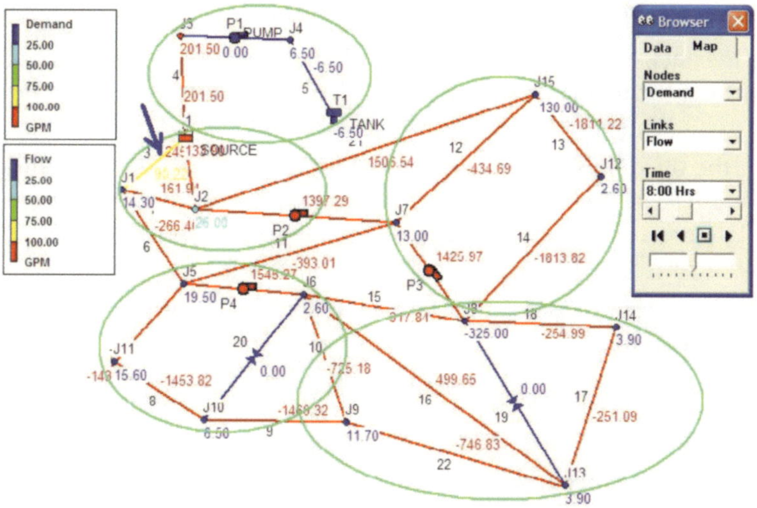

Fig. 3. A more complex topology and node groupings in EPANET

Link Results at 1:00 Hrs:

Link ID	Flow GPM	VelocityUnit fps	Headloss ft/Kft	Status
1	135.65	0.28	0.05	Open
2	69.84	0.20	0.03	Open
3	34.66	0.22	0.06	Open
4	75.00	0.48	0.25	Open
5	-2.50	0.02	0.00	Open
6	-175.31	0.50	0.16	Open
7	-1364.58	3.87	7.33	Open
8	-1370.58	3.89	7.39	Open

Fig. 4. Link information from full report

Node Results at 1:00 Hrs:

Node ID	Demand GPM	Head ft	Pressure psi	Quality
J1	5.00	1000.29	173.45	0.00
J2	10.00	1000.15	260.04	0.00
J3	75.00	998.77	216.12	0.00
J4	2.50	833.99	58.06	0.00
J5	7.50	1000.46	216.85	0.00
J6	1.00	1024.65	97.34	0.00
J7	5.00	1001.11	87.14	0.00
J8	-100.00	1023.99	391.70	0.00

Fig. 5. Node information from full report

simulation of the cyber layer of a WDN, as the decision support algorithms used are typically implemented in a distributed fashion.
ns-2 USC Information Sciences Institute (2011), a public-domain discrete event simulator, is the tentative choice for representing the communication network, an aspect of the cyber infrastructure that is yet to be investigated.

3.3 Challenges in linking simulators for the cyber and physical networks

Accurate simulation of a CPS hinges on correctly recreating the information flow of Fig.1, through the following iterative procedure:

1. Simulating the operation of the physical infrastructure.
2. Extracting the data, e.g., water pressure in various pipes, required by the decision support algorithms from the report generated in Step 1, and converting this data to an acceptable input format for the simulator for the cyber infrastructure.
3. Simulating the operation of the cyber (computing) infrastructure, including the data of Step 2 as input. This data may be supplemented by other information, e.g., historical averages. The goal of this step is generation of settings for control elements, e.g., valves, in the physical layer.
4. Converting the output of Step 3 to a format acceptable as input by the simulator for the physical infrastructure.
5. Providing the data from Step 4 as input to the simulator for the physical infrastructure.
6. Repeat Step 1.

The procedure described above is repeated iteratively for the duration of the simulation. After the initial setup, all steps are expected to take place without user intervention, as would be the case with using a single simulator. As described in Section 1, differences in temporal resolution and data representation, and the lack of interoperability, especially in interfaces, pose considerable challenges in linking cyber and physical simulators in a fashion that accurately represents the CPS as a whole. Our approach to overcoming these challenges is discussed in Section 4, which describes the simulation of an intelligent WDN using Matlab and EPANET.

4. Integrated cyber-physical simulation of intelligent WDNs

One of the main contribution of this book chapter is in developing a procedure for simulation of an intelligent WDN, such that cyber (computing) and physical aspects of the CPS are accurately and precisely represented. As described in Section 3, Matlab and EPANET, respectively, are used to simulate the computing and physical infrastructures of an intelligent WDN. The procedure described in Section 3.3 is necessary, as it would be for a CPS from any other domain. Fig. 6 depicts this procedure for the specific case of simulation of an intelligent WDN with EPANET and Matlab. The numbers identify the corresponding step from the procedure described in Section 3.3.

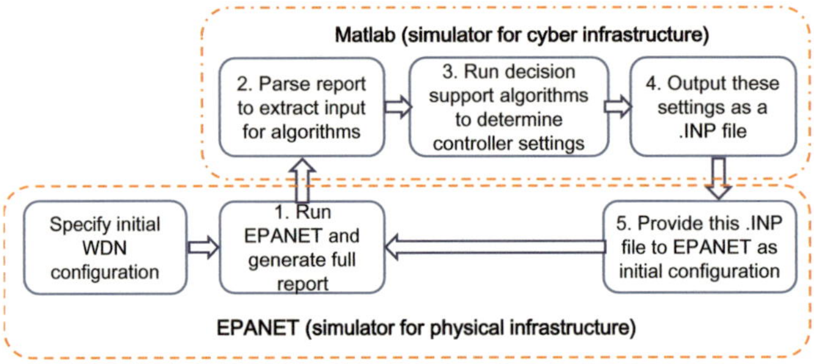

Fig. 6. Procedure for simulation of an intelligent WDN

The first step in simulating an intelligent WDN is to specify the duration to be simulated and the configuration of the physical infrastructure, e.g., topology and demand values, in

EPANET. A 24-hour duration was selected for the simulation presented in this section. After simulating the system for the specified duration, EPANET generates a full report that includes information for all links and nodes for each time step (one hour by default), as shown in Figs. 4 and 5. The full report generated as the output file of EPANET is automatically saved as a plain-text .NET file. This information includes values required as input by the decision support algorithms of the cyber infrastructure, which in turn determine settings for physical control elements such as valves.

To simulate the provision of sensor readings and other information about the physical infrastructure to the cyber control system, the full report generated as output by EPANET needs to be provided as input to Matlab. This necessitates pre-processing of the file, and parsing of the data into the matrix form required by Matlab. A script using the *textscan* and *cell2mat* commands can be defined within Matlab to carry out this pre-processing to generate a separate matrix from the EPANET data for each entity (node or link) for each simulation time step recorded in the full report, e.g., hour 1:00.

For simplicity, the simulation illustrated in this section was focused on node flow. The controller (pump or valve) settings were determined by averaging the node demand within a node group, which is a subset of nodes defined in EPANET. Fig. 3 shows a number of groups. The same parsing approach can be used to extract additional data, e.g., water pressure or concentration of a given chemical, from the EPANET report, as required by more sophisticated decision support algorithms.

Each node group can reflect an associated group of consumers, such as residential nodes in the south of a city. The only requirement is that each node group include at least one controller (pump or valve), so controller settings determined by the cyber infrastructure can be utilized in water allocation. The focus of the simulation in this section was integrated simulation of the CPS, and as such, a simplistic approach was taken to water allocation, with the goal of distributing the water as equitably as possible, subject to physical constraints on the nodes. More intelligent decision support can be achieved through game-theoretic approaches Yu-Peng Wang & Thian (2006), and it will be elaborated in Section 5.

Matlab generates a matrix of controller settings, which need to be provided to EPANET, as they would be to the physical control elements in an actual WDN. A .INP file is required, in a format identical to the original input provided to EPANET in the first step of the simulation, with controller values updated to reflect the settings determined by the decision support algorithm. A Matlab script utilizing the *dlmwrite* and *fprintf* commands can be used to generate a .INP file with the format expected by EPANET.

```
[TITLE]
EPANET INPUT FILE

[JUNCTIONS]
; ID        Elev      Demand        Pattern
1           600       5         1
2           400       -4.5      1
3           500       25        1
4           700       2.5       1
5           500       4.3       1
6           800       1         1
7           800       -19.5     1
8           120       -100      1
```

Fig. 7. EPANET input file generated by MATLAB

In the final stage of the simulation, the .INP file generated by Matlab, which specifies settings for various control elements, is used to initiate another execution of EPANET, closing the physical-cyber-physical loop. The process can be repeated as necessary to simulate operation of the WDN over multiple cycles of cyber control. Fig. 7 shows the file resulting from execution of the water allocation algorithm for the node groups of Fig. 3. The result of executing EPANET with the .INP file generated by Matlab is shown in Fig.8. As an example of the manifestation of cyber control, the flow in the link connecting Junction1 (J1) and SOURCE, marked with an arrow, has been reduced from 75-100 GPM (yellow) in Figure 3 to 50-75 GPM (green) in Figure 8.

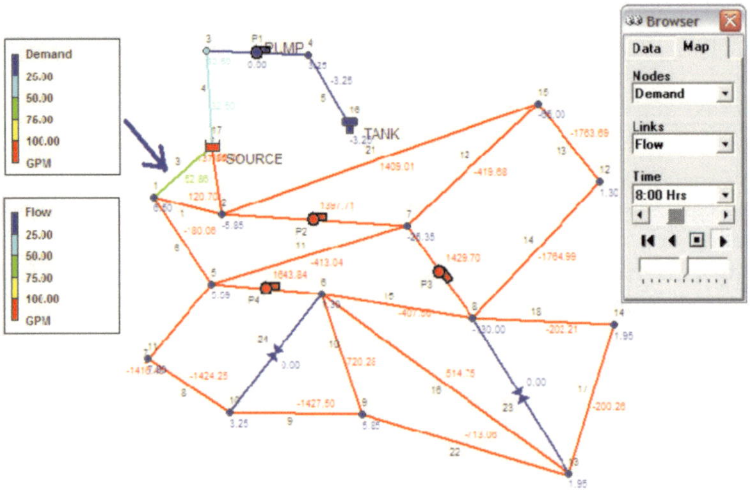

Fig. 8. Complex topology after applying cyber control

5. Intelligent water allocation as a game

In this section, we present an agent-based framework for intelligent environmental decision support. Among the techniques available for modeling intelligent environmental decision support systems (EDSSs), agent-based modeling holds particular promise in surmounting the challenges of representing both cyber and physical components, with high fidelity, in one system; and characterizing their interaction quantitatively. This is due to the capability of an agent-based model to encapsulate diverse component attributes within a single agent, while accurately capturing the interaction among autonomous, heterogeneous agents that share a common goal achieved in a distributed fashion. Sensors are key to this approach, as they provide situational awareness to the agents and enable them to function based on the semantics of their mission and the specifics of their environment.

The specific environmental management problem addressed in our work is water distribution, i.e., the allocation of water to different consuming entities by an intelligent WDN. The work presented in this section investigates the adoption of game theory as the algorithmic technique used for agent-based decision support in an intelligent WDN. The focus is on management of the quantity of water allocated to each consuming entity. Our proposed approach is based on the utilization of game theory for resource sharing and service provision in peer-to-peer networks Gupta & Somani (2005).

5.1 Model of the service game

In this section, we model the interaction among selfish agents, the consuming entities, as a service game, using the notation of Gupta & Somani (2005), where the service game presented models resource sharing in peer-to-peer networks. We divide time, t, into discrete numbered slots, e.g., $t = 0$ or $t = 1$. During each time slot, each agent can receive requests for service from other agents, or request their services for itself. The service in question here is the provision of water. The quality of the water provided is beyond the scope of this book chapter; our focus is on quantity. The model presented in this book chapter is a first step that seeks to demonstrate the feasibility of an agent-based implementation of an EDSS based on game theory. In this preliminary model, we assume an unlimited water supply. This assumption is justified in cases where water resources are not scarce, and the aim of decision support is to facilitate more efficient water distribution. Future work will investigate the application of game theory to a WDN with limited water supply.

Each request issued by an agent can be sent to more than one service provider (peer agent), to increase the probability that the request will be fulfilled. For a service provider, the incoming requests can arrive either in parallel or in sequence. A request will stop propagating among the agents when any of the providers agree to serve, at which point the request is considered to have been fulfilled. For simplicity, we assume that an agent can submit only one service request and can accommodate only one service request during a time slot. An agent's status for a given time slot is labeled as $\{Srv\}$ if it fulfills any of the requests received during the time slot. The status of all agents and requests is propagated throughout the system. The cycle of service request and provision repeats indefinitely, which corresponds to an infinitely repeated game, G^{∞}, where the basic game being repeated is G.

More specifically, the basic game, G, is defined in terms of the following items:

- Players: all peer agents that participate in water allocation; for tractability, peer agents are assumed to be identical.
- Actions: each agent can decide for or against service provision, denoted as $\{Srv\}$ and $\{Dcln\}$, respectively.
- Preference of each player: represented by the expected value of a payoff function determined by the action taken. When service is received by an agent, the payoff value of the agent denoted as utility, U; when the agent provides service, the payoff value is denoted as cost, C.

The reputation of a player, i, in a given time slot, t, is denoted by $R(t,i)$, and depends on whether or not it provides service, both in the current time period and in prior periods, as represented by Equation 1:

$$R(t,i) = R(t-1,i) * (1-a) + (w * a),\ 0 \leq a \leq 1, t \geq 2 \quad (1)$$

If service is provided by player i in time period t, w is set to 1, otherwise 0. The reputation of all players is initialized as 0 at time $t = 0$, and is defined as w at $t = 1$. Therefore, $0 \leq R(t,i) \leq 1$ is always maintained. In Equation 1, parameter a is a constant that captures the strength of the "memory of the system," i.e., the relative importance of current vs. past behavior of an agent in determining its reputation. The notion of reputation is key in the game model, as it affects the probability of receiving service for a player, and forms the incentive mechanism to contribute service in the system. More detailed discussion is presented in Section 6.

5.2 Nash equilibrium of the game

In this section, we investigate the Nash equilibrium action profile of the service game defined above. Per the Nash Folk theorem, investigating this equilibrium for a single iteration of the game G will suffice, as G^{∞} will have the same equilibrium Fudenberg & Maskin (1986). The results of this section follow from the service game model, and as such, are based on Gupta & Somani (2005).

In the game model, the utility that a player gains increases with the player's contribution to the system, as the probability of receiving service is determined by the reputation of a player, which improves (increases) as the player provides service. Each player wants to gain the maximum benefit from the model, leading to a non-cooperative game. Nash equilibrium is reached when competition ends among the players. This occurs when the collective set of actions taken by the players with respect to service provision is locally optimum, i.e., no player can improve its utility by electing a different strategy. The two types of Nash equilibria are *Pure* and *Mixed*.

5.2.1 Pure Nash equilibrium

Pure Nash equilibrium results when every player declines to serve, i.e., elects the action $\{Dcln\}$. This is easily proven. If only one player, i, elects to serve, then its payoff is $-C$, as compared to the (higher) payoff of 0 that would result from declining to serve. Every other player has declined to serve, and as such the serving player, i, is unable to utilize its increased reputation to obtain service from others, discouraging further provision of service. This action profile leads to a stalemate, where no service is provided anywhere in the system, and as such is considered a trivial equilibrium.

The opposite case, where all players elect to serve is not a local optimum, and hence not a Nash equilibrium action profile. If every other player is providing service, then the best strategy for any single player is to decline service, resulting in a payoff of U instead of $U - C$.

5.2.2 Mixed Nash equilibrium

The agents responsible for decision support in a WDN are considered to be peers, and members of a homogeneous population, in terms of capabilities and responsibilities. As such, it is assumed that the Nash equilibrium reached will be symmetric, i.e., all players will choose the same strategy. This enables us to drop the player index i in referring to parameters in the discussion below.

The symmetric equilibrium action profile of interest is mixed-strategy, where players elect to serve in some time periods and decline service in others. As previously mentioned, the pure-strategy equilibrium of no service throughout the system is not a sustainable operational state for a WDN.

In the mixed-strategy symmetric Nash equilibrium action profile, each player, i, elects to serve with probability p and declines service with probability $1 - p$, with $p > 0$, meaning that either action is possible. We assume that each player can provide service prior to requesting it.

The expected payoff value of electing to serve during time period t is defined as:

$$\text{Payoff}(Srv) = p * (-C + R(t, Srv) * U) \tag{2}$$

In Equation 2, the term $(-C + R(t, Srv) * U)$ illustrates the tradeoff inherent to service provision, namely, that cost of providing service as compared to the benefit of receiving service. The term $R(t, Srv) * U$ reiterates that the probability of obtaining service in the current time period depends on a player's reputation. This payoff value of a player not only reflects its current payoff after providing service, but also captures the potential to obtain service in the next period, through the inclusion of $R(t, Srv)$, which can be used as a health indicator that reflects the capability of the player to gain service in the near future. When service is provided, $w = 1$, and per Equation 1:

$$R(t, i) = R(t-1, i) * (1-a) + a \tag{3}$$

Similarly, the payoff value of selecting the action $\{Dcln\}$ is:

$$\text{Payoff}(Dcln) = (1-p) * (R(t, Dcln) * U) \tag{4}$$

The equation reflects the "no contribution, no cost" case. When service is declined, $w = 0$, and per Equation 1:

$$R(t, i) = R(t-1, i) * (1-a) \tag{5}$$

In a mixed-strategy Nash equilibrium of finite games, each player's expected payoff should be the same for all actions. In other words, the respective payoff values for $\{Srv\}$ and $\{\text{Dcln}\}$ are equal:

$$\text{Payoff}(Srv) = \text{Payoff}(Dcln) \tag{6}$$

Substituting from Equations 2 and 4 yields:

$$p * (-C + R(t, Srv) * U) = (1-p) * (R(t, Dcln) * U) \tag{7}$$

Incorporating the iterative definition of reputation, from Equations 3 and 5, the probability of service provision, p, is determined as:

$$p = \frac{R(t-1) * U(1-a)}{-C + 2R(t-1) * U(1-a) + Ua} \tag{8}$$

Several noteworthy points arise from the equations above. Firstly, p changes during each time period, and is a function of the agent's reputation at the end of the immediately preceding period, $R(t-1)$. Secondly, recall that this is a mixed-strategy Nash equilibrium action profile, where all players have the same p. Thirdly, we contend that this equilibrium is more stable than the pure-strategy equilibrium discussed above, as self-interest will motivate agents to eventually provide service in order to increase their chances of receiving service.

6. Design of experimental validation

In this section, we present experimental validation of the game-theoretic approach to water allocation described in the previous section. Matlab simulation was implemented with the three interacting peer agents shown in Fig. 9.

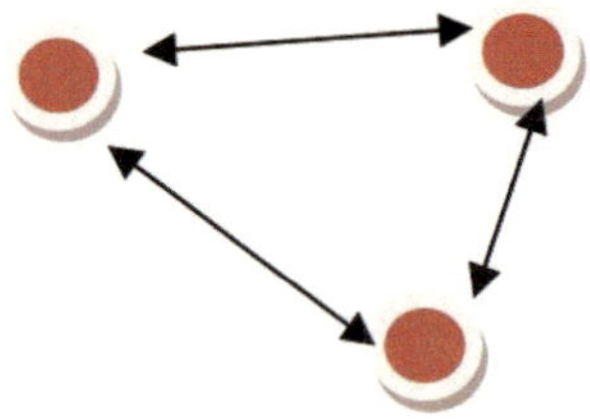

Fig. 9. Interaction among three peer agents.

The agents are labeled Node i, Node j, and Node k, respectively. For each agent, the service strategy is as shown in Table ??. The strategy shown in Table ?? does not exhaustively capture all actions that could be taken by the three agents, but it provides a representative set of actions over a non-trivial duration of ten time slots.

Time t	Node i	Node j	Node k
1	Serve j	Serve k	Decline
2	Decline	Serve i	Decline
3	Serve k	Decline	Decline
4	Decline	Decline	Serve i
5	Serve k	Decline	Serve i
6	Serve j	Decline	Serve i
7	Serve j	Serve i	Decline
8	Decline	Decline	Decline
9	Decline	Decline	Serve j
10	Serve k	Serve i	Decline

Table 1. Strategy for service game.

According to the Table ??, we can summarize the strategy of each player, i, as W_i below:

- $W_i = [1\,0\,1\,0\,1\,1\,1\,0\,0\,1]$
- $W_j = [1\,1\,0\,0\,0\,0\,1\,0\,0\,1]$
- $W_k = [0\,0\,0\,1\,1\,1\,0\,0\,1\,0]$

The configuration of initial values for the utility of obtaining service U and the cost of providing service C is $U/C = 80$, with $U = 800$ and $C = 10$. The main reason to adopt the ratio of utility to cost, $U/C = 80$, rather than their difference, $U - C$, is the normalization inherent to use of the ratio. In civil engineering literature, water pricing has been approached from a supply and demand perspective Brown & Rogers (2006); Cui-mei & Sui-qing (2009), which is what U and C try to capture.
The U/C ratio can reflect whether the water resource is scarce or sufficient. U/C is low when water is scarce, as serving a limited resource to other agents while maintaining sufficient resources for own usage purpose will be expensive for an agent, leading to high C; and gaining utility from other agents is difficult, leading to low U. Similarly, U/C is high when sufficient water exists for all peer agents. Our initial choice of $U/C = 80$ for the simulation reflects a non-draught situation. Simulation results for other values of U/C are presented in Lin et al. (2011, to appear).

7. Integration of game theory and Cyber-Physical Simulator

In this section, we apply the game theory in the cyber networks implemented by Matlab, which issues the control command to EPANET based on the computed result by equilibrium strategy. This is an effort to combine the game theory and the CPS simulator, which is expected to reflect the dynamic behavior of the CPS and reveal the interdependencies across the cyber-physical boundary.

7.1 The topology for the integrated simulation

The topology that we create for investigating the combination of game theory in Section5 and the integrated CPS simulator in Section4 is shown in Fig. 10. The principle that we follow to create this topology is to easy the application of game theory, which is applied on three agents to collaborate on water allocation.

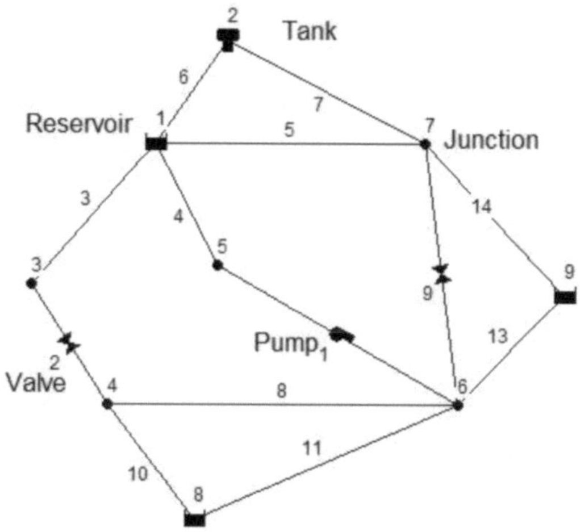

Fig. 10. Simple topology for integrating game theory.

The main criteria for creating the topology include two aspects: the water distribution network should have at least 3 actuators, either pump or valve, in charge of three different areas, respectively; the water distribution network should have 3 reservoirs, representing three agents to provide or retrieve water from their neighbors. Fig. 11 shows the grouped nodes in the topology, which indicates what components are incorporated in the scope managed by the particular agent. Each scope managed by one agent has one actuator.

7.2 Initial configuration

For the grouped components in Fig. 11, reservoir 1, tank 2, junction 5 and 7, pump 1 are in the same group; reservoir 8, valve 2, junction 3 and 4 are in the same group; reservoir 9, junction 6 and valve 9 are in the same group. After running EPANET as introduced in Fig. 6, the simulation results in the first hour (the time step that we configure for simulation is 1 hour) are summarized in Fig. 12 and Fig. 13.

Fig. 11 is a snapshot of the node demand in EPANET simulation at 1 hour, and from the result we can tell that at 1 hour, reservoir 1 is providing water (indicated by the negative demand value) and reservoir 8 and reservoir 9 are retrieving water (indicated by the positive demand value). Similarly as in the game theory experimental validation in Section6, we use 1

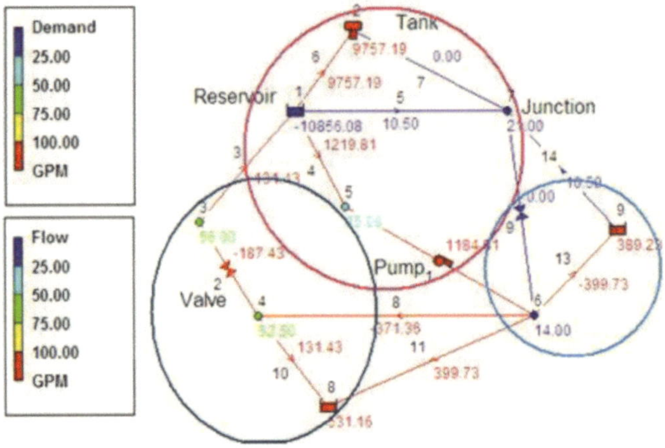

Fig. 11. Grouped nodes in the topology.

Network Table - Nodes at 1:00 Hrs

Node ID	Demand GPM	Head ft	Pressure psi
Junc 3	56.00	999.99	129.99
Junc 4	52.50	999.99	216.65
Junc 5	35.00	999.99	173.32
Junc 6	14.00	1000.00	216.65
Junc 7	21.00	1000.00	173.32
Resvr 1	-9846.97	1000.00	0.00
Resvr 8	-54.78	1000.00	0.00
Resvr 9	-33.95	1000.00	0.00
Tank 2	9757.19	720.00	8.67

Fig. 12. Node demand (in GPM) at 1 hour.

to represent the state of serving water in one agent and 0 to represent the state of declining to serve water (including retrieving water from other agents). Accordingly, in the first simulation period, the script played by three agents is (1, 0, 0). Similarly as shown in the topology of Fig. 9, we suppose the reservoir 1 is node i, and reservoir 8 and 9 are node j and node k, respectively.

In terms of implementation, the water attributes (demand, pressure, head, flow, etc.) in EPANET are controlled by the actuators (pump and valve). By sending the control command to the actuator from the cyber infrastructure (implemented in MATLAB), we can configure the serve/decline to serve operation of the node (reservoir). Because there are three actuators in Fig. 11 with the open/close options, we can have totally 8 different combinations, shown in Fig. 14.

The initial configuration (constraints) of the components (pump, valve, tank, node) can affect the simulation result, and we set the initial values as following:

Network Table - Links at 1:00 Hrs

Link ID	Flow GPM	Velocity fps	Unit Headloss ft/Kft	Status
Pipe 3	37.80	0.11	0.01	Open
Pipe 4	35.00	0.10	0.01	Open
Pipe 5	16.97	0.05	0.00	Open
Pipe 6	9757.19	27.68	280.00	Open
Pipe 7	0.00	0.00	0.00	Closed
Pipe 8	-32.90	0.09	0.01	Open
Pipe 10	-37.80	0.11	0.01	Open
Pipe 11	-16.97	0.05	0.00	Open
Pipe 13	16.97	0.05	0.00	Open
Pipe 14	16.97	0.05	0.00	Open
Pump 1	0.00	0.00	0.00	Closed
Valve 2	-18.20	0.05	0.00	Open
Valve 9	12.95	0.04	0.00	Open

Fig. 13. Flow in the link (in GPM) at 1 hour.

Reservoir	**1**	**8**	**9**	**Result at the 0:00 hr**
Actuator	Pump 1	Valve 2	Valve 9	
Status of actuator	Open	Open	Open	Error. Pump 1 open but exceeds max flow at 0:00 hr.
	Open	Open	Close	Reservoir 1 is serving, others are not. (1, 0 , 0)
	Open	Close	Open	Error. Pump 1 open but exceeds max flow at 0:00 hr.
	Close	Open	Open	All the three reservoirs are serving at 0:00 hr. (1, 1, 1)
	Close	Close	Open	All the three reservoirs are serving at 0:00 hr. (1, 1, 1)
	Close	Open	Close	All the three reservoirs are serving at 0:00 hr. (1, 1, 1)
	Open	Close	Close	Reservoir 1 and 9 are serving, reservoir 8 is not. (1, 0, 1)
	Close	Close	Close	All the three reservoirs are serving at 0:00 hr. (1, 1, 1)

Fig. 14. Result at 0:00 hr with different configuration of actuators.

- All the three reservoirs (1, 8 and 9) have the total head of 1000 feet and elevation of 1000 feet.
- Valve 2 has 12 inch diameter, the type is PRV, loss coefficient is 0, and the fixed status is set as none, as it can be open or closed.
- Pump 1 has pump curve 1 and the initial status is set as open.
- Valve 9 has 12 inch diameter, the type is PRV, loss coefficient is 0, and the fixed status is set as none, as it can be open or closed.
- Tank 2 has elevation of 10 feet(the elevation above a common datum in feet of the bottom shell of the tank) of 700 feet, initial level (the height of the water surface above the bottom elevation of the tank at the start of the simulation), minimum level of 0 feet(the minimum height in feet of the water surface above the bottom elevation that will be maintained; the tank should not be allowed to drop below this level), maximum level of 20 feet (the maximum height in feet of the water surface above the bottom elevation that will be maintained; the tank should not be allowed to rise above this level) and 50 inch diameter.
- Junction 3 has elevation of 700 feet, base demand of 80 gpm, and its actual demand is shown during simulation.
- Junction 4 has elevation of 500 feet, base demand of 75 gpm, and its actual demand is shown during simulation.
- Junction 5 has elevation of 600 feet, base demand of 50 gpm, and its actual demand is shown during simulation.
- Junction 6 has elevation of 500 feet, base demand of 20 gpm, and its actual demand is shown during simulation.
- Junction 7 has elevation of 600 feet, base demand of 30 gpm, and its actual demand is shown during simulation.

Subjected to the limited cases that actuators can manipulate the water flow and the constraints of the capacity of pipe and node, such as the maximum flow the pipe can sustain for pump 1, when we use the game theory to control the water resource on the EPANET, we need to take these constraint factors into consideration and make decision accordingly.
Indicated by Fig. 14, we should avoid the failures generated by the two types of configuration of the actuators. In another words, EPANET can not continue the simulation if pump 1, valve 2 and valve 9 are in the status of (open, open, open) or (open, close, open). This shows that the command issued from the cyber simulator for controlling the actuators can lead to the errors or malfunction of the underlying simulator for the physical network, and in this case, it is EPANET.
According to Fig. 14, three patterns (strategy of the player) of water resource provision are repeated consecutively, and they are (1, 0, 0), (1, 1, 1) and (1, 0, 1). We define the pattern as serving pattern and the serving strategy similarly as Table **??** is the combination of the three patterns. For example, if the initial serving pattern is (1, 0 ,0), the we configure the next serving pattern as (1, 1, 1). There are multiple actuator setting methods to achieve this serving pattern, for this case, we select the combination of (close, open, open), mapping with pump 1, valve 2 and valve9. All the rest of the configuration remains the same as initial configuration. The generated control command file (input .INP file to EPANET) by MATLAB is shown in the snapshot of as Fig. 15, which captures the part of actuator configuration. As shown in the .INP file, the three actuators are configured as (close, open, open).

```
[TAGS]

[DEMANDS]
;Junction                Demand

[STATUS]
;ID                      Status/Setting
 1                       Closed
 2                       Open
 9                       Open
```

Fig. 15. The configuration for actuator in .INP file.

7.3 Result and analysis

The topology in Fig. 16 shows the simulation result after actuators are configured as (close, open, open), which leads to the scenario that all reservoirs are serving. In Fig. 16, all the serving reservoirs are indicated by blue color with negative value of demand in GPM.

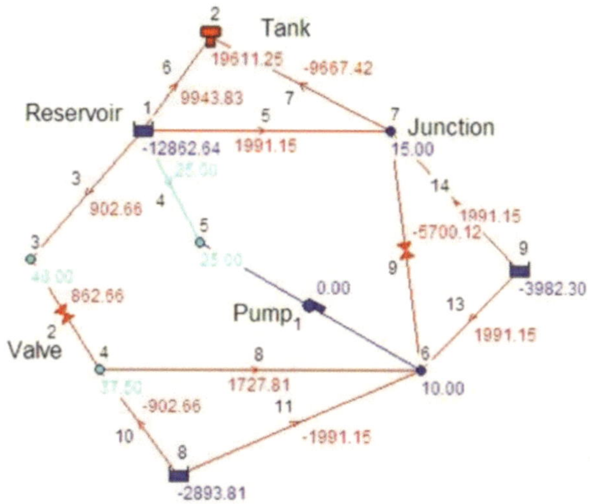

Fig. 16. Topology of simulation for all reservoirs are serving.

After we run EPANET based on the configuration set in MATLAB, the simulation results in the very first hour (0:00 hr) are presented as Fig. 17 and Fig. 18.

We further investigate the case that three reservoirs are consistently providing water, i.e. throughout the total 10 simulation periods, all the three reservoirs are always providing water. Fig. 19 summarizes the demand values (in GPM) of each reservoir in time series.

Given the current initial configuration, the EPANET can run successfully and can generate the simulation values for each reservoir provided above. At time 0:00hr, all the reservoirs are providing water, but the water quantity provided by reservoir 1 is much higher than the quantity provided by reservoir 8 and 9. Since 1:00 hr, the water quantity provided by reservoir 8 and 9 have dramatically decreased, whereas the majority of water is provided by reservoir 1. The simulation results gain some insights of the role that the advanced algorithm play and show some limitations of the integrated simulation, which are summarized as following:

1. The EPANET simulator, or the physical water network in real world, has certain capability to regulate water by itself to achieve stable status without cyber control or manipulation. Some other factors can play role in achieving the stable status, such as gravity.

Network Table - Nodes at 0:00 Hrs

Node ID	Demand GPM	Head ft	Pressure psi
Junc 3	40.00	996.59	128.51
Junc 4	37.50	996.59	215.17
Junc 5	25.00	1000.00	173.32
Junc 6	10.00	985.25	210.26
Junc 7	15.00	985.25	166.93
Resvr 1	-12862.64	1000.00	0.00
Resvr 8	-2893.81	1000.00	0.00
Resvr 9	-3982.30	1000.00	0.00
Tank 2	19611.25	710.00	4.33

Fig. 17. Node demand (in GPM) at 0 hour when all three reservoirs are serving.

Network Table - Links at 0:00 Hrs

Link ID	Flow GPM	Velocity fps	Unit Headloss	Status
Pipe 3	902.66	2.56	3.41	Open
Pipe 4	25.00	0.07	0.00	Open
Pipe 5	1991.15	5.65	14.75	Open
Pipe 6	9943.83	28.21	290.00	Open
Pipe 7	-9667.42	27.42	275.25	Open
Pipe 8	1727.81	4.90	11.34	Open
Pipe 10	-902.66	2.56	3.41	Open
Pipe 11	-1991.15	5.65	14.75	Open
Pipe 13	1991.15	5.65	14.75	Open
Pipe 14	1991.15	5.65	14.75	Open
Pump 1	0.00	0.00	0.00	Closed
Valve 2	862.66	2.45	0.00	Open
Valve 9	-5700.12	16.17	0.00	Open

Fig. 18. Flow in the link (in GPM) at 0 hour when all three reservoirs are serving.

Time Series Table - Node 1

Time Hours	Demand GPM	Head ft
0:00	-12862.64	1000.00
1:00	-9846.97	1000.00
2:00	-9911.10	1000.00
3:00	-9872.62	1000.00
4:00	-9821.32	1000.00
5:00	-9846.97	1000.00
6:00	-9911.10	1000.00
7:00	-9872.62	1000.00
8:00	-9821.32	1000.00
9:00	-9846.97	1000.00
10:00	-9911.10	1000.00

Time Series Table - Node 8

Time Hours	Demand GPM	Head ft
0:00	-2893.81	1000.00
1:00	-54.78	1000.00
2:00	-93.90	1000.00
3:00	-70.43	1000.00
4:00	-39.13	1000.00
5:00	-54.78	1000.00
6:00	-93.90	1000.00
7:00	-70.43	1000.00
8:00	-39.13	1000.00
9:00	-54.78	1000.00
10:00	-93.90	1000.00

Time Series Table - Node 9

Time Hours	Demand GPM	Head ft
0:00	-3982.30	1000.00
1:00	-33.95	1000.00
2:00	-58.20	1000.00
3:00	-43.65	1000.00
4:00	-24.25	1000.00
5:00	-33.95	1000.00
6:00	-58.20	1000.00
7:00	-43.65	1000.00
8:00	-24.25	1000.00
9:00	-33.95	1000.00
10:00	-58.20	1000.00

Fig. 19. Demand value changes in reservoir 1, 8 and 9.

2. The reservoir in EPANET has the ability to provide infinite quantity of water, which could be infeasible in real application case.
3. Although all the three reservoirs are providing water, the magnitude of provided water quantity is different. Compared with reservoir 1, the water provided by reservoir 8 and

9 can almost be neglected, although at the beginning reservoir 8 and 9 are providing more quantity of water. This change actually indicates the condition for reaching the equilibrium in a water distribution network, i.e. the case that all the reservoirs (or players) are consistently providing water is not an equilibrium or stable case, which conforms to our previous analysis in subsection 5.2.1 on the pure equilibrium case.

4. The game theory in MATLAB is an supplemental intelligence onto the EPANET, and it is an artificial manipulation for controlling the water rather than the hydraulic or physic law. The purpose to define the reputation of player and the expected payoff value is to investigate how the incentive mechanism for contributing service in the system can affect the equilibrium in the water allocation. The more the player serves, the higher reputation it can gain, and the higher probability it can gain water from other players. The parameters in the game theory configure how the game will play among the players, such as the probability that one player will serve in the next phase, but the strategy for service game played among the players (i.e. which player serve and which player decline to serve) determines the actual water allocation. In the combination of game theory and the integrated CPS simulator, we directly use the strategy played among the players, and set the configuration of actuators accordingly.

The effort of combining the CPS simulator and game theory shows the chain effect that the advanced algorithm can issue a command of controlling the actuator, and the configuration of the actuator can affect the simulation on the physical network. Sometimes the configuration of the actuators may cause failures as indicated in Fig. 14, and this is due to the fact that the physical components, such as pipes or tanks are subjected to the constraints which are configured initially. The simulation reveals the risk that in real application, the calculated configuration of the actuators can lead to the malfunctions of physical components, because of the multiple constraints exerted on the components. This discovery can be used to develop mitigation techniques that harden the WDN against failures, specifically, the design of advanced computing algorithm on the cyber network needs to consider the multiple constrains in the physical network, in order to ensure that adding the cyberinfrastructure to support the operation of critical infrastructure will not bring serious reliability issues.

8. Conclusion and future work

The CPSs are an recently emerging research area that incorporates the physical infrastructure and the cyber networks together. The simulation of the complicated system is the preliminary step towards assessing the impact that cyber control brings to the existing infrastructure system. However, the tools for their modeling and simulation are very limited. A number of related challenges were discussed in this book chapter, with focus on integrated simulation of CPSs, where the goal is to accurately reflect the operation and interaction of the cyber and physical networks that comprise the system, and reflects the interdependencies between the physical and cyber infrastructures. In this book chapter, we address one of the major challenges that is to accurately and precisely represent the features and operation of the physical infrastructure by adopting the domain-specific tool EPANET, a simulator for WDNs. A method was described and illustrated for using Matlab and EPANET in integrated simulation of intelligent WDNs, which make use of intelligent decision support to control the quantity and quality of water.

To quantitatively analyze the distribution of water quantity, we investigate the sophisticated algorithm, game theory, as the intelligent decision support facilitated by CPSs to revolutionize environmental management. An agent-based EDSS was presented that utilized game theory for allocation of water among consuming entities. The design of experiment was proposed to validate the model. Based on the created integrated simulator, we apply the game theory in the cyber networks for making decision to control the actuators on the physical network represented in EPANET. The result shows some of the limitation of the simulator, and what is more important, it reveals that if the decision support algorithms do not consider the constraints of the physical components (such as the maximum flow that pipe can sustain or tank capacity), the control command sent to the actuators can lead to the failures on the physical network. The combination effort reflects the interdependencies between the physical and cyber infrastructures that comprise a CPS. Understanding these interdependencies is a critical precursor to any investigation of CPS, especially with respect to reliability, and can be used to develop mitigation techniques to prevent failures caused by improper design of decision support algorithms.

The integrated simulation technique presented in this book chapter is a preliminary step that will facilitate further research towards CPS-based simulation and environmental decision support. Insights gained from the WDN domain will be used to extend the models and simulation techniques developed to other CPS domains, with the ultimate goal of creating CPS models that are broadly applicable, yet capable of accurately reflecting attributes specific to each physical domain. Future extensions to this work will involve refinements to the game-theoretic algorithm, incorporating sensor data into the decision support and taking the various constraints of physical components into consideration. The multi-objective optimization issue will be investigated in such case.

9. References

Ahmad, I. & Luo, J. (2006). On using game theory to optimize the rate control in video coding, *IEEE Transaction on Circuits and System for Video Technology* 16.

Al-Hammouri, A., Liberatore, V., Al-Omari, H., Al-Qudah, Z., Branicky, M. S. & Agrawal, D. (2007). A co-simulation platform for actuator networks, *Proceedings of the 5th International Conference on Embedded Networked Sensor Systems (SenSys '07)*, ACM, New York, NY, USA, pp. 383–384.

Brown, C. & Rogers, P. (2006). Effect of forecast-based pricing on irrigated agriculture: A simulation, *Journal of Water Resources Planning and Management* 132(6): 403–413.

Cui-mei, L. & Sui-qing, L. (2009). Water price forecasting method based on marginal-cost theory: a case study in China, *World Environmental and Water Resources Congress 2009*, ASCE.

Dutch Ministry of Economics (2011). Waterspot.
URL: *http://www.waterspot.nl/*

Fudenberg, D. & Maskin, E. (1986). The Folk theorem in repeated games with discounting or with incomplete information, *Econometrica* 54: 533–554.

Gupta, R. & Somani, A. K. (2005). Game theory as a tool to strategize as well as predict node's behavior in peer-to-peer networks, *Proceedings of the 11th International Conference on Parallel and Distributed Systems (ICPADS '05)*.

Haimes, Y. Y. & Jiang, P. (2001). Leontief-based model of risk in complex interconnected infrastructures, *Journal of Infrastructure Systems* 7(1).

Kainuma, M., Nakamori, Y. & Morita, T. (1990). Integrated decision support system for environmental planning, *IEEE Transactions on Systems, Man and Cybernetics* 20: 777 – 790.

Kim, J. E. & Mosse, D. (2008). Generic framework for design, modeling and simulation of cyber physical systems, *ACM SIGBED Review* 5(1): 1–2.

Lin, J., Sedigh, S. & Miller, A. (2011, to appear). Investigating the application of game theory to resource allocation in cyber-physical systems, *Proceedings of the 44th Hawaii International Conference on System Sciences (HICSS '44)*, Kauai, HI.

MacKenzie, A. B. & Wicker, S. B. (2001). Game theory in communications: Motivation, explanation, and application to power control, *Proceedings of the IEEE Global Telecommunications Conference (GLOBECOM '01)*.

National Center for Supercomputing Applications (2011). RiverWeb.
URL: *http://destiny.mbhs.edu/riverweb/riverweb.html*

National Institute of Standards and Technology (2011). GAMS.
URL: *http://gams.nist.gov/*

Pederson, P. (2006). Critical infrastructure interdependency modeling: The survey of U.S. and international research.

Rennolls, K., Richards, T., Fedorec, A., Ibrahim, M., McManus, K. & Butler, A. (2004). Models and tools for an integrated european environmental management and decision support system (IEEMDSS), *Proceedings of the 15th International Workshop on Database and Expert Systems Applications (DEXA '04)*.

Rinaldi, S. M. (2004). Modeling and simulating critical infrastructures and their interdependencies, *Proceedings of the 37th Hawaii International Conference on System Sciences*.

Serment, J., Espinasse, B. & Tranvouez, E. (2006). Environmental decision support system for hydraulic management of the Camargue: Functionalities and software architecture, *Proceedings of the 1st International Symposium on Environment Identities and Mediterranean Area (ISEIMA '06)*.

Simoes, M., Gilson, A. P., Singh, D., Singh, K. P., Heitor, L. C. C., Fraga, E., Berroir, J. P., Herlin, I., Vieira, H. V. & Santos, U. P. (2003). Remote sensing and spatial decision support system for environmental degradation monitoring, *IEEE International Geoscience and Remote Sensing Symposium*.

Svendsen, N. K. & Wolthusen, S. D. (2007). Analysis and statistical properties of critical infrastructure interdependency multiflow models, *Proceedings of the IEEE Information Assurance and Security Workshop (IAW '07)*, pp. 247–254.

Tu, M. Y., Hsu, N. S. & W.G.Yeh, W. (2003). Optimization of reservoir management and operation with hedging rules, *Journal of Water Resources Planning and Management* 129.

United States Environmental Protection Agency (2011a). EPANET.
URL: *http://www.mathworks.com/products/parallel-computing/*

United States Environmental Protection Agency (2011b). EPANETmanual.
URL: *http://www.epa.gov/nrmrl/wswrd/dw/epanet/EN2manual.PDF*

United States Environmental Protection Agency (2011c). Ground Water and Rainmaker Simulators.
URL: *http://www.epa.state.oh.us/ddagw/SWEET/sweet simulators.html*

United States Environmental Protection Agency (2011d). Water Quality Analysis Simulation Program.
URL: *http://www.epa.gov/athens/wwqtsc/html/wasp.html*

USC Information Sciences Institute (2011). ns-2.
URL: *http://nsnam.isi.edu/nsnam/index.php/User Information*

Wang, B. & Cheng, H. (2010). Regional environmental risk management decision support system based on optimization model for minhang district in shanghai, *International Conference on Challenges in Environmental Science and Computer Engineering*.

Xiao, L. & Yimit, H. (2008). Environmental decision support system development for soil salinization in the arid area oasis, *Proceedings of the International Seminar on Business and Information Management*, IEEE Computer Society.

Xu, Y., Chen, W., Cao, Z. & Letaief, K. B. (2008). Game-theoretic analysis for power allocation in frequency-selective unlicensed bands, *Proceedings of the IEEE Global Telecommunications Conference (GLOBECOM '08)*.

Yu-Peng, W., Jian-Cang, X., Lintao, C., Ker, K. & Yew-Gan, T. (2006). Game analysis in water resources optimal allocation, *Proceedings of the International Conference on Hybrid Information Technology (ICHIT '06)*.

Yu-Peng Wang, Jian-Cang Xie, L. C. K. K. & Thian, Y.-G. (2006). Game analysis in water resources optimal allocation, *2006 International Conference on Hybrid Information Technology (ICHIT '06)*.

8

A Novel Wide Area Protection Classification Technique for Interconnected Power Grids Based on MATLAB Simulation

Moustafa, Mohammed Eissa and Masoud, Mohammed El-Shahat
Helwan University at Helwan/Faculty of Engineering
Egypt

1. Introduction

More recent technological advancements in microprocessor relays, combined with GPS receivers for synchronization and accurate time stamping, is providing users advanced relay systems with synchronized measurements, called synchrophasor measurements (IEEE Power System Relaying Committee, 2002; Phadke, 2002; Marek, 2002). Synchrophasor measurements together with advancements in digital communications, provides users with the power system state at a rate of twenty times per second. Synchrophasor measurements from different network locations when combined and processed in a central computer system will provide users with the absolute phase angle difference between distant network buses with an accuracy of tenths of an electrical degree. These types of central computer systems, equipped with wide-area protection and control algorithms, will be able to better address future system out-of-step conditions and other system problems because they will have a better knowledge of what happens throughout the power system. In addition, knowledge of online generation and load demand provided from synchrophasor measurement systems will aid in balancing better the generation and load during islanding, as well as minimizing load and generation shedding in order to preserve stability during major system disturbances. Time synchronized phasor measurements provide a dynamic view of a power system, combining these measurements in a central protection system (CPS); this capability is used to set up a wide area control, protection and optimization platform by means of new communication systems and (GPS), integrated application design is shown in Figure 1. Figure 1 shows an integrated application design based on phasor measuring units. When the system operates in extreme conditions, load shedding, generation shedding, or system islanding must occur to prevent total system collapse (Thorp et al., 1988; Centen et al., 1993; Guzman et al., 2002; Guzman et al., 2002). Typical causes of system collapse are voltage instability or transient angle instability. These instabilities can occur independently or jointly. In most cases, system wide-area disruptions begin as a voltage stability problem. Because of a failure to take proper actions for the system to recover, this voltage stability problem evolves into an angle stability problem. New monitoring, protection, and communications technologies allow us to implement economical local- and wide-area protection systems that minimize risk of wide-area system disruptions or total system collapse.

A real-time monitoring system collects "real-time information" of the transmission system that consists of measurements of selected system elements that are collected by SCADA and/or Intelligent Electronic Devices (IEDs) at various time intervals. These measurements are taken at generators, substations, and at selected other points on the system, and could be used, stored in local computer databases, or sent by telecommunication lines to remote computer databases. A real-time monitoring system should provide operators with real-time information about the transmission system's "functional status," (i.e., real-time information about the operational status of the transmission system and its components). This information includes direct measurements such as switching status of the transmission line (i.e., in service/out of service), amount of sag on the line, power flow in the line, and interconnection frequency. Other information is calculated from measurements such as whether equipment is being overloaded (Gjerde el at., 2001; Larsson et al., 2002; Zima et al., 2003; Rehtanz et al., 2002).

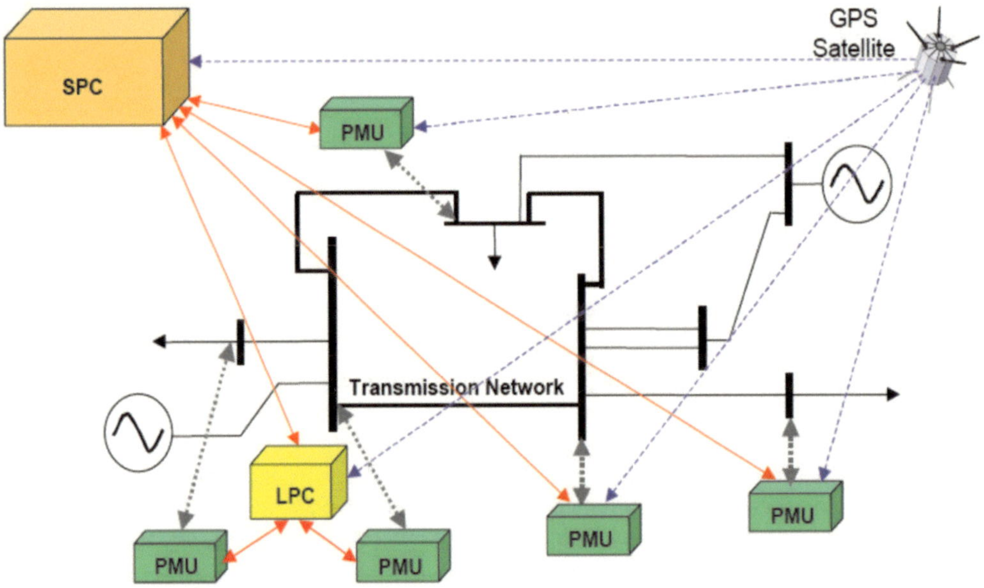

Fig. 1. An integrated application design based on Phasor measuring units.

Fault detection and classification are very challenging task for a transmission line with interconnected system. Different attempts have been made for fault classification using wavelet transform, the Kalman filtering approach, and neural network (Rehtanz, 2001; Zhang et al., 2004; Lin et al., 2004; Yu, 2003).

The electricity supply industries need tools for dealing with system-wide disturbances that often cause widespread catastrophic blackouts in power system networks. When a major disturbance occurs, protection and control measures overtake a greatest role to prevent further degradation of the system, restore the system back to a normal state, and minimize the impact of the disturbance. Continuous technological development in Information and Communication Technology (ICT), novel sensors and measurement principles in general have promoted the utilization of Phasor Measurement Unit (PMU), which is a technological enabler of Wide-Area Measurement Systems (WAMS) in power system protection and control for better management of the system security through advanced control and protection strategies.

The electricity supply industries need tools for dealing with system wide disturbances that often cause cascading outages and widespread blackouts in power system networks. When a major disturbance occurs, protection and control measures overtake the greatest role to prevent further degradation of the system, restore the system to a normal state, and minimize the impact of the disturbance. Electrical measurements of the system, which may include synchronized phasors, are supplied to one or more wind farm controllers, which in turn perform a control function improving the damping of electromechanical oscillations or voltage performance in the utility system. The benefits are improved damping to electromechanical oscillations and better voltage profile and ultimately more efficient utilization of assets, reducing the necessity for installing new assets. Wide-area protection is becoming an important issue and a challenging problem in the power industry (Wang et el., 2005).

This study proposes a novel technique based on wide-area measurements for a power system. The study is very vital and needed in the current state regarding the electrical utility and the society as well to face future expansion of the electrical grid and to cover the demand of the increasing growth and solving the problem of peak period. The study is very beneficial also from the stability and security of the grid viewpoint in case of interconnection with other countries.

This study presents a new approach for fault detection and classification for interconnected system using the time synchronized phasor measurements. The scheme is depending on comparing positive sequence voltage magnitudes for specified areas and positive sequence current phase difference angles for each interconnected line between two areas on the network. The chapter will cover all fault events for fault classification. The Matlab/simulink program is extensively used to implement the idea. It uses to simulate the power system, phase measurement unit function, synchronization process, fault detection and classification.

2. Conventional protection schemes and a wide-area backup protection system

According to recent studies, the mal-operation or fail-to trip of protection is determined as one of the origins to raise and propagate major power system disturbances. A vast majority of relay mal-operations are unwanted trips and have been shown to propagate major disturbances. A CIGRE study found that 27% of bulk power system disturbances resulted from false trips of the protection system. The major reason of these conventional solutions lies in that local protection devices are not considering a system view and are therefore not able to take optimized and coordinated actions. Backup protections in fault clearance system have the task to operate only when the primary protection fails to operate or when the primary protection is temporarily out of service. The recent complexity and enlargement of power systems makes it difficult to coordinate operation times and reaches among relays especially. In the existed relay protection system, mal operations of backup protection contribute a lot to system security and stability; furthermore, they are main reasons to system cascade tripping. To solve this problem, one proposal is to add an intelligent analyzing and controlling function in key process of protection functionality. In the areas of power system automation and substation automation, there are two different trends:

centralization and decentralization. More and more dynamic functions are moving from local and regional control centers toward central or national control centers. At the same time we also observe more "intelligence" and "decision power" moving closer towards the actual power system substations. Greater functional integration is being enclosed in substation hardware. In view of global security of power systems, the action algorithms of conventional backup protections possibly are not best choices because the operations of individual relays are hardly coordinated each other. Therefore, the principle of the protection design needs innovation to overcome the above problem (Yan et al., 2008; Xiaoyang et al., 2008; Yangguang et al., 2010; Hui, et al., 2009).

Modem protection devices have sufficient computing and communications capabilities to allow the implementation of many novel sophisticated protection principles. Therefore, a novel wide-area backup protection system with fault classification is reported in this chapter. This system is capable of acting as the substitution of conventional distributed backup protections in substation. The architecture and algorithm of the system are also introduced. To ensure the fast responsibility of such a system to the emergent events, the communication requirements are discussed as well. Conclusively, the proposed system is designed by two ways. First, in substation, concentrate some conventional backup protection functions to an intelligent processing system; second, concentrate the coordinated and optimized processing and controlling arithmetic of all backup protection in a region into a regional processing unit. The communication of data among them is carried via optic-fiber networks (Zhiyuan et al., 2009; 2009).

The proposed system comprises a master system and several local units. The system is arranged as three layers. The bottom layer consists of PMUs with additional protection functionality. The next layer consists of several Local Backup Protection Centers (LBPCs), each of which interfaces directly with a number of PMUs. The top layer, System Backup Protection Center (SBPC), acts as the coordinator for the LBPCs. Connected together via fiber-optic communication links, these devices can process intelligent algorithms based on data collected locally. The structure can be seen as Figure 2 (Seong et al., 2008).

Local part of the proposed wide-area backup system comprises PMUs and LBPC, which are both installed in the station. PMUs are made up of DSP (Digital Signal Processor) and GPS (Global Positioning System). The DSP measures instantaneous voltages and currents of protected power system in real-time, and calculates the state variables, which provide vital information for backup protection system. Then, power system variable data is transferred to LBPC, LBPC samples digital inputs, and pre-processes the analog and digital signals, and then deliver pre processed results to SBPC via fiber-optic communications between the substation and SBPC. SBPC will be installed at Regional Control Center, and integrates various well-developed functions, such as data acquisition via communication, system monitoring, fault location, security analyzing, making tripping strategy and descending strategy to LBPCs, also, SBPC can do post-event playback and post-event data analyses. These functions employ PMUs to fulfil real-time demand (Testa et al., 2004).

LBPCs perform the correlative operations on the spot when receiving the strategy from SBPC, then fault will be isolated rationally. While it is not possible to prevent all contingencies that may lead to power system collapse, a wide area backup protection system that provides a reliable security isolated scheme and optimized coordinated actions is able to mitigate or prevent large area disturbances.

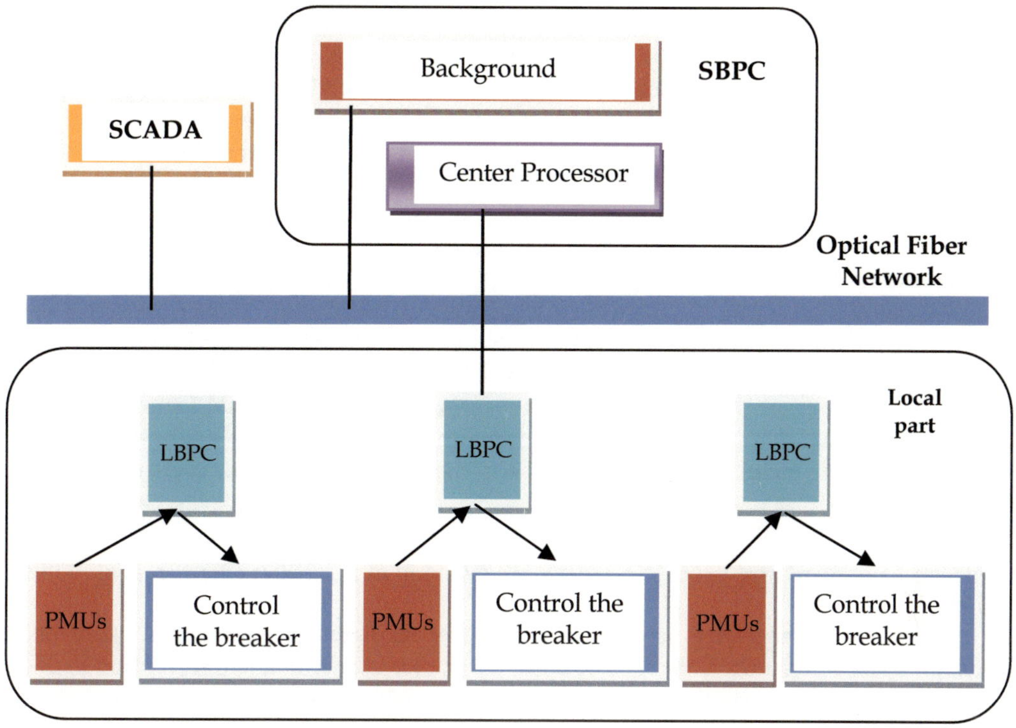

Fig. 2. General configuration of wide-area backup protection system General configuration of wide-area backup protection system.

3. Technology issues in wide area protection

3.1 Monitoring and protection for wide area disturbances

The disturbance in the power system usually develops gradually; however some phenomena, such as transient instability, can develop in a fraction of second. Regardless of the phenomena and available measures, any protection/control procedure during an emergency should consist of the following elements:

Identification and prediction - A fast identification of the specific phenomena, from the power system parameters and from the predisposing factors, is required to start the procedure to return the power system to a healthy state. An emergency may be identified from the primary consequences which are either directly or not-directly observable from local measurements (Begovic et al., 2004). Further, secondary consequences need to be predicted to avoid adverse impact of protection/control measures.

Classification - Disturbance classification is based on the constraints that are violated, severity and combination of violations, time scale of the phenomena, and utility control policy. Classification should include identification of the place of a disturbance (eg. the procedure may be different if a disturbance is caused by an internal or an external event).

Decisions and actions - The choice of the measures is strongly related to the level of priority during emergency. These levels are:

- stop the degradation of the system,
- return the system to a secure state, and
- Consider the economical and social impacts.

Coordination - Different measures may be used to solve different problems. An uncoordinated action may not be economical or secure (e.g. trip of the plant on under-frequency protection before operation of the last step of the system under-frequency control). An intelligent coordination of the protection and control actions is a major challenge and a major requirement for any successful emergency procedure (Terzija et al., 2010).
Corrections - After control measures have been applied, the system can be in an improved but unsatisfactory state. This is acceptable, since it may be advantageous to implement initial measures to stop further degradation of the system and then to continue with more optimal actions when time allows. For example, initial load can be shed merely to stop rapid frequency decline; and additional load, required to return frequency to normal, can be calculated more accurately (Terzija et al., 2011).
Time scale - For any of the previous elements, available time is a vital factor in selecting appropriate actions. A trade-off between optimal methods and time is very often required. The decision time includes selection of the remedial measure and implementation of remedial measure.

3.2 Inputs to control and protection systems (Moxley et al., 2007; Phadke et al., 2009; Jetti et al., 2006)

The state of the power system is represented by several network parameters. Thresholds, trends, patterns, and sudden changes of these parameters provide key information to detect an emergency. Some of the key system parameters which constitute the possible inputs to improved protection and control systems are:
Active power flows in the network - If the limits on active power are violated, the system is in a viability crisis. For the overloaded transformer, a loss-of-life occurs. Thus guidance for loading is established to assure a long life. The limit for the transmission line loading is set by transient and steady-state stability conditions (usually long lines), voltage collapse conditions (usually medium lines), and thermal conditions (usually short lines).
Voltage magnitude and reactive power flows - The voltages in the power system as well as sudden voltage changes need to be contained within a small range. The voltage and reactive power and their rate-of-change can provide valuable information on voltage instability.
Angles between buses - Stability limits for every line will be satisfied, if the difference in angles across the line does not exceed a certain limit. Detection of the out-of-step condition can prevent instability, and, consequently, cascading.
Impedance - Unstable swing, stable swing, and fault condition may be detected and distinguished by observing behavior of the impedance loci at the local bus. A typical out-of-step blocking or tripping scheme is accomplished by "blinders" or circles in R-X diagram and timers.
Resistance and rate-of-change of resistance - These parameters may be used to speed-up the out-of-step detection.
Frequency - Frequency deviation from the nominal value is a result of power imbalance. In modern interconnected systems, frequency deviation usually occurs in the islanded area (a definite indicator of "in extremis" crisis).
Rate of change of frequency - Unlike frequency, rate of change of frequency is an instantaneous indicator of power deficiency in the islanded area. The oscillatory nature of the rate of change of frequency needs to be considered in utilizing this feature.

Spinning reserve - The spinning reserve quantity, distribution, and the speed of its' dynamical response are factors that influence the effectiveness of the spinning reserve during an emergency. The speed of the dynamic response for the hydro units the first few seconds after a demand is made is relatively slow compared to thermal units. Consequently, the spinning reserve needs to be distributed throughout the system on both hydro and thermal units. The spinning reserve needs to be considered in load shedding schemes to optimize shed load.

Load - Load is a non-linear function of voltage and frequency. These changes in load impact power system imbalance and frequency behavior. Further, load changes with the season and the time of the day. In addition, underfrequency load shedding programs specify percent of the total load that should be shed at each step. As load changes, actual load for shedding does not correspond to planned load.

Relays and breaker status - Operation of the protective relays (desired or undesired) and network configuration have an essential impact to disturbance propagation. If undesired operation may be avoided by detecting hidden failures or by adapting relay settings to prevailing system conditions, unwanted transition of the system to a less desirable emergency state may be prevented. Further, equipment unavailability because of maintenance and testing needs to be recognized and considered.

Modeling of the power network is required to simulate disturbances and to choose features that will be extracted. The disturbance in the power network usually develops gradually; however some phenomena, such as a rise of transient instability, can develop in a fraction of second. Selection of appropriate power network analysis tools is important (load flow, transient stability, mid and long term dynamic models, EMTP, etc.).

3.3 Performance requirements for wide area measuring system sensors

It is very important to understand the functionality, limitations, and various relevant performance requirements of wide area measuring systems (WAMS). This information is helpful in:

- Understanding the application benefits and limitations of WAMS for protection and emergency control of power systems.
- Detailed specification of WAMS.

Following is a sample list of parameters that are important in the application and use of WAMS. For certain applications of WAMS, some parameters will be more or less important than for other applications of WAMS. Similarly, some parameters may have stricter specifications for some applications than for other applications. The following types of applications could be considered as general broad categories (Yi et al., 2006):

- System operation (Real time applications, for system protection, or for manual or automatic control)
- System maintenance (applications such as disturbance analysis)
- System planning (applications such as model validation)

4. Wide Area Protection (WAP)- A strategy to counteract large area disturbances (Wenxin et al., 2006; Xiupeng et al., 2007; Zhang et al., 2010; Moraes et al., 2008)

In view of the increasing probability for outages due to the system overloads, which are caused by the ever-increasing demand for electric power, utilities are examining what modern information technology can contribute to improve this situation. Our proposal to review the present protection strategy to counteract large area disturbances addresses the potentials that are derived from the advances in system operational, protection and control techniques. It will be explained how the application of numerical technology can avoid catastrophic disturbances to occur or at least to keep the impact of single fault within certain limits.

In contrast to the requirements for protection relays designed to protect individual plant objects, system protection schemes intended to prevent voltage or frequency instabilities have to cope with the loss of generation on a large scale and/or loss of one or more transmission lines. Information technology offers digital applications, in terms of numerical adaptive protection relays, integrated disturbance recorders and fast broadband communication much greater functionality and overall efficiencies than conventional analogue techniques.

5. Phasor measurement technology

The technology of synchronized phasor measurements is well established. It provides an ideal measurement system with which to monitor and control a power system, in particular during conditions of stress. A number of publications are available on the subject. The essential feature of the technique is that it measures positive sequence (and negative and zero sequence quantities, if needed) voltages and currents of a power system in real time with precise time synchronization. Fig. 3 shows the connections of PMU in the bay level.

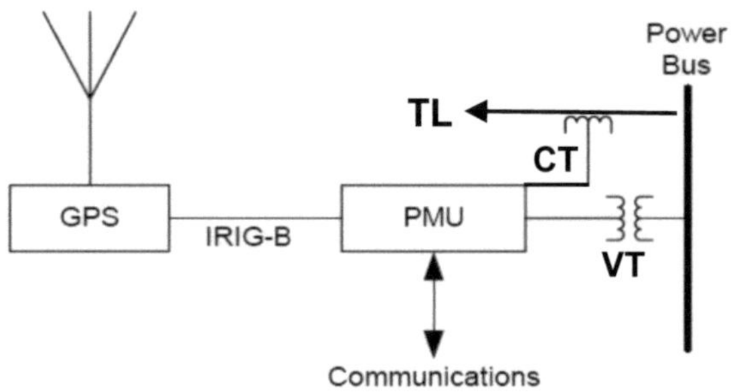

Fig. 3. Phasor measuring unit connections.

Precise time synchronization allows accurate comparison of measurements over widely separated locations as well as potential real-time measurement based control actions. Very fast recursive Discrete Fourier Transform (DFT) calculations are normally used in phasor calculations. The synchronization is achieved through a Global Positioning Satellite (GPS) system.

5.1 Discrete fourier transform technique

The Discrete Fourier Transform (DFT) technique is a short-time variation of the Fourier analysis. Like the Fourier analysis, the DFT assumes that a signal is made up of a fundamental frequency and harmonics of that frequency. While the Fourier transform is applied to signals in the continuous time domain, the DFT is applied to time-domain signals represented by sequences of numbers. Another major difference is that in the Fourier transform, the signal is assumed to exist from time - to + but in the DFT, the signal exists for a small duration of time (called window). The components of different frequencies determined by the DFT analysis can be combined to recreate the original waveform.

6. Phasor measurement unit simulation (Sybille et al., 2000)

Figure 4 shows a typical synchronized phasor measurement system configuration. The GPS transmission is received by the receiver section, which delivers a phase-locked sampling clock pulse to the Analog-to-Digital converter system. The sampled data are converted to a complex number which represents the phasor of the sampled waveform. Phasors of the three phases are combined to produce the positive sequence measurement. Figure 4 shows the Matlab\Simulink simulation of the PMU.

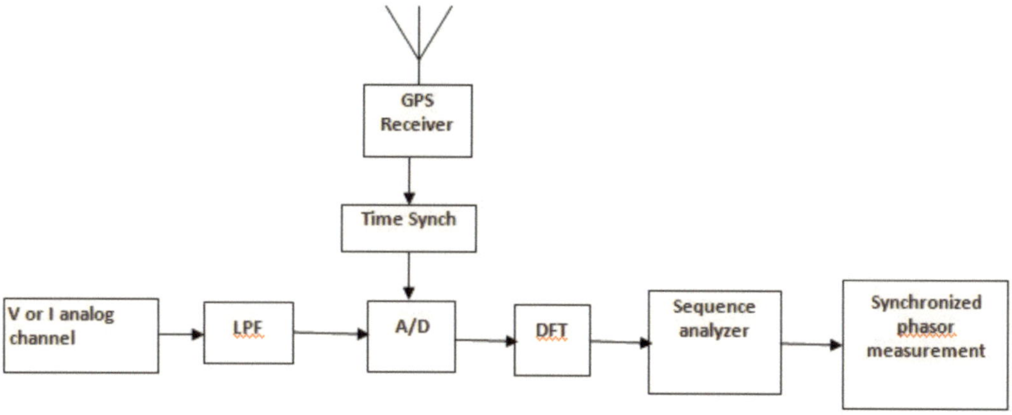

Fig. 4. Block diagram of the Synchronized Phasor Measurement System (PMU).

The basic Phasor measurement process is that of estimating a positive-sequence (also negative and zero are available), fundamental frequency phasor representation from voltage or current waveforms. As indicated by Fig. 3, the analog power signal is converted into digital data by the analog to digital converter. For example, if the voltage is needed to be measured, the samples are taken for each cycle of the waveform and then the fundamental frequency component is calculated using (DFT). The positive sequence phasor can be calculated as follows;

$$V = 1/3\,(Va + \alpha.\,Vb + \alpha 2.\,Vc) \quad (1)$$

Where $\alpha = j \angle 120°$ and Va, Vb, and Vc are the DFT phasor coefficients of each of the three phases.

Figure 5 shows a simple block diagram explaining the procedure of measured voltage or current analog signal. The external time source is an absolute time reference from a global positioning system (GPS) receiver, which delivers a phase-locked sampling clock pulse to the Analog-to-Digital converter system. The sampled data are converted to a complex number which represents the phasor of the sampled waveform. Phasors of the three phases are combined to produce the positive sequence measurement. A time stamp is generated to associate with the comtrade report via communication port to phasor data concentrator. The figure includes a hardware low-pass filter (Hardware LPF) for anti-aliasing and an analog-to-digital (A/D) converter for analog-to-digital conversion. The system of supervision permits capturing records of the same event at different points in the power system with a unique time reference, the phasor measurement units at present are located strategically, with the purpose of capturing information on the impact of contingencies at the local or system level.

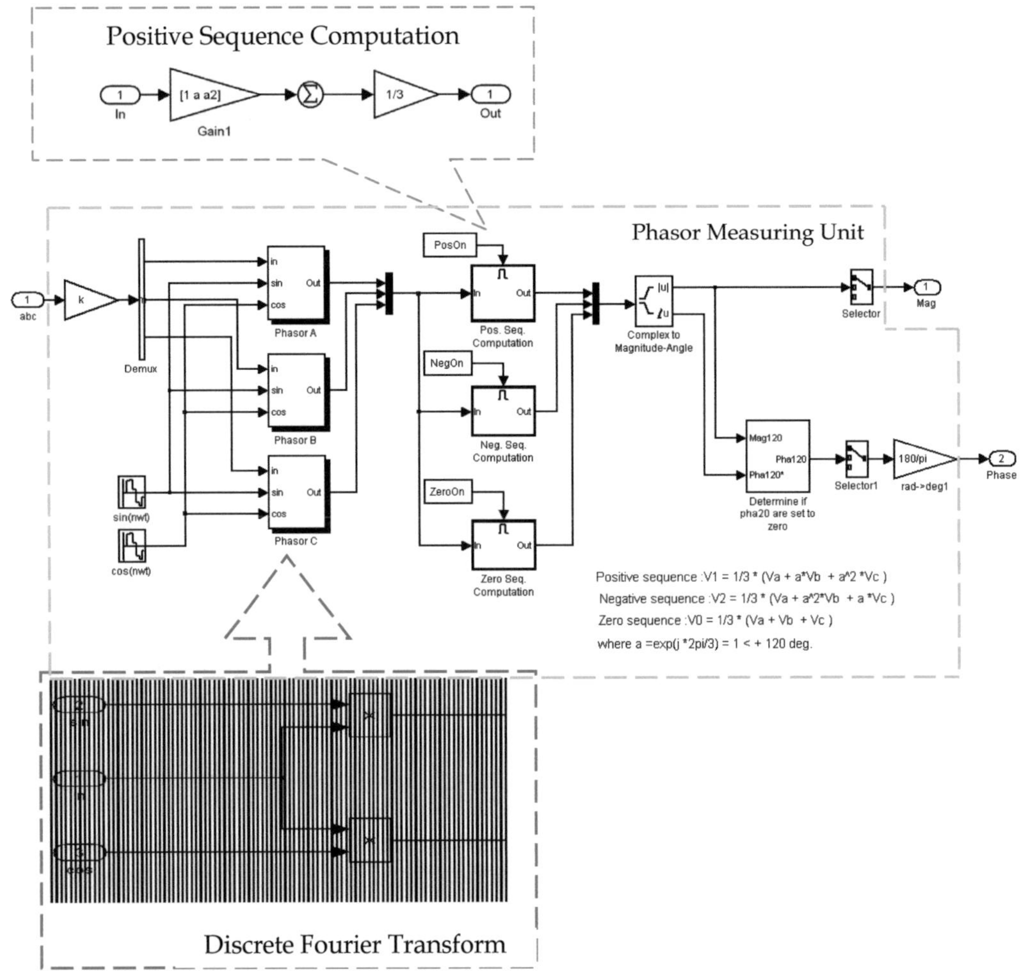

Fig. 5. PMU block diagram using Matlab/Simulink.

7. Communication issues (De La Ree et al., 2010; Hall et al., 2003; Naduvathuparambil et al., 2002; Klump et al., 2005)

Standard communication systems are adequate for most phasor data transmission. The issue for data communications includes speed, latency and reliability. Communication speed (data rate) depends on the amount of Phasor data being sent. Communication links used by WAPS include both wired (telephone lines, fiber-optics, power lines) and wireless (satellites) options. Delays associated with the link act as a crucial indicator to the amount of time-lag that takes place before action is initiated. The delays are an important aspect and should be incorporated into any power system design or analysis, as excess delays could ruin any control procedures adopted to stabilize the power grid.

Although more and more control systems are being implemented in a distributed fashion with networked communication, the unavoidable time delays in such systems impact the achievable performance. Delays due to the use of PMUs and the communication link involved are due primarily to the following reasons:

Transducer delays: Voltage transducers (VT) and current transducers (CT) are used to measure the RMS voltages and currents respectively, at the instant of sampling.

Window size of the DFT: Window size of the DFT is the number of samples required to compute the phasors using DFT.

Processing time: The processing time is the time required in converting the transducer data into phasor information with the help of DFT.

Data size of the PMU output: Data size of the PMU message is the size of the information bits contained in the data frame, header frame and the configuration frame.

Multiplexing and transitions: Transitions between the communication link and the data processing equipment leads to delays that are caused at the instances when data is retrieved or emitted by the communication link.

Communication link involved: The type of communication link and the physical distance involved in transmitting the PMU output to the central processing unit can add to the delay.

Data concentrators: Data concentrators are primarily data collecting centers located at the central processing unit and are responsible for collecting all the PMU data that is transmitted over the communication link.

8. Phasor data concentrators PDC

A Phasor Data Concentrator is a logical unit that collects phasor data, and discrete event data from PMU's and other PDC's, and transmits data to other applications. PDC's should have storage capability to buffer data for a reasonable time to allow data alignment and other vital tasks. Thus, a PDC is capable of receiving, aligning, storing and transmitting GPS-synchronized data.

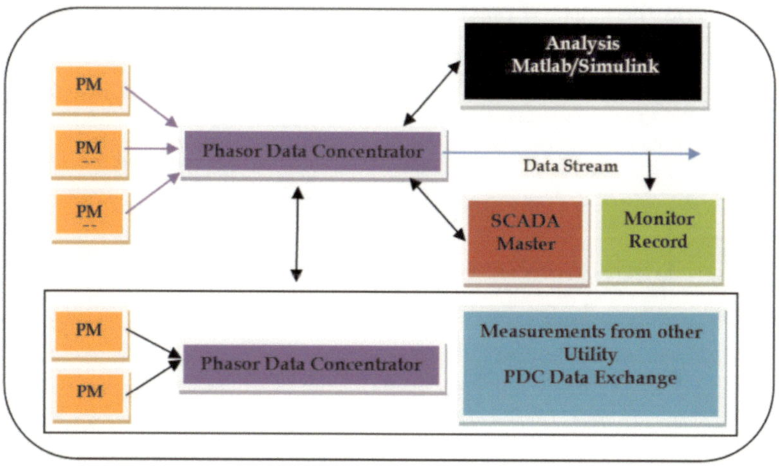

Fig. 6. Phasor data concentrator.

Specification	Suggested Minimum Requirement
Input Data Format	IEEE1344, upgrade to PC37.118 in 2005 if available Optional: COMTRADE, OPC
Output Data Format	COMTRADE. IEEE 1344. Upgrade to PC37.118 in 2005 if available. (Optional: PDC Stream, PDCxchng)
Data Alignment	Adopt BPA standard*
Output Data Rate	It should support IEEE1344 and PC37.118 (future). Default value: 30 samples per second
Streaming Channels	User Defined Configuration
Continuous Data Retention	32 Days

Table 1. Phasor data concentrator suggested minimum requirements.

Table 1 summarizes the minimum requirements for a phasor data concentrator. The minimum requirements enable applications of streaming phasor data and event capturing. Figure 6 shows the PDC (Bhargava et al., 2008).

It is important to note that it is possible that a PDC may receive data from PMUs from different manufacturers. Aligning data from different manufacturer PMUs may be a complex task that requires knowledge of the characteristics of each unit. For application level one, the alignment of data is done on the basis of the time tag that each PMU data has. This may result in misalignments of several microseconds. For streaming data applications and event capturing applications, this misalignment is not critical. For other applications it may be critical.

9. Conventional problems

The distance relays which are widely applied in the protection today and involve the determination of impedance achieve operating times of the order of a period of the power system frequency. A distance relay is designed to only operate for faults occurring between the relay location and the selected reach point, and remains stable for all faults outside this region or zone (Horowitz et al., 2009).

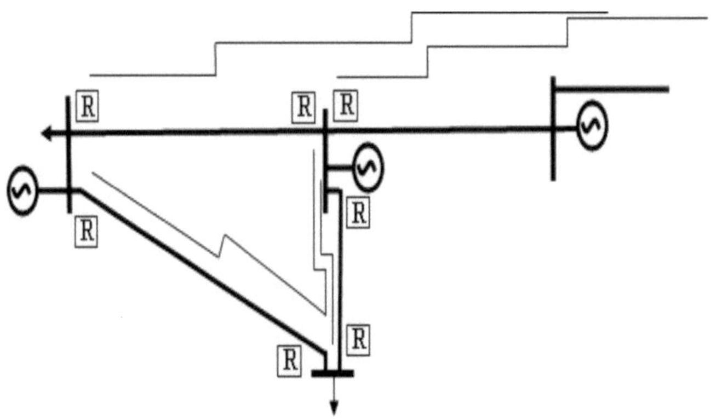

Fig. 7. Three zones of operation for each stand alone relay.

The resistance of the fault arc takes the fault impedance outside the relay's tripping characteristic and, hence, it does not detect this condition. Alternatively, it is only picked up either by zone 2 or zone 3 in which case tripping will be unacceptably delayed (Eissa, 2009). The distance relays are based on standalone decision, while each relay operates independently according to three different zone of operation, see Figure 7.

The mal-operation or fail-to trip of protection is determined as one of the origins to raise and propagate major power system disturbances (Tang, et al., 2006). A vast majority of relay mal-operations is unwanted trips and have been shown to propagate major disturbances. Backup protections in fault clearance system have the task to operate only when the primary protection fails to operate or when the primary protection is temporarily out of service. The recent complexity and enlargement of power systems makes it difficult to coordinate operation times and reaches among relays. In the areas of power system automation and substation automation, there are two different trends: centralization and decentralization. More and more dynamic functions are moving from local and regional control centers toward central or national control centers. At the same time we also observe more "intelligence" and "decision power" moving closer towards the actual power system substations. Greater functional integration is being enclosed in substation hardware. In view of global security of power systems, the action algorithms of conventional backup protections possibly are not best choices because the operations of individual relays are hardly coordinated each other. Therefore, the principle of the protection design needs innovation to overcome the above problem. Modern protection devices have sufficient computing and communications capabilities to allow the implementation of many novel sophisticated protection principles. Therefore, a novel wide-area backup protection system is reported in this paper.

This system is capable of acting as the substitution of conventional distributed backup protections in substation. To ensure the fast responsibility of such a system to the emergent events, the communication requirements are discussed as well. Conclusively, the proposed system is designed by two ways. First, in substation, concentrate some conventional backup protection functions to an intelligent processing system; second, concentrate the coordinated and optimized processing and controlling arithmetic of all backup protection in a region into a regional processing unit.

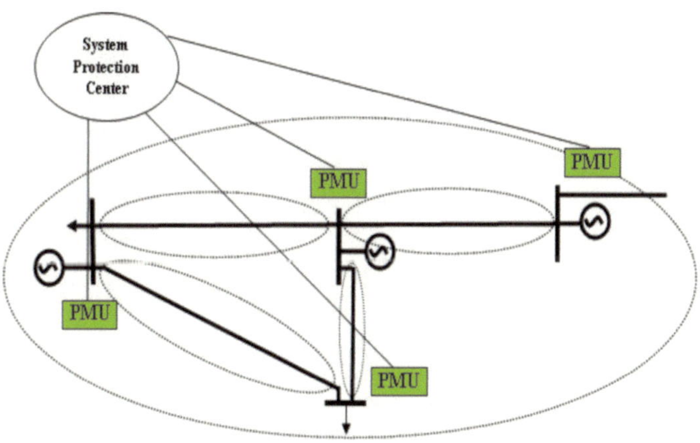

Fig. 8. The new protected zones of the proposed relay.

The communication of data among them is carried via optic-fiber networks. The relay decision is based on collected and shared data through communication network. The suggested technique satisfies high degree of reliability and stability while it is based on shared decision rather than stand alone decision. The suggested technique can see all the power system area and can deal with the transmission lines as unit protection, see Figure 8. The primary purpose of these systems is to improve disturbance monitoring and system event analysis. These measurements have been sited to monitor large generating sites, major transmission paths, and significant control points. Synchronized Phasor measurements provide all significant state measurements including voltage magnitude, voltage phase angle, and frequency.

10. The proposed solution

The proposed technique is based mainly on two components to identify the faults on the transmission lines. The first component is the voltage reduction due to fault occurrence. The second component is the power flow direction after fault occurrence. The phase angle is used to determine the direction of fault current with respect to a reference quantity. The ability to differentiate between a fault in one direction or another is obtained by comparing the phase angle of the operating voltage and current. The voltage is usually used as the reference polarizing quantity. The fault current Phasor lies within two distinct forward and backward regions with respect to the reference Phasor, depending on the power system and fault conditions (Eissa 2008, 2009, 2005). The normal power flow in a given direction will result in the phase angle between the voltage and the current varying around its power factor angle$\pm\phi$. When power flows in the opposite direction, this angle will become ($180°\pm \phi$). For a fault in the reverse direction, the phase angle of the current with respect to the voltage will be ($180°- \phi$) (Dissertation, 2008).

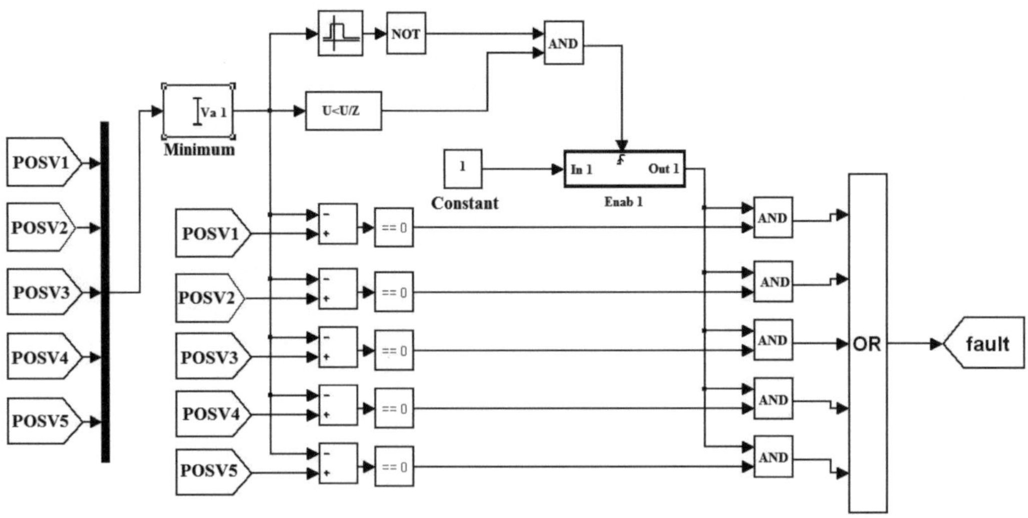

Fig. 9. Matlab/Simulink block diagram shows selecting the minimum value.

The main idea of the proposed technique is to identify the faulted area. This can be achieved by comparing the measured values of the positive sequence voltage magnitudes at the main bus for each area. This can result in the minimum voltage value that indicates the nearest area to the fault. In addition to that, the absolute differences of the positive sequence current angles are calculated for all lines connected with the faulted area. These absolute angles are compared to each other. The maximum absolute angle difference value is selected to identify the faulted line. The above two keys of operation can be mathematically described as follows:

$$\text{Min}\{|V1|, |V2|,.. |Vm|, ...|Vn|\} \tag{2}$$

where $|Vn|$ is the positive sequence voltage magnitude measured by PMU and located at area "1", "2", "3",...,"m" , to "n". Figure 9 shows the Matlab simulink block diagram responsible of the selection of the nearest area to the fault based on comparing positive sequence voltage magnitudes. POSV1, POSV2... POSV5 are the input signals of positive sequence voltage magnitudes collected from 5 areas on the network. The minimum voltage magnitude is indicated by the Minimum block which identifies the value and/or position of the smallest element in each column of the input, or tracks the minimum values in a sequence of inputs over a period of time.

The Minimum block output is shown in Figure 10. The graph shows the o/p from the Matlab/Simulink simulation, which is the minimum positive sequence voltage magnitude during fault. Any decrease in the signal magnitude is indicated by the Detect Decrease block which determines if the input signal is strictly less than its previous value or not, the status can be recognize as:

- The output is "1", when the input signal is less than its previous value.
- The output is "0", when the input signal is greater than or equal to its previous value.

The threshold value of the input signal is detected by the Interval Test block which outputs "1" if the input is between the values specified by the Lower limit and Upper limit parameters. The block outputs "0" if the input is outside those values.

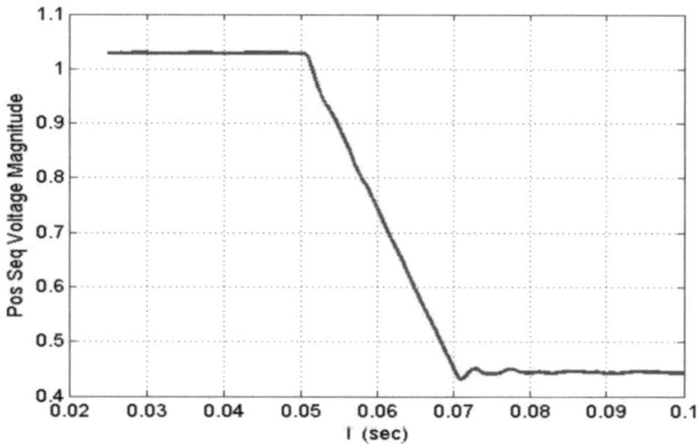

Fig. 10. The Minimum block output from the Matlab/Simulink.

For a fault occurred on the grid, the output from (2) is the minimum positive sequence voltage magnitude which indicates the nearest area to the fault. Suppose that the nearest area to the fault is indicated by number "m". The next step is to compare the absolute differences of positive sequence current angles for all lines connecting area "m" with all other neighboring areas and then selecting the max one. This can be explained as:

$$\text{Max}\,\{|\Delta\phi m1|,\ |\Delta\phi m2|\ldots,|\Delta\phi mn|\} \tag{3}$$

where $|\Delta\phi mn|$ is the absolute difference of positive sequence current angle for a transmission line connecting area "m" with area "n". This can be described by (4).

$$|\Delta\phi mn| = |\phi mn - \phi nm| \tag{4}$$

Figure 11 shows the Matlab/Simulink block diagram responsible of the selection of the faulted line from all lines connecting to the faulted areas; the absolute difference between positive sequence current angles at line terminals for each line is given. The maximum current angle difference is indicated by the Maximum block which identifies the value and/or position of the largest element in each column of the input, or tracks the maximum values in a sequence of inputs over a period of time.
Figure 12 shows the output from the Maximum block shown in Figure 11. The graph shows the maximum absolute difference of positive sequence current angle during internal fault. The threshold value of the input signals is detected by the Interval Test block. Figure 13 shows the maximum absolute difference of positive sequence current angle during external fault. Discrete on/off delay timer block given in Figure 11 is used to ignore big changes in angle difference which associated with change in current direction in any line due to external faults.

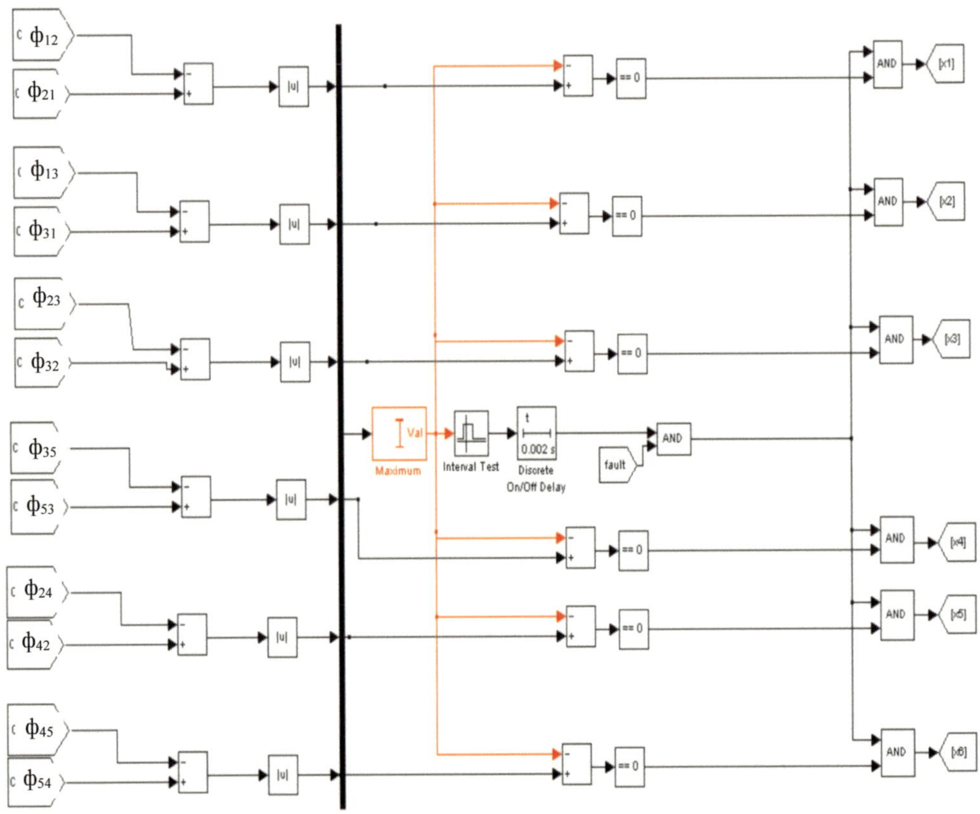

Fig. 11. The Matlab/Simulink block diagram responsible of the selection of the faulted line.

Part of the 500/220 kV Egyptian interconnected electrical network is used for the study; five main buses that represent five different areas with 500 kV are selected to verify the suggested technique. Figure 14 shows the selected five areas from the overall network. In the single line diagram, each bus represents the selected area in the simulation that can connect the 500 kV network with 220 kV network through three single phase 500/220 kV power transformers. The system is simulated using the Matlab/Simulink with a sampling frequency of 20 kHz for a system operating at a frequency of 50 Hz. By means of measuring positive sequence magnitude of three phase to ground voltage and positive sequence current angle difference between sending and receiving ends, we make a new criteria to deal with faults (single, double and three phase to ground faults). This new criteria will detect faults and select the nearest area to the fault. Also, the new criteria will distinguish between internal and external faults in the interconnected lines.

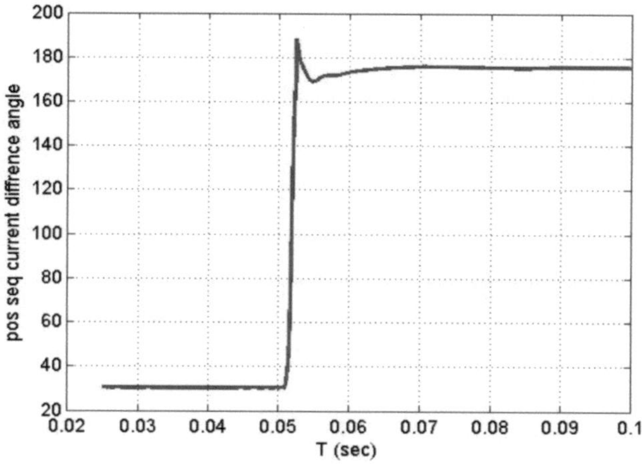

Fig. 12. Maximum absolute difference of positive sequence current angle due to internal fault.

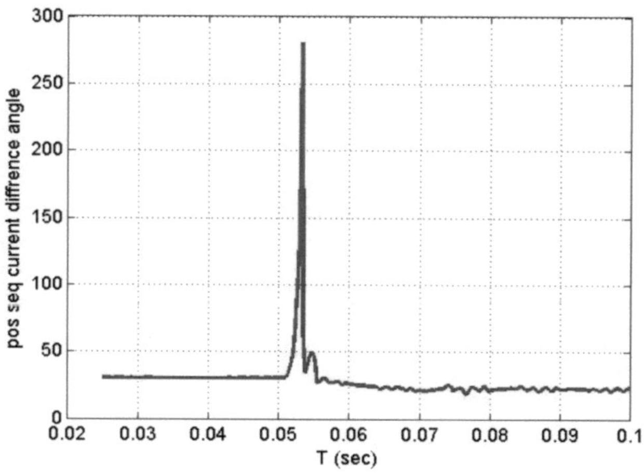

Fig. 13. Maximum absolute difference of positive sequance current angle due to external fault.

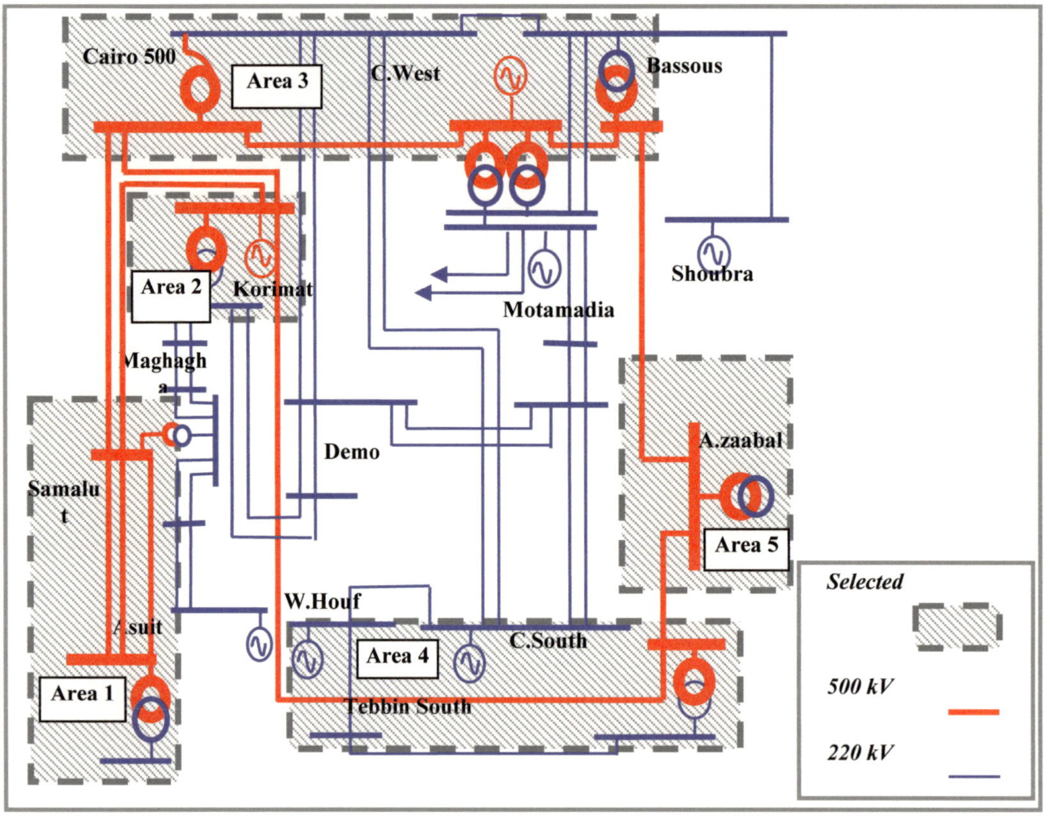

Fig. 14. The selected five areas from the overall network.

11. Case study

An extensive series of study is examined on the power system given in Figure 15. All fault events are studied and a sample of the results is given here. As mentioned above, the studied network is classified into 5 neighboring areas. The 5 areas are connected with each others by six lines. Three phases to ground fault are located on line 1 which connecting area "1" with area "2", see Figure 15. Fault location is placed away from area "1" and area "2" by 100 and 45 km respectively.

11.1 Short circuit on transmission line 1(Samalot-Kurimat)

The suggested technique is used to be verified under different fault conditions, the fault data is generated from power system configuration simulated using the Matlab/Simulink. A short circuit is located on transmission line (TL1) as shown in Figure 15.The total length of the faulted transmission line is 145 Km. Each fault type (three phase, double phase and single phase to ground fault) is tested. Different locations of fault along the transmission line are tested to affirm the criteria as being effective and operate successfully.

11.2 Three phase to ground fault

A three-phase to ground fault is located on transmission line (TL1) .The distance between fault location on the transmission line and the nearest bus (Kurimat) is 45 Km. The 3-phase voltage signals measured from Kurimat bus bar is recorded and displayed in Figure 16. The 3-phase current signals for all transmission lines away from Kurimat are recorded and displayed in Figure 17.

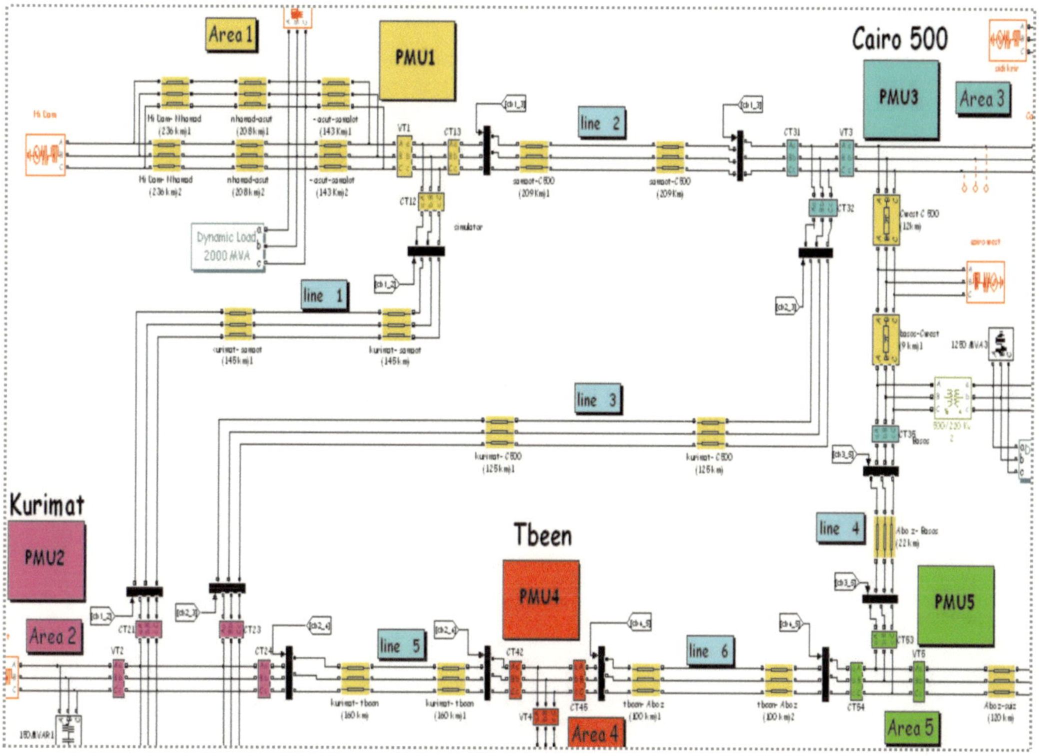

Fig. 15. Matlab/Simulink Block diagram of the interconnected network.

Figure 18 shows the five positive phase sequence voltage magnitudes (PSVM), minimum value is selected which indicates the nearest area to the fault area (2). Figure 19 shows the absolute differences of positive phase sequence current angles (PSCA) for all lines connecting to the faulted area (2) with all neighboring areas (1, 3, and 4). The angles difference of line (1) terminals is the maximum (=180°), this means that the current is reversed from one terminal only, and then it is clear that the fault is internal on transmission line TL1.

12. Fault type classification technique

All faults are identified as a phase fault or a ground fault, one parameter, λzero, is derived for fault classification:

$$\lambda_{zero} = \frac{1}{3}\left|I_a + I_b + I_c\right| \tag{5}$$

The fault is classified as a ground fault if λ_{zero} is greater than threshold value. Once the fault has been classified, the specific fault type is determined by comparing all rate of change of phase currents with an predetermined disturbance detection pickup, The fault typing software module is employed when the measured parameter exceeds a prescribed threshold (e.g., when a measured correct exceeds an overcurrent pickup).

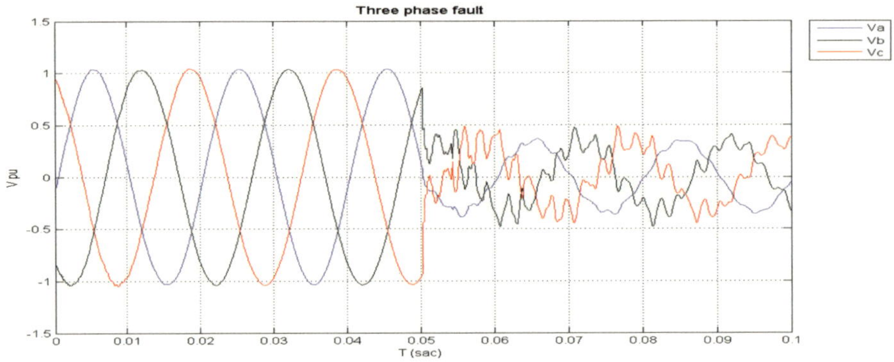

Fig. 16. Three phase voltage signals at Kurimat busbar.

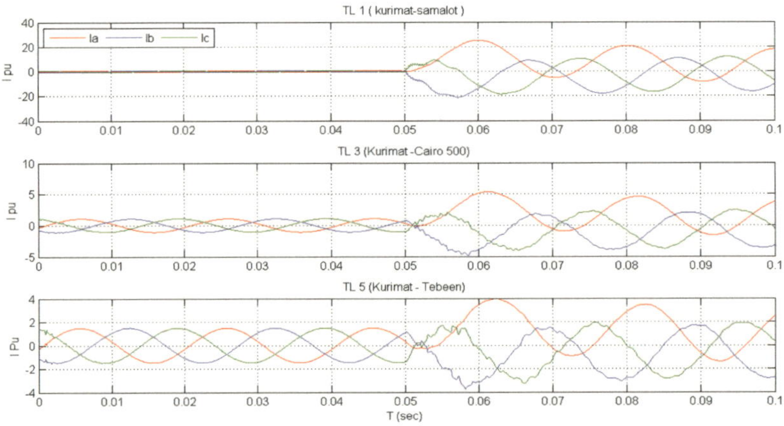

Fig. 17. Three phase current signals for all lines connected to Kurimat.

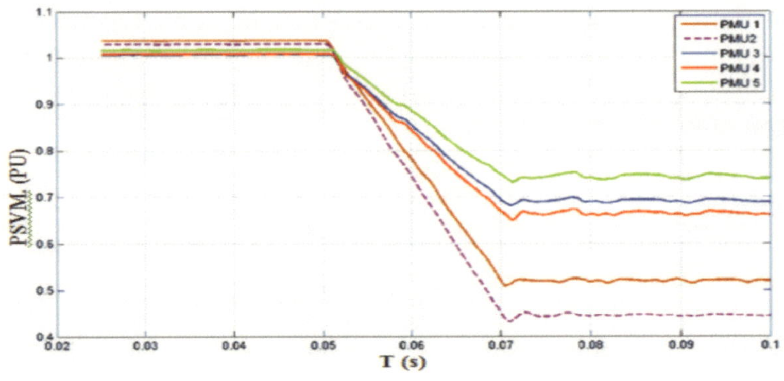

Fig. 18. Positive sequence voltage magnitudes.

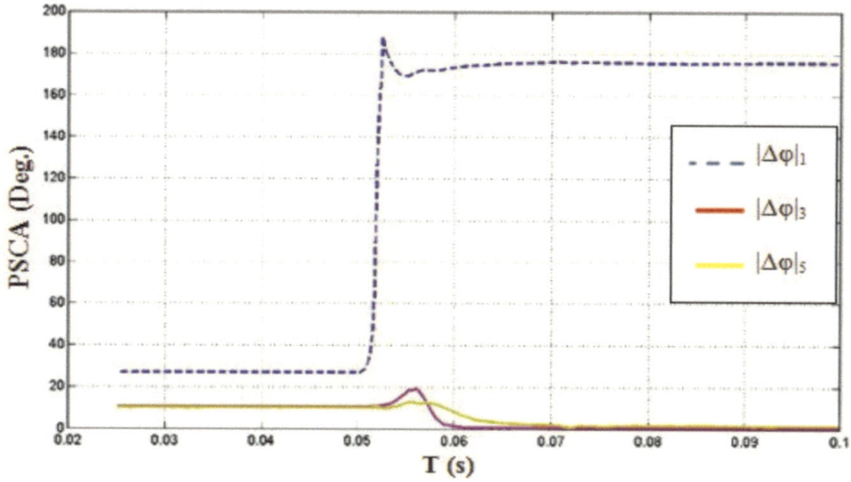

Fig. 19. Positive sequence current angle absolute differences for all lines connected to the faulted area.

Discrete Fourier transform block computes the fundamental value of the input phase current signal over a running window of one cycle of the specified fundamental frequency as shown in Figure 20. First and second outputs return respectively the magnitude and phase degrees of the fundamental. The magnitude is taken as a percentage from its steady state value. The rate of change of this percentage is compared with a threshold value. For the first cycle of simulation, the outputs are held constant to the value specified by the parameter "Initial input".
As shown in Figure 21, the input three-phase current is used to calculate zero sequence components to classify the fault type. Then each phase current signal is taken as a percentage from its steady state value. Then the rate of change of the percentage of phase current magnitude is compared by a threshold value to identify the faulted phase.

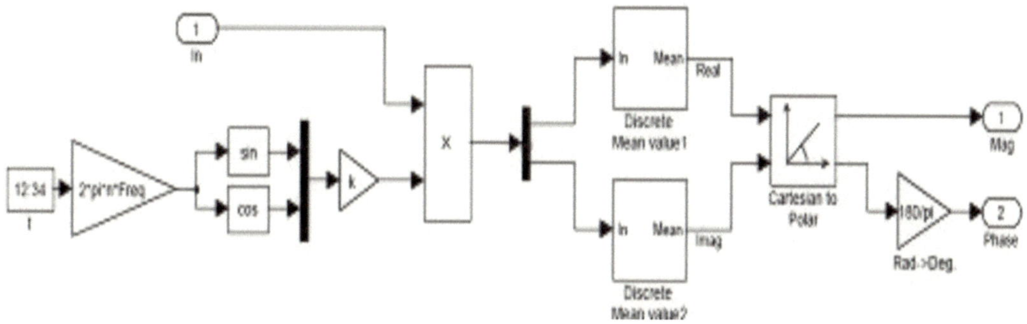

Fig. 20. Discrete Fourier block set.

Three phase fault is applied on TL1 Samalout-Kurimat. Fault resistance = 50 Ω. Fault Distance = 50 %, Figure 22 shows fault recorder display at each terminal of the faulted transmission line. The fault is recorded as symmetrical fault. As shown in Figure 23, zero sequence current magnitude is zero.

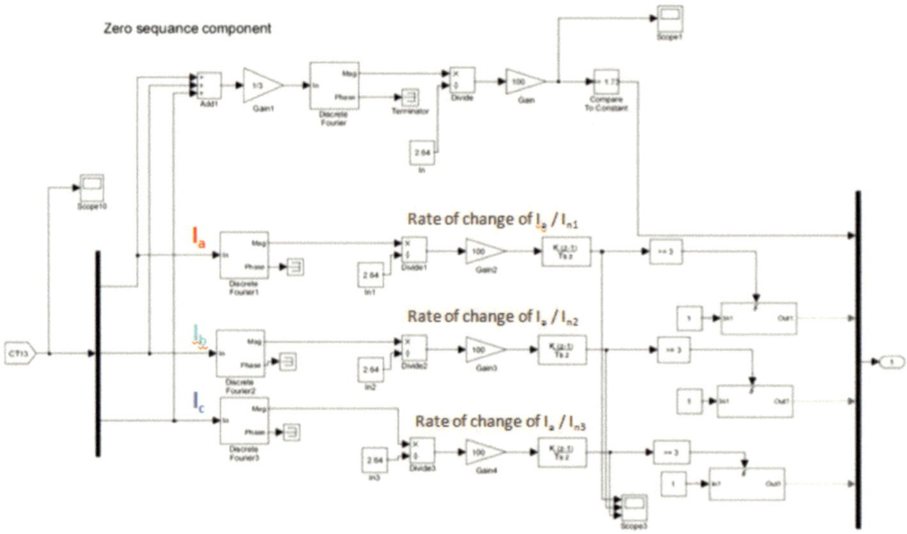

Fig. 21. Fault Classification Blockset.

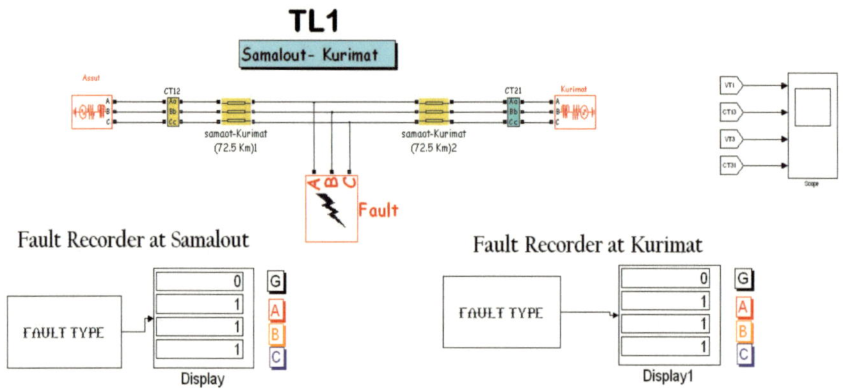

Fig. 22. Fault recorder at each terminal display that fault type is three phase fault.

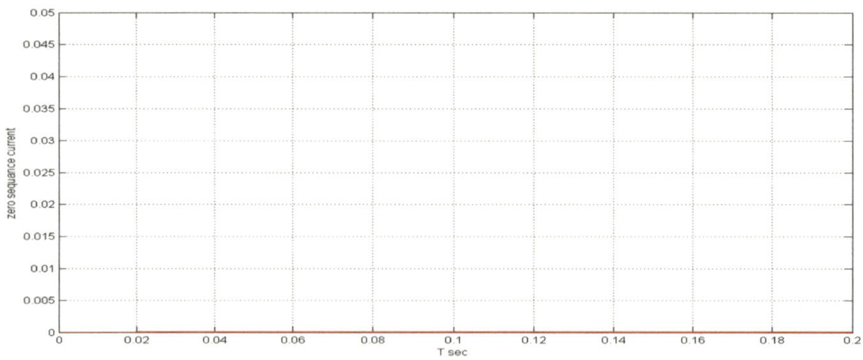

Fig. 23. Zero sequence component current magnitude during fault.

13. Conclusion

The chapter outlines a novel idea for fault detection and classification using Phasor measurement units in a wide area system. The idea has successfully identified the faulted line on a large power interconnected system. The idea descried in this paper represents a new state-of-art in the field of interconnected grid protection and classification. The idea is based on sharing data from many PMUs. The new idea also calssified the fault types for the interconnected system. The idea used a center protection unit for collecting the data and issued the tripping signal. The idea is implemented and investigated using the powerful Matlab/Simulink package. Power system configuration, fault detection, fault calculation, discrimination, and classification are achieved through the Matlab/Simulink program.

14. Acknowledgment

This chapter is written, revised and analyzed by the author. Some parts of the chapter are cited from MSc dissertation done in Helwan University-Faculty of Engineering-Cairo-Egypt by Eng. Mohamed Magdy. The MSc dissertation is supervised by Prof. Mohammed El Shahat Masoud and the author of the chapter.

15. References

Phadke, A. (2002). Synchronized Phasor Measurements a historical over view. *Virginia Polytechnic Institute and American Electric Power Bhargava*.0-7803-7525-4/02/IEEE

Marek Zima. (2002). Special Protection Schemes in Electric Power Systems. *Literature survey*, (June 2002).

Thorp, J. S; Phadke A. G; Horowitz, S. W. & Begovic, M. M. (1988). Some Applications of Phasor Measurements to Adaptive Protection. *IEEE Transactions on Power Systems*, Vol. 3, No. 2, (May 1988).

Centeno, V; De La Ree, J; Phadke, A. G.; Mitchell, G; Murphy, J; Burnett, R; (1993). Adaptive Out-of-Step Relaying Using Phasor Measurement Techniques. IEEE Computer Applications in Power, (October 1993).

Guzman, A & Tziouvaras, D (2002). Local and Wide-Area Network Protection Systems improve power system reliabili, *Schweitzer Engineering Laboratories, E. O. ty. Inc. Pullman, WA, USA, Ken E. Martin Bonneville Power Administration Vancouver*, WA, USA, Aviable from, www.naspi.org/resources/archive/prtt/waps_wprc04.pdf

Guzman, A; Mooney, J. B; Benmouyal, G; Fischer, N. (2002). Transmission Line Protection System for Increasing Power System Requirements. *55th Annual Conference for Protective Relay Engineers, College Station, Texas,* (April 2002).

Gjerde, P. O & Mangelrod, R. (2001). Optimisation of Protection Performance During System Disturbances. *CIGRE 2001 SC 34 Colloquium*, (Septemper 2001).

Larsson, M & Rehtanz, C. (2002). Predictive Frequency Stability Control Based on Wide-Area Phasor Measurements. *Proc. 2002 IEEE Power Engineering Society Summer Meeting, (2002).*

Zima, M; Korba, M & Andersson, G. (2003). Power Systems Voltage Emergency Control Approach Using Trajectory Sensitivities. *2003 IEEE Conference on Control Application, CCA, Istanbul*, (June 2003).

Rehtanz C & Westermann, D. (2002). Wide Area Measurement and Control System for Increasing Transmission Capacity in Deregulated Energy Markets. *Proc. 2002 Power Systems Computation Conference in Sevilla,* (2002).

Rehtanz, C. (2001). Wide Area Protection System and Online Stability Assessment based on Phasor Measurements. Bulk Power System Dynamics and Control - V, *Onomichi City, Japan,* (Augest 2001).

Zhang, N & Kezunovic, M. Verifying the Protection System Operation Using An Advanced Fault Analysis Tool Combined with the Event Tree Analysis. *Northern American Power Symposium, NAPS 2004 Moscow, Idaho,* (August 2004).

Lin, Y. L; Liu, C. W. & Chen, C. S. (2004). A new PMU-based fault detection/location technique for transmission lines with consideration of arcing fault discrimination—Part I: Theory and algorithms. *IEEE Trans. Power Del.,* Vol. 19, No. 4, (October 2004), pp. 1587–1593.

Yu, C. S; Liu, C. W; Yu, S. L. & Jiang, J. A. (2002). A new PMU-based fault location algorithm for series compensated lines. *IEEE Transaction on Power Deivery,* Jan. 2002, Vol. 17, No. 1, pp. 33–46.

Wang, et el. (2005). Design of a novel wide-area backup protection system, *Proceedings of IEEE/PES Transmission Distribution Conference Asia Pac. Dalian, China, (2005), pp. 1-6.*

Yan Wang; Yan-Xia Zhang; Song-Xiao Xu; (2008). Wide-area protection against chain over-load trip based on multi-agent technology, *Interntional Conference on Machine Learning and Cybernetics,* pp. 1548 - 1552, Volume: 3, Digital Object Identifier: 10.1109/ICMLC.2008.4620652, 2008.

Xiaoyang Tong; Xiaoru Wang; Li Ding (2008). Study of information model for wide-area backup protection agent in substation based on IEC61850, *Third International Conference on Electric Utility Deregulation and Restructuring and Power Technologies,* pp. 2212 - 2216, Digital Object Identifier: 10.1109/DRPT.2008.4523778

Yangguang Wang; Xianggen Yin; Dahai You; (2010). Agent-based wide area protection with high fault tolerance, *International Conference on the Modelling, Identification and Control (ICMIC),* (2010), pp. 739 - 744

Hui Sun; Qianjin Liu (2009). Research of the Structure and Working Mechanisms of Wide-Area Backup Protection Agent. *1st International Conference on Information Science and Engineering (ICISE),* (2009), Digital Object Identifier: 10.1109/ICISE.2009.926, (2009), pp. 5037 - 5042.

Zhiyuan Duan; Zhang, C.; Hu, Z.; Sun, Y. (2009). Design of Robust Controller of Interconnected Power System Considering Signals Transmission Delay. *International Workshop on Intelligent Systems and Applications,* (2009). ISA 2009. Digital Object Identifier: 10.1109/IWISA.2009.5072823, (2009), pp. 1 - 5

Zhiyuan Duan; Chengxue Zhang; Zhijian Hu; Yuanyuan Zhang (2009). Robust Control of Interconnected Power System Based on WAMS Considering Signals Transmission Delay, *Power and Energy Engineering Conference,* (2009). APPEEC 2009, Asia-Pacific, Digital Object Identifier: 10.1109/APPEEC.2009.4918729, (2009), pp. 1 – 4

Seong-Jeong Rim; Seong-Il Lim; Seung-Jae Lee (2008). Multi-agent based reliability enhancement scheme for IEC61850 substation, *Transmission and Distribution Conference and Exposition,* (2008), T&D. IEEE/PES, Digital Object Identifier: 10.1109/TDC.2008.4517294, (2008), pp. 1 - 6

Testa, S. & Chou, W. (2004). The distributed data center: front-end solutions, *IT Professional* Conference, Vol. 6, No. 3, Digital Object Identifier: 10.1109/MITP.2004.24, (2004), pp. 26 – 32

Begovic, M. (2004). Wide area protection and emergency control. *Power Systems Conference and Exposition,* (2004). IEEE PES Digital Object Identifier: 10.1109/PSCE.2004.1397488, (2004), pp. 1776 - 1777

Terzija, V.; Cai, D.; Valverde, G.; Regulski, P.; Vaccaro, A.; Osborne, M. & Fitch, J. (2010). Flexible Wide Area Monitoring, Protection and Control applications in future power networks Developments in Power System Protection (DPSP 2010), *10th IET International Conference on Managing the Change,* Digital Object Identifier: 10.1049/cp.2010.0361 (2010), pp. 1 – 5

Terzija, V.; Valverde, G.; Deyu Cai; Regulski, P.; Madani, V.; Fitch, J.; Skok, S.; Begovic, M. M. & Phadke, A. (2011). Wide-Area Monitoring, Protection, and Control of Future Electric Power Networks, *Proceedings of the IEEE,* Vol. 99, No. 1, Digital Object Identifier: 10.1109/JPROC.2010.2060450, (2011), pp. 80 - 93

Moxley, R. & Wronski, M. (2007). Using time error differential measurement in protection applications, *Power Systems Conference: Advanced Metering, Protection, Control, Communication, and Distributed Resources,* 2007. PSC 2007 Digital Object Identifier: 10.1109/PSAMP.2007.4740918, (2007), pp. 278 - 283

Phadke, A. G. & Kasztenny, B. (2009). Synchronized Phasor and Frequency Measurement Under Transient Conditions, *IEEE Transactions on Power Delivery,* Vol. 24, No. 1, Digital Object Identifier: 10.1109/TPWRD.2008.2002665, (2009), pp. 89 - 95

Jetti, S. R. & Venayagamoorthy, G. K. (2006). Real-Time Implementation of a Dual Function Neuron based Wide Area SVC Damping Controller, *Industry Applications Conference,* (2006), 41st IAS Annual Meeting. Conference Record of the 2006 IEEE, Vol. 2, Digital Object Identifier: 10.1109/IAS.2006.256598, (2006), pp. 672 - 678

Yi Hu & Novosel, D. (2006). Challenges in Implementing a Large-Scale PMU System Power System Technology, *International Conference on Power Con 2006.* Digital Object Identifier: 10.1109/ICPST.2006.321829, (2006), pp. 1 - 7

Wenxin Liu; Cartes, D. A. & Venayagamoorthy, G. K. (2006). Particle Swarm Optimization based Defensive Islanding of Large Scale Power System, *International Joint Conference on Neural Networks,* IJCNN, (2006), Digital Object Identifier: 10.1109/IJCNN.2006.246642
(2006), pp. 1719 - 1725

Xiupeng Guan; Yuanzhang Sun & Lin Cheng (2007). A load parameter identification method based on wide area measurement, *International Power Engineering Conference,* 2007. IPEC 2007, (2007), pp. 431 - 436

Zhang, G.; Lee, S.; Carroll, R.; Jian Zuo; Beard, L. & Yilu Liu (2010). Wide area power system visualization using real-time synchrophasor measurements, *Power and Energy Society General Meeting,* 2010 IEEE Digital Object Identifier: 10.1109/PES.2010.5588188, (2010), pp. 1 - 7

Moraes, R.; Volskis, H. & Yi Hu (2008). Deploying a large-scale PMU system for the Brazilian interconnected power system, Third International Conference on Electric Utility Deregulation and Restructuring and Power Technologies, (2008), DRPT 2008, Digital Object Identifier: 10.1109/DRPT.2008.4523392, (2008), pp. 143 - 149

Sybille, G. & Hoang Le-Huy (2000). Digital simulation of power systems and power electronics using the MATLAB/Simulink Power System Blockset, *IEEE Power Engineering Society Winter Meeting,* (2000), Vol. 4 Digital Object Identifier: 10.1109/PESW.2000.847358, (2000), pp. 2973- 2981

De La Ree, J.; Centeno, V.; Thorp, J.S. & Phadke, A. G. (2010). Synchronized Phasor Measurement Applications in Power Systems, *IEEE Transactions on Smart Grid,* Vol. 1, No. 1, Digital Object Identifier: 10.1109/TSG.2010.2044815, (2010), pp. 20 - 27

Hall, I.; Beaumont, P.G.; Baber, G.P.; Shuto, I.; Saga, M.; Okuno, K. & Uo, H. (2003), New line current differential relay using GPS synchronization, *Power Tech Conference Proceedings, 2003 IEEE Bologna,* Vol. 3 Digital Object Identifier: 10.1109/PTC.2003.1304464, 2003

Naduvathuparambil, B; Valenti, M. C. & Feliachi, A. (2002). Communication delays in wide area measurement systems, *Lane Dept. of Comp. Sci. & Elect. Eng., West Virginia University, Morgantown, WV,* 2002. Avialble from
www.csee.wvu.edu/~mvalenti/documents/SSST_02.pdf

Klump R. & Wilson, R. E. (2005). Visualizing real-time security threats using hybrid SCADA/PMU measurement displays, *Proc. 38th Hawaii Int. Conf. System Sci.,* 2005, p. 55c.

Bhargava, B. & Salazar, A. (2008). Use of Synchronized Phasor Measurement system for monitoring power system stability and system dynamics in real-time, Power and Energy Society General Meeting-Conversion and Delivery of Electrical Energy in the 21st Century, 2008 IEEE Digital Object Identifier: 10.1109/PES.2008.4596963, 2008, pp. 1 - 8

Horowitz S. H. & Phake A. G. (2009). Power System Relaying, *Taunton Somerset, U.K.* Research Studies Press

Eissa, M. M. (2009). New principle for transmission line protection using phase portrait plane. *IET Generation Transmission Distribution,* (2009), Vol. 3, No. 1, pp. 49–56

Tang J. & McLaren, P. G. (2006). A wide area differential backup protection scheme for Shipboard application, *IEEE Transaction on Power Delivery,* (2006), Vol. 21, No. 3, pp. 1121-1129

Eissa, M. M. (2008). Development and investigation of a new high-speed directional relay using field data, *IEEE Transaction on Power Delivery,* (2008), Vol. 23, No.3, pp. 1302–1309.

Eissa, M. M. (2009). A new digital feed circuit protection using directional element, *IEEE Transaction on Power Delivery,* (2009), Vol. 24, No. 2, pp. 531–537

Eissa, M. M. (2005). Evaluation of a new current directional protection technique using field data, *IEEE Transaction on Power Delivery,* (2005), Vol. 20, No. 2, pp. 566–572

Protection of Interconnected Electrical Networks Using Phasor Synchronized Measuring Technique, Ph.D. dissertation, Helwan University-Faculty of Engineering at Helwan, Cairo, Egypt, (2008)

9

Simulated Performance of Conical Antennas Using Matlab-Based Finite-Difference Time Domain (FDTD) Code

George S. Kliros
Hellenic Air-Force Academy, Department of Aeronautical Sciences, Division of Electronics and Communication Engineering
Greece

1. Introduction

The need of ultrawideband (UWB) antennas with omni-directional coverage is increasing for both military and commercial applications (Wiesbeck *et. al.*, 2009; Minin, 2010). The UWB radio technology promises high resolution radar applications, sensor networks with a large number of sensors for industrial or home surveillance as well as high data-rate communication over short range for personal area networks. With a need for antennas with the characteristics of broad bandwidth and small electrical size, conical antenna structures have been a focus of research because of its broad bandwidth and omni-directional radiation pattern (Maloney & Smith, 1993; Sandler & King, 1994; Yu & Li, 2008; Palud *et. al.*, 2008). The bi-conical antenna exhibits a very stable omni-directional radiation pattern in the plane normal to the dipole axis together with an excellent transient response. However, the feeding with a usual coaxial cable requires a balun, which transforms the asymmetric mode of the feed line into a symmetric mode at the feed point. For the coaxial balun the ultra wide bandwidth demands very high precision in the manufacturing process in order to get a good and stable matching especially for the high frequencies. The mono-cone antenna as asymmetric structure does not need any balun for an asymmetric feed line but it needs an infinite ground plane, which in reality can only be approximated. The theory of wide-angle conical antennas has been developed sufficiently to permit calculation of the transfer functions relating source voltage to radiated field and incident field to load voltage over the range of frequencies required in the study of transients. Such calculations were demonstrated in (Harrison & Williams, 1965).

Due to their three-dimensional configurations, conical antennas are bulky and difficult to fabricate, integrate, and reconfigure. Moreover, since conventional conical antennas comprise of free-standing metal, they are typically heavy in order to achieve sufficient mechanical stability. Several configurations have been proposed to improve conical antennas' mechanical performance (Ma *et. al.*, 2009; Zhou *et. al.*, 2009, Kliros *et. al.*, 2010a). Resistive loading for conical antennas, which is investigated in (Maloney 1993), does not constitute the optimal solution as it reduces the antennas' efficiency. Recently, investigations have been carried out on configurations that employ a dielectric or magnetic material to cover the conical antenna (Gentili *et. al.*, 2004, Lu, 2007). Dielectric and magnetic coating of the radiating cone, enables making the antenna electrically smaller and more rugged while maintaining a wide band input impedance.

In this chapter, we present a Finite Difference Time Domain (FDTD) code in spherical coordinates implemented in MATLAB in order to simulate the performance of dielectric covered conical antennas. MATLAB provides an interactive environment for algorithm development, data post-processing and visualization. The spherical FDTD equations can be found using a modified Yee cell in spherical coordinates (Fusco, 1990). Spherical Berenger's perfectrly matched layer (PML) is applied as absorbing boundary condition where a parabolic conductivity profile in the spherical PML-region is used (Berenger, 1996). A unique feature of the PML is that electromagnetic waves of arbitrary incidence, polarization and frequency are matched at the boundary in a reflectionless manner. Results concerning time evolution of the radiated electromagnetic field, the return loss, input impedance, maximum gain as well as far-field radiation patterns across an extended bandwidth, are presented. A time domain study has also been performed to characterize the antenna's behaviour in case an UWB pulse is used. For evaluating waveform distortions caused by the antenna, we examine the degree of similarity between source pulse and received pulse waveforms in several propagation directions. The effect of the dielectric spherical cover on the antenna's performance is investigated. The author mostly worked in MATLAB version 7.4 and the related sample codes are provided in the Appendix.

2. Conical antenna design and analysis

In this section, we present the design of a conical antenna covered by a dielectric material with hemispherical shape and describe the FDTD algorithm in spherical coordinates for the analysis of the radiation as well as the time-domain characteristics of the antenna. Dielectric coating of the metallic radiating cone enables making the antenna electrically smaller and more rugged while maintaining a wide band input impedance. Moreover, dielectric coating enables the design of a quasi-planar structure with approximately omni-directional radiation pattern. Therefore, this antenna can be easily integrated with planar circuits.

2.1 Conical antenna geometry

The dielectric covered conical antenna is illustrated in Fig. 1 and can be described by two parameters: the half-cone angle (flare angle) θ_0 and the length of the cone's arm antenna length) ℓ. The spherical dielectric cover is made of homogeneous material with permittivity $\varepsilon_r\varepsilon_0$ and permeability $\mu_r\mu_0$, where ε_0 and μ_0 are the permittivity and permeability of free space, respectively. The addition of the dielectric cover provides mechanical support to conical radiator and enables physical size reduction of the antenna. The bottom side of the dielectric is coated by metal and behaves as the ground plane. The metallic cone and the ground plane jointly form a mono-cone radiator. The antenna is fed by a coaxial connector, with its outer and inner conductors connected to the ground plane and the cone tip respectively.

The radiation mechanism of this dielectric covered antenna is similar to the conventional mono-conical antenna (Liang & Wah, 2000). Since the feed is located at the center of a revolutionarily symmetric structure, spherical transverse electromagnetic (TEM) wave is launched in the dielectric material. When the TEM wave hits the end of the cone, it is reflected and scattered. The reflection and scattering attenuate as frequency increases and therefore, the antenna approaches a semi-infinitely long transmission line for high frequencies. Compared to conventional mono-conical antennas, the addition of the dielectric cover introduces some complications (Lu *et. al.*, 2007):

a. The wavelength within the dielectric material is shorter than that in the air and as a result, the electrical length of the antenna increases. This affects the UWB performance of the antenna.
b. The dielectric-air interface results in more reflection and scattering of the outgoing TEM wave, making the antenna less matched to free space.
c. The dielectric material forms a cavity that stores energy, hence would reduce the antenna's bandwidth.
d. The conductivity of the dielectric cover would reduce the antenna's efficiency and low dielectric loss should be another criterion for the antenna's cover.

Consequently, it is not easy to predict the effect of the dielectric cover on the performance of the conical antenna for UWB applications.

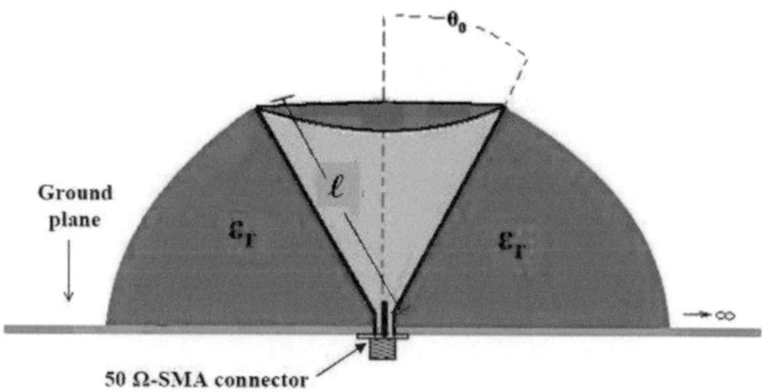

Fig. 1. Geometry of the dielectric covered conical antenna.

2.2 FDTD Method in spherical coordinates

FDTD method is very suitable for analysing and optimising the antenna for UWB radio technology. The method becomes one of the attractive methods due to its programming simplicity and flexibility in analyzing wide range of electromagnetic structures. Cartesian-grid FDTD technique utilizes a cubic prism as a unit cell. Thus, it may produce significant errors when modelling perfect electric conductors with curved surfaces and edges because of the staircase approximation introduced in the process. In this section, the FDTD algorithm in spherical coordinates is described following the lines of (Liu & Grimes, 1999; Brocato, 2004). The Maxwell's equations in finite difference form, the suitable absorbing boundary conditions and the input voltage source model are presented.

2.2.1 Spherical FDTD Equations for a conical antenna

The FDTD equations are derived directly from Maxwell's curl equations in the time domain. Taking into account the medium properties, Maxwell's curl equations can be written as:

$$\nabla \times \vec{E} = -\mu \cdot \frac{\partial \vec{H}}{\partial t} - \sigma^* \cdot \vec{H} \tag{1}$$

$$\nabla \times \vec{H} = \varepsilon \cdot \frac{\partial \vec{E}}{\partial t} + \sigma \cdot \vec{E} \tag{2}$$

where ε and μ are the permittivity and permeability respectively and, σ and σ* the electric and magnetic conductivity of the propagation space respectively. These two vector equations are the general equations governing the antenna operation. Because the conical antenna is a revolutionary symmetric structure, the three dimensional problem can be reduced to two-dimensional problem. In spherical coordinates, due to rotational symmetry, Eq. (1) and (2) lead to the following three scalar partial differential equations:

$$\frac{\partial H_\phi}{\partial t} = -\frac{\sigma^*}{\mu} \cdot H_\phi - \frac{1}{\mu \cdot r \cdot \sin\theta}\left(\sin\theta \frac{\partial}{\partial r}(r \cdot E_\theta) - \frac{\partial}{\partial \theta}(\sin\theta \cdot E_r) \right) \tag{3}$$

$$\frac{\partial E_r}{\partial t} = -\frac{\sigma}{\varepsilon} \cdot E_r + \frac{1}{\varepsilon \cdot r \cdot \sin\theta} \frac{\partial}{\partial \theta}\left(\sin\theta \cdot H_\phi\right) \tag{4}$$

$$\frac{\partial E_\theta}{\partial t} = -\frac{\sigma}{\varepsilon} \cdot E_\theta - \frac{1}{\varepsilon \cdot r} \frac{\partial}{\partial r}\left(r \cdot H_\phi\right) \tag{5}$$

To obtain a discrete set of the continuous differential equations, the central difference approximation is used on both the time and space first-order partial derivatives. The entire computational space is a collection of modified Yee unit cells (Yee, 1966). In our modified Yee's scheme, the computational space is subdivided by using an orthogonal mesh in spherical coordinates. The electric fields are located along the edges of the cells, while the magnetic fields are positioned at the centers of these cells. Using the well-known half time step notation in all locations and after some rearrangements, a set of finite difference field forms for Eqs. (3)-(5) follows (Kliros *et. al.*, 2010a, 2010b):

$$E_r^{n+1}(i,j) = C_a(i) E_r^n(i,j) + \frac{C_b(i)}{(i+1/2)\Delta\theta} \cdot \left[\frac{\sin((j+1/2)\,\Delta\theta)}{\sin((j-1/2)\,\Delta\theta)} H_\phi^{n+\frac{1}{2}}(i,j) - H_\phi^{n+\frac{1}{2}}(i,j-1) \right] \tag{6}$$

$$E_\theta^{n+1}(i,j) = C_a(i) E_\theta^n(i,j) + C_b(i) \cdot \left[H_\phi^{n+\frac{1}{2}}(i-1,j) - \left(\frac{i+1/2}{i-1/2} \right) \cdot H_\phi^{n+\frac{1}{2}}(i,j) \right] \tag{7}$$

$$\begin{aligned} H_\phi^{n+\frac{1}{2}}(i,j) = D_a(i) H_\phi^{n-\frac{1}{2}}(i,j) + \frac{D_b(i)}{(i+1/2)\Delta\theta} \cdot \left[\frac{\sin((j+1)\Delta\theta)}{\sin(j\Delta\theta)} E_r^n(i,j+1) - E_r^n(i,j) \right] \\ - D_b(i) \left[\left(\frac{i+1}{i} \right) E_\theta^n(i+1,j) - E_\theta^n(i,j) \right] \end{aligned} \tag{8}$$

where

$$C_a(i) = \frac{1 - \dfrac{\sigma(i)\Delta t}{2\varepsilon(i)}}{1 + \dfrac{\sigma(i)\Delta t}{2\varepsilon(i)}}, \quad C_b(i) = \frac{\dfrac{\Delta t}{\varepsilon(i)\Delta r}}{1 + \dfrac{\sigma(i)\Delta t}{2\varepsilon(i)}} \tag{9}$$

$$D_a(i) = \frac{1 - \dfrac{\sigma^*(i)\Delta t}{2\mu(i)}}{1 + \dfrac{\sigma^*(i)\Delta t}{2\mu(i)}}, \quad D_b(i) = \frac{\dfrac{\Delta t}{\mu(i)\Delta r}}{1 + \dfrac{\sigma^*(i)\Delta t}{2\mu(i)}} \tag{10}$$

and Δr , $\Delta\theta$ represent the step size in the *r*- and *θ*- directions, respectively. Superscript n signifies that the quantities are to be evaluated at $t = n\Delta t$, and, i and j represent the point $(i\Delta r, j\Delta\theta)$ in the spherical grid. The half time steps indicate that the fields E and H are calculated alternately. The maximum time step is limited by the stability Courant's criterion (Fusco, 1990):

$$\Delta t \le \min \frac{r(\Delta r)(\Delta\theta)}{c\sqrt{(\Delta r)^2 + (r\Delta\theta)^2}} \tag{11}$$

where c is the velocity of the light in free space.

2.2.2 Absorbing Boundary Conditions (ABC) treatment

In order to study antenna matching and pulse fidelity in the time domain, any spurious reflections had to be eliminated using suitable absorbing boundary conditions (ABC). Because we treat the problem using spherical coordinates, the absorbing boundary layer should be spherically symmetric as shown in Fig. 2. The purpose of the PML is to simulate an infinite simulation space, that is, outgoing waves are absorbed by the PML and cannot reflect back into simulation space. A unique feature of the PML is that plane waves of arbitrary incidence, polarization and frequency are matched at the boundary in a reflection-less manner. The boundary of the computational space must be sufficiently far from the antenna, usually in a distance at least ten times the free space operating wavelength.

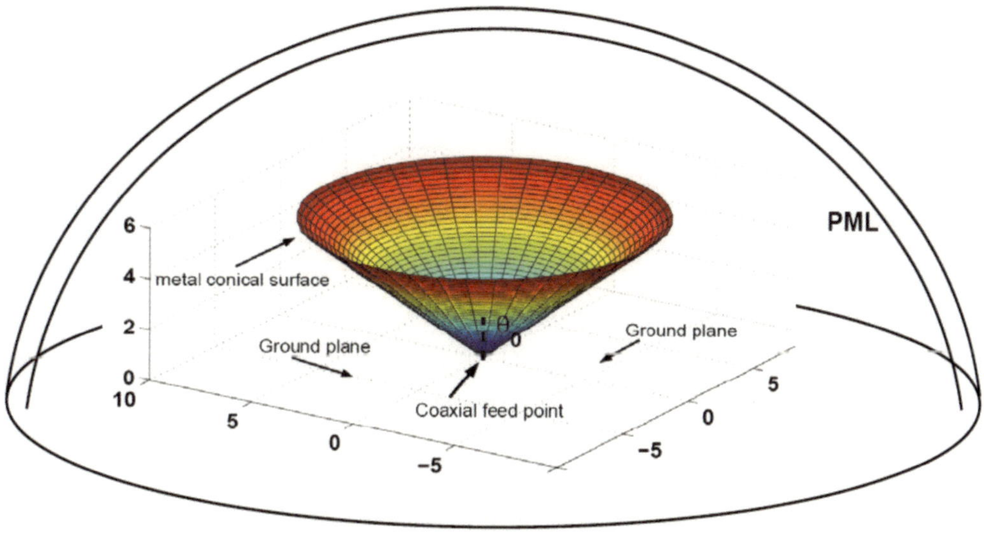

Fig. 2. Spherical perfectly matched layer at the edge of the simulation space.

In order to determine a spherical PML, the following steps must be taken:

i. Splitting of the magnetic field component H_{ϕ} into two sub-components $H_{\phi r}$ and $H_{\phi\theta}$ in the coupled Maxwell equations, as follows:

$$\frac{\partial H_{\phi\theta}}{\partial t}=\frac{1}{\mu}\left[-\sigma_{\theta}^{*}H_{\phi\theta}+\frac{1}{r\sin\theta}\frac{\partial(E_r\sin\theta)}{\partial\theta}\right] \tag{12}$$

$$\frac{\partial H_{\phi r}}{\partial t}=-\frac{1}{\mu}\left[\sigma_r^{*}H_{\phi r}+\frac{1}{r}\frac{\partial(r\cdot E_{\theta})}{\partial r}\right] \tag{13}$$

$$\frac{\partial E_r}{\partial t}=\frac{1}{\varepsilon}\left[-\sigma_{\theta}E_r+\frac{1}{r\sin\theta}\frac{\partial\left(\left(H_{\phi r}+H_{\phi\theta}\right)\sin\theta\right)}{\partial\theta}\right] \tag{14}$$

$$\frac{\partial E_{\theta}}{\partial t}=-\frac{1}{\varepsilon}\left[\sigma_r E_{\theta}+\frac{1}{r}\frac{\partial\left(r\left(H_{\phi r}+H_{\phi\theta}\right)\right)}{\partial r}\right] \tag{15}$$

ii. Create spherical FDTD equations from the above revised Maxwell equations:

$$H_{\phi\theta}^{n+\frac{1}{2}}(i,j)=D_{a\theta}(i)H_{\phi\theta}^{n-\frac{1}{2}}(i,j)+\frac{D_{b\theta}(i)}{(i+1/2)\Delta\theta}\cdot\left[\frac{\sin((j+1)\Delta\theta)}{\sin(j\Delta\theta)}E_r^n(i,j+1)-E_r^n(i,j)\right] \tag{16}$$

$$H_{\phi r}^{n+\frac{1}{2}}(i,j)=D_{ar}(i)H_{\phi r}^{n-\frac{1}{2}}(i,j)-D_{br}(i)\left[\left(\frac{i+1}{i}\right)E_{\theta}^n(i+1,j)-E_{\theta}^n(i,j)\right] \tag{17}$$

$$E_r^{n+1}(i,j)=C_{\alpha\theta}(i)E_r^n(i,j)+\frac{C_{b\theta}(i)}{(i+1/2)\Delta\theta}\cdot\left[\frac{\sin((j+1/2)\,\Delta\theta)}{\sin((j-1/2)\,\Delta\theta)}H_{\phi}^{n+\frac{1}{2}}(i,j)-H_{\phi}^{n+\frac{1}{2}}(i,j-1)\right] \tag{18}$$

$$E_{\theta}^{n+1}(i,j)=C_{ar}(i)E_{\theta}^n(i,j)+C_{br}(i)\cdot\left[H_{\phi}^{n+\frac{1}{2}}(i-1,j)-\left(\frac{i+1/2}{i-1/2}\right)\cdot H_{\phi}^{n+\frac{1}{2}}(i,j)\right] \tag{19}$$

where

$$C_{\alpha r}=\frac{1-\dfrac{\sigma_r\Delta t}{2\varepsilon}}{1+\dfrac{\sigma_r\Delta t}{2\varepsilon}},\quad C_{br}=\frac{\dfrac{\Delta t}{\varepsilon\Delta r}}{1+\dfrac{\sigma_r\Delta t}{2\varepsilon}} \tag{20}$$

$$D_{ar}=\frac{1-\dfrac{\sigma_r^{*}\Delta t}{2\mu}}{1+\dfrac{\sigma_r^{*}\Delta t}{2\mu}},\quad D_{br}=\frac{\dfrac{\Delta t}{\mu\Delta r}}{1+\dfrac{\sigma_r^{*}\Delta t}{2\mu}} \tag{21}$$

$$C_{a\theta} = \frac{1 - \frac{\sigma_\theta \Delta t}{2\varepsilon}}{1 + \frac{\sigma_\theta \Delta t}{2\varepsilon}}, \quad C_{b\theta} = \frac{\frac{\Delta t}{\varepsilon \Delta \theta}}{1 + \frac{\sigma_\theta \Delta t}{2\varepsilon}} \tag{22}$$

$$D_{a\theta} = \frac{1 - \frac{\sigma_\theta^* \Delta t}{2\mu}}{1 + \frac{\sigma_\theta^* \Delta t}{2\mu}}, \quad D_{b\theta} = \frac{\frac{\Delta t}{\mu \Delta \theta}}{1 + \frac{\sigma_\theta^* \Delta t}{2\mu}} \tag{23}$$

and $H_\phi = H_{\phi r} + H_{\phi\theta}$ in the last two equations.

iii. for a given number N of PMLs, calculation of free-space conductivities, σ_0 and σ_0^*, the final conductivities σ_N and σ_N^* and the conductivity profile of each PML.

According to (Berenger, 1996), for a desired conductivity profile $\sigma(r)$ of thickness δ, the reflection factor at normal incidence R(0) is given by:

$$R(0) = \exp\left(-\frac{2}{\varepsilon c} \int_0^\delta \sigma(r)\, dr \right) \tag{24}$$

and consequently, the reflection factor for a wave at arbitrary incidence, θ, is

$$R(\theta) = R(0)^{\cos\theta} \tag{25}$$

Assuming a parabolic conductivity profile and extending the results of (Berenger, 1996) for spherical PMLs, we obtain the following equations for the desired conductivities:

a) free space conductivity:

$$\sigma_0 = -\frac{\varepsilon_0 c \ln\left(R(0)\right)}{2^4 \Delta r\, N_{PML}^3} \tag{26}$$

b) conductivity of each layer (i):

$$\sigma(i) = \sigma_{\max} \left(\frac{i}{\delta} \right)^2, \quad \sigma_{\max} = 24 \sigma_0 N_{PML} \tag{27}$$

The correct conductivity profile is calculated automatically in our code for any desired reflection factor and number of perfectly matched layers.

2.2.3 Resistive voltage source model

Antennas modelled using FDTD are often excited by a "hard" voltage source in which the internal source resistance is zero. However, a "hard" voltage source generates non-physical reflections. To avoid such problems, the base of the antenna is driven by a voltage signal $V_s(t)$ with internal resistance R_s through a coaxial line with inner and outer conductor's diameters a and b respectively. Fig. 3 illustrates the equivalent circuit for a voltage source which includes an internal source resistance R_s.

The electric driving field E_θ, resulting from the input voltage, is given by (Liu, 1999).

$$E_\theta^n(i,j) = -\frac{V_s(t) - I_{in}(t) R_s}{b \sin(\theta) \ln(b/a)} \tag{28}$$

where

$$I_{in}(t) = (2\pi r \sin\theta) H_\phi(r,\theta,t) \tag{29}$$

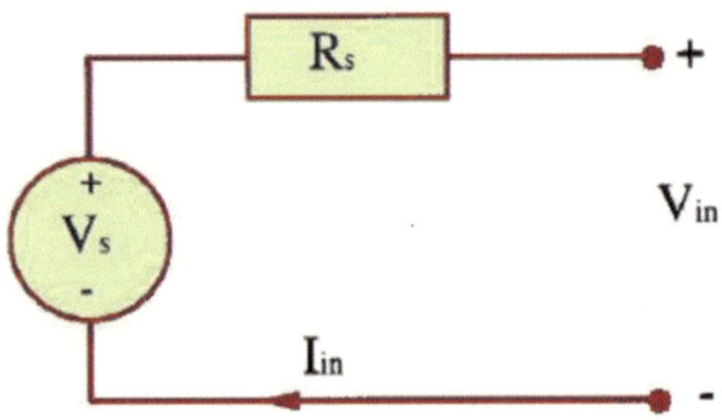

Fig. 3. Equivalent circuit of the FDTD input source.

A voltage source that corresponds to electric field of Eq. (28) can be generated in a certain mesh location ($i\Delta r$, $j\Delta\theta$) within the source region and, therefore, the electric field in the source region can be written in FDTD form as

$$E_\theta^n(i,j) = -\frac{V_s(n\Delta t) - R_s I_{in}^{n-1/2}(i,j)}{b \cdot \sin(j\Delta\theta)\ln(b/a)} \tag{30}$$

$$I_{in}^{n-1/2}(i,j) = 2\pi(i\Delta r)\sin\left((j+1/2)\Delta\theta\right) \cdot H_\phi^{n-1/2}(i+1/2, j+1/2) \tag{31}$$

The above field is a spherical source extending from the inner conductor of the coaxial line to the outer conductor. Consequently, as the voltage $V_s(t)$ steps forward in time, it drives the base of the conical antenna with the above spherical field. Then, the antenna radiates the resulting wave following the time evolution described by Eq. (6)-(8).

2.3 Antenna characteristics

There are general factors determining the antenna performance for UWB applications (Stuzman & Thiele, 1997). Those are input matching represented by the input impedance, Voltage Standing Wave Ratio (VSWR) and Return Loss, frequency dependence of the maximum gain, radiation pattern determining the available beam angle for distortionless wave received from the transmitter, as well as, waveform fidelity which describes the distortion of radiated impulses. All the necessary frequency domain parameters can be calculated from the time domain parameters using a Fast Fourier Transformation code in MATLAB.

The input impedance of the antenna Z_{in} is calculated in the center of feeding line over a range of frequencies. It is determined from the ratio of the Fourier transform of the voltage wave and that of the input current wave

$$Z_{in}(f) = \frac{V_{in}(f)}{I_{in}(f)} \exp(-j\pi f \Delta t) \tag{32}$$

where the exponential term accounts for the half-time step difference between the electric and magnetic field computation.

The results of input impedance are then used to obtain the return loss characteristics of the antenna. Thus, the Return Loss S_{11} (dB) of the antenna is given by

$$S_{11}(dB) = 20\log\left|\Gamma(f)\right| \tag{33}$$

where

$$\Gamma(f) = \frac{Z_{in}(f) - Z_{line}}{Z_{in}(f) + Z_{line}} \tag{34}$$

is the frequency dependent reflection coefficient. From the calculated reflection coefficient, the VSWR can be calculated as follows:

$$VSWR = \frac{1+\left|\Gamma(f)\right|}{1-\left|\Gamma(f)\right|} \tag{35}$$

The bandwidth of the antenna is the frequency range corresponding to a reflection coefficient of the antenna less than or equal to 1/3 that leads to VSWR ≤ 2.
To calculate the conical antenna gain, the far electric field in the desired direction must be determined as a function of frequency. Since the electric far-field is computed so that the 1/r amplitude factor and the propagation delay are suppressed, the antenna gain relative to a lossless isotropic antenna in θ_m - direction is given by

$$G(f,\theta_m) = \frac{1}{2\eta}\frac{\left|E(f,\theta_m)\right|^2}{P_{in}/4\pi} \tag{36}$$

where $E(f,\theta_m)$ is the peak value of the Fourier transform of the pulsed far field radiated in the θ_m-direction, η the characteristic space impedance and P_{in} the steady-state input power at each frequency given by

$$P_{in}(f) = \frac{1}{2}\mathrm{Re}\left[V_{in}(f)I_{in}^*(f)\right] \tag{37}$$

Directivity curves can be also computed. Directivity of an antenna is defined as the ratio of the radiation intensity in a given direction from the antenna to the radiation intensity averaged over all directions. The directivity in θ_m-direction is given by the ratio of the integral of Poynting vector with the value of electric field $E(f,\theta_m)$ to the actual value of the integral:

$$D(f,\theta_m) = \frac{2\left|E(f,\theta_m)\right|^2}{\int_0^\pi E^*(f,\theta)E(f,\theta)\sin\theta\, d\theta} \tag{38}$$

3. Simulation of the conical antenna characteristics

Parametric studies concerning both time domain and frequency domain characteristics of the dielectric covered conical antenna were performed using the above described spherical-coordinate FDTD algorithm implemented in MATLAB. A flowchart of the FDTD algorithm is given in Fig.4.

The FDTD cell dimensions are Δr=3 mm and $\Delta\theta$=1°. The antenna sits on top of a perfectly conducting ground plane that extends 360° in all directions for a distance of R_m=10 ℓ. Just before the maximum radial distance R_m is reached, the simulation space is terminated by a PML section of thickness 20Δr. The maximum reflection coefficient at normal incidence is chosen to be $R(0) = 10^{-14}$. The time step is taken Δt=0.2 psec, sufficient to satisfy Courant's criterion. An UWB Gaussian pulse (FWHM = 64 psec) modulated by a continuous sine wave carrier of frequency f_c is used in our simulations, that is,

$$V_s(t) = V_m \exp\left(-\frac{(t-t_0)^2}{t_d^2}\right)\sin\left(2\pi f_c (t-t_0)\right) \tag{39}$$

where $\tau = 64\,p\text{sec}$, $t_0 = 4\times\tau$, $f_c = 6.5\,GHz$ and $V_m = 0.1V$. The UWB excitation pulse driving the conical antenna is depicted in Fig.5.

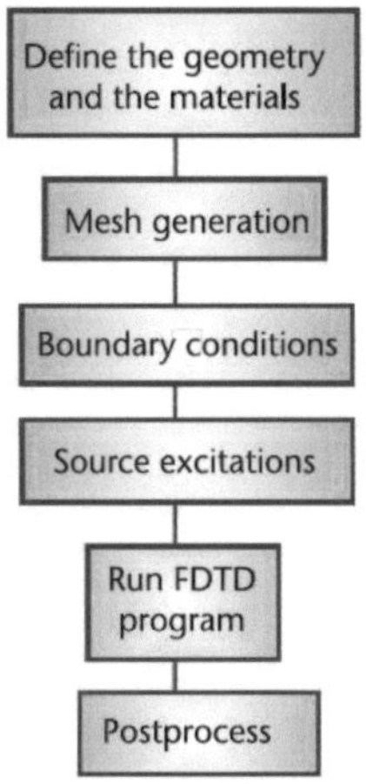

Fig. 4. Flowchart of the FDTD algorithm.

To verify the FDTD steady-state calculations, time-domain fields are transformed to the frequency domain by a Fast Fourier Transform routine. The MATLAB code was run for a wide range of different antenna's parameters combinations in an effort to find the antenna with the best match to a 50 Ω SMA-connector. FDTD has the ability to get the frequency response in one run. Accurate simulations require 2^{14}= 16384 time steps to achieve a complete decay of the fields in the structure. The code was run on a computer equipped with an AMD Athlon 64X2 Dual Core Processor at 1.9 GHz and 2 GB of RAM memory and the computing time required to obtain a result, for specific antenna's parameters, is less than 3.5 minutes.

In the following sub-sections, we present both time-domain and frequency-domain results for a spherically dielectric covered antenna with arm's length ℓ=45 mm (~$\lambda_c=c_0/f_c$), for different loading dielectrics ε_r and different flare angles θ_0. In all simulations the antenna is a small cone made of copper with conductivity of $5.8\text{x}10^7$ mhos/m place at the center of the simulation space. The simulations were performed in spherical coordinates and then re-mapped to Cartesian coordinates. Finally, the Fourier transforms forward and backward are the operations to switch from frequency domain to time domain, and vice versa.

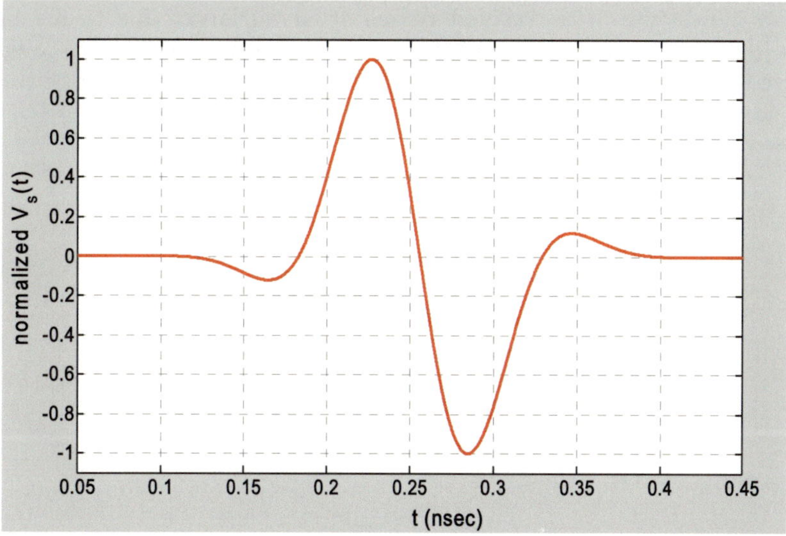

Fig. 5. Excitation UWB pulse driving the conical antenna.

3.1 Time domain characteristics

In general, our FDTD simulation provides very useful visualization of the dynamic field distributions that can help identify undesired radiation and reflection sources. Here we consider an antenna with length ℓ =45 mm, flare angle θ_0=47° and dielectric cover ε_r=3. As you can see from Fig.6(a) the UWB pulse has started to travel out from the base of the conical antenna. The snapshot is taken after 2000 time steps or at t=0.4 nsec. After 5000 time steps, i.e., at t=1 nsec, the UWB pulse is propagating out of the conical antenna forming its far-field pattern shape as it is shown in Fig.6(b). The wave reflection at the dielectric - free space interface produces a wave that travels back to the antenna. The mismatch between the antenna and the feed produces a second reflection but the resulting standing wave dampens out very slowly. Figure 6(c) shows the field distribution after 9000 time steps, i.e. t=1.8 nsec. The main Gaussian UWB pulse has been absorbed by the PML surrounding the simulation space but we see some small ringing arising from the imperfect mismatch between source and antenna impedances. These are not reflected from the PML region and within another 2000 steps (i.e. at t=2.2 nsec) have been totally absorbed.

The main purpose of a Time-Domain study is to characterize the distortion introduced by the antenna, in terms of the angular coordinates and the excitation waveform. In narrow-band operation, it is assumed that the antenna radiates identical signals in all directions. In UWB operation, this cannot be taken for granted. The UWB antenna is excited by an incident signal whose waveform undergoes a distortion induced by the antenna. This distortion can be quantified using the correlation between the incident signal and the radiated one in certain direction, which illustrates the fidelity of the antenna in that direction (Sibille et. al., 2006). For evaluating waveform distortions caused by our dielectric covered conical antenna, we examine the degree of similarity between source pulse and received pulse waveforms in several propagation directions. Figure 7 shows that the radiated pulses, in several elevation angles θ_V, is not very different from the excitation signal and therefore, antenna's fidelity in the time-domain have been achieved. Nevertheless, a late-time ringing is observed which can be attributed to the nonlinear far-field phase over the frequency bandwidth. The received pulses are a bit larger due to the fact that the antenna has filtered all frequencies outside the impedance bandwidth. The longer duration of the received pulses indicates lower achievable data-rates while the shape distortion can make the detection process more difficult. Proper channel models can be used to study these effects (Molisch, 2003).

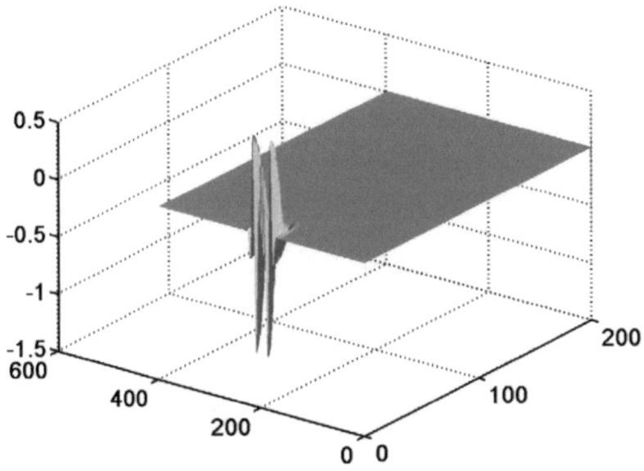

(a)

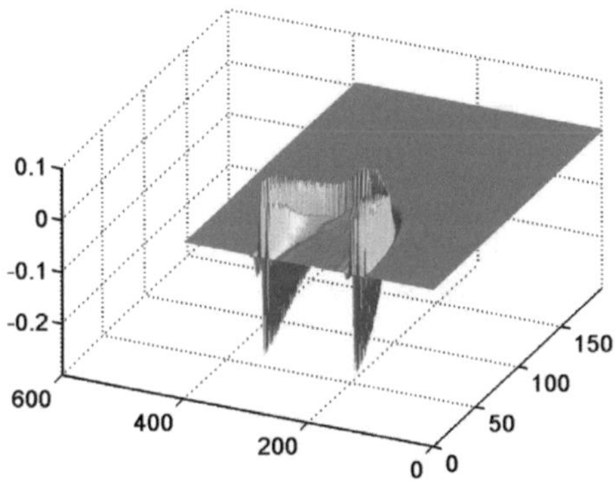

(b)

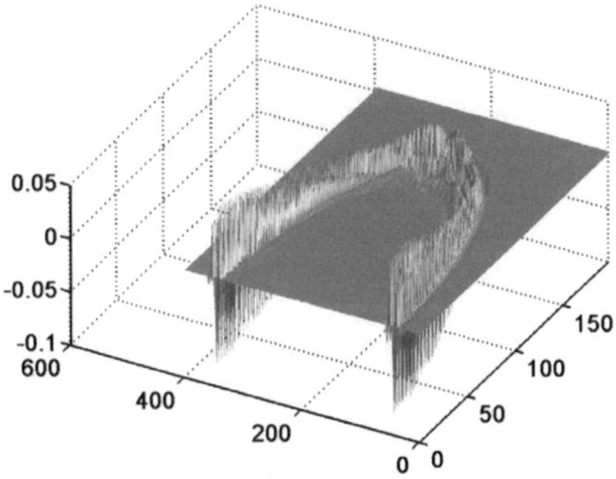

(c)

Fig. 6. FDTD simulation snapshots of the electric field strength after 2000 time steps (a), 5000 time steps (b) and 9000 time steps (c).

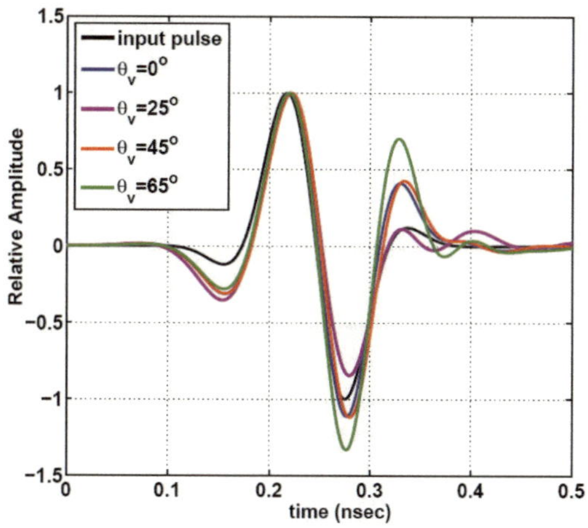

Fig. 7. Excitation and radiated pulses versus the elevation angle. It can clearly be seen that the radiated signals are elevation angle dependent.

3.2 Frequency domain characteristics

In this subsection, we present our parametric study concerning the impedance, VSWR and maximum gain of the spherically covered conical antenna varying the dielectric constant ε_r of the cover material or the cone flare angle.

As it is seen in Fig.9, the impedance bandwidth (VSWR < 2 or input return loss S_{11}< -10 dB) of the covered antenna, with dielectric of ε_r=3, increases as the flare angle increases until reaches its maximum at θ_0=47°. As it is expected, the corresponding real part of input impedance (Figure 8) varies with the flare angle. It is observed that an optimum flare angle θ_0=47° exists for 50 Ω matched impedance in a frequency band from about 5.5 to 17 GHz. Therefore, the designed antenna can provide more than 100% impedance bandwidth.

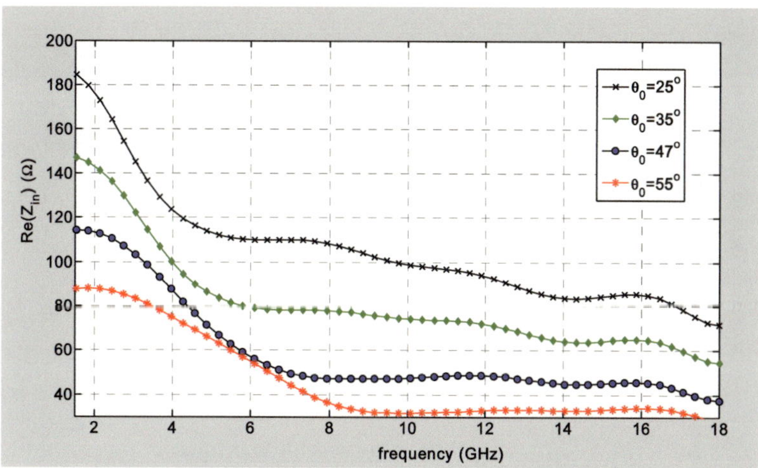

Fig. 8. Input impedance for various flare angles and ε_r=3.0.

Figure 10, shows the evolution of maximum gain in the elevation plane (E-plane) versus frequency. Gain gradually increases with frequency from 10 dBi to about 14 dBi in the frequency range from 5.5 to 8.5 GHz and remains almost frequency independent at 14 dBi in the frequency range from 8.5 to 17 GHz.
Furthermore, the power radiation patterns in the elevation plane are calculated in the above frequency range, although for brevity, only the patterns at 4.5, 6.5, 8 and 10 GHz are shown in Fig.11. Obviously, the power radiation patterns present quasi-perfect omni-directional (monopole-like) behaviour but gradually degrade with increasing frequency. The radiation lobe enlarges downwards up to 6.5 GHz, and above 10 GHz a 'null' appears near θ=35° while the beamwidth decreases slowly with frequency. These variations are attributed to the fact that the antenna's electrical size increase with frequency. It is also observed that the radiation patterns are slightly upward looking. This feature could be useful for radar sensor network applications.

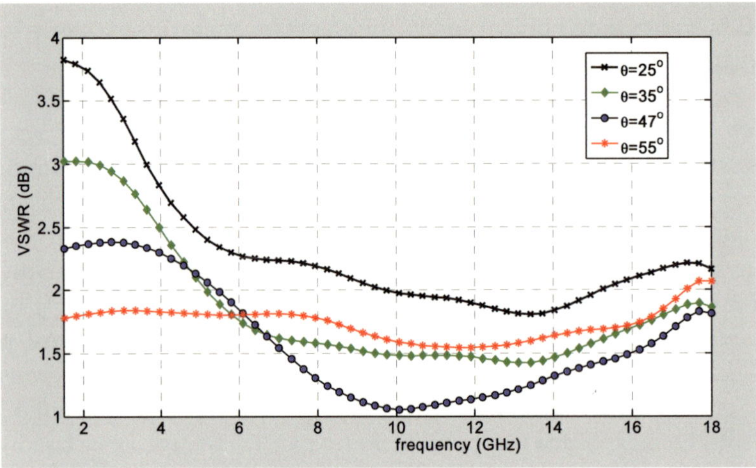

Fig. 9. Simulated VSWR for various flare angles and ε_r=3.0.

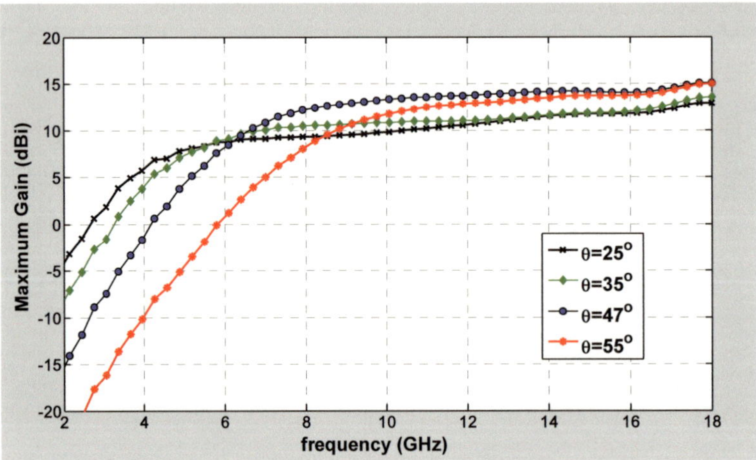

Fig. 10. Maximum gain for various flare angles and ε_r=3.0.

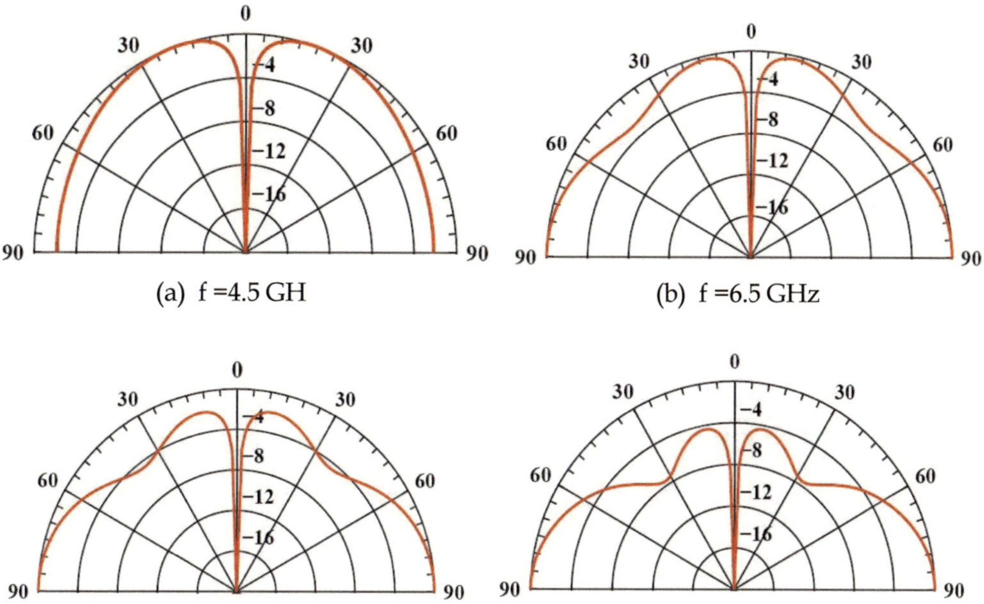

(a) f =4.5 GH (b) f =6.5 GHz

(c) f = 8 GHz (d) f =10 GHz

Fig. 11. Computed radiation patterns in the elevation plane at f=4.5, 6.5, 8.0, 10.0 GHz. The flare angle and relative dielectric constant are taken to be to θ=47° and ε_r=3, respectively.

The influence of the dielectric cover on the frequency domain characteristics of the designed antenna are investigated next. For a conical antenna with fixed flare angle θ_0=47°, five materials of increasing dielectric constants ε_r = 1, 2.2, 3, 4.4 and 9.8 have been considered.

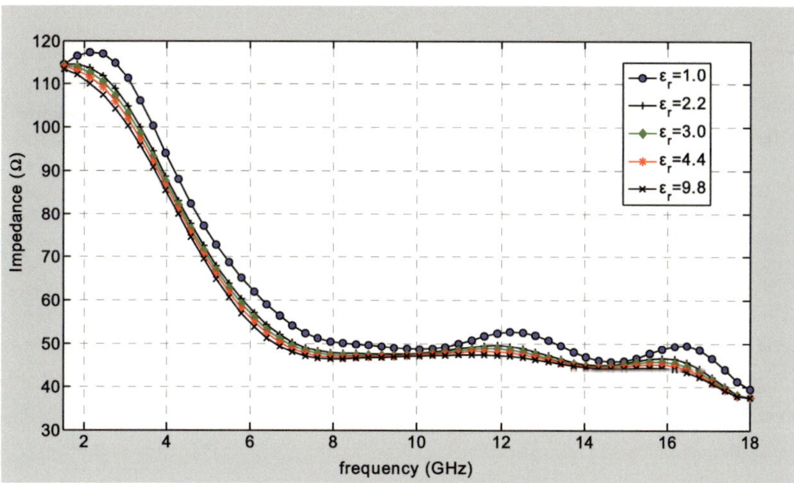

Fig. 12. Input impedance for various flare angles and ε_r=3.0.

As it is seen in Figs.12 and 13, the ultra wide-band characteristics of the antenna are not sensitive to the variation of dielectric constant ε_r. Some ripples appeared in both real part of impedance and VSWR are smoothed out when the dielectric cover is present. As it is seen, when ε_r is reasonably small, the antenna's input impedance remains close to a constant (~50 Ω) within a wide frequency band. However, because of the dielectric-air interface, the reflection and scattering at the end of the conical radiator is stronger making the antenna less matched to free space. Consequently, a wide range of dielectric materials can be used to construct the spherical cover of the antenna. Obviously, low conductivity material is preferred in order to minimize the dielectric loss. Figure 14 illustrates the frequency dependence of the maximum gain for covers of different dielectric constant. As it is seen, the maximum gain remains almost frequency independent in a wide range of frequency for all materials. However, as the dielectric constant increases, the maximum gain decreases.

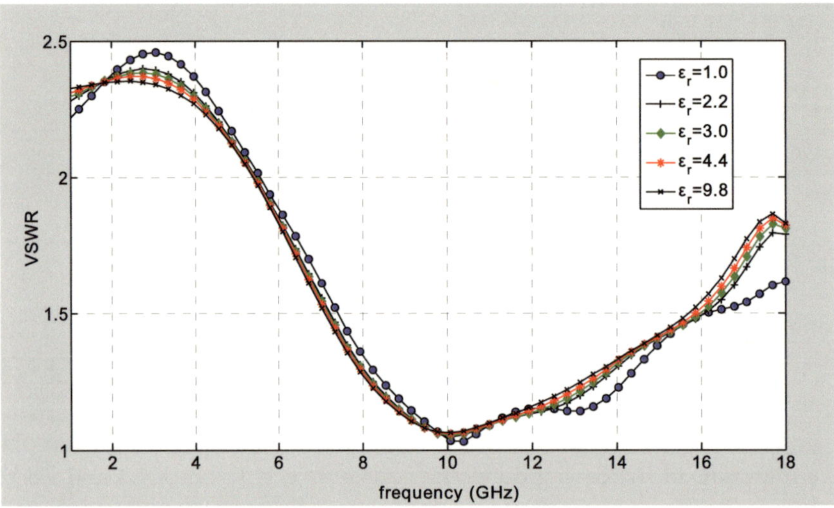

Fig. 13. Simulated VSWR for various flare angles and ε_r=3.0.

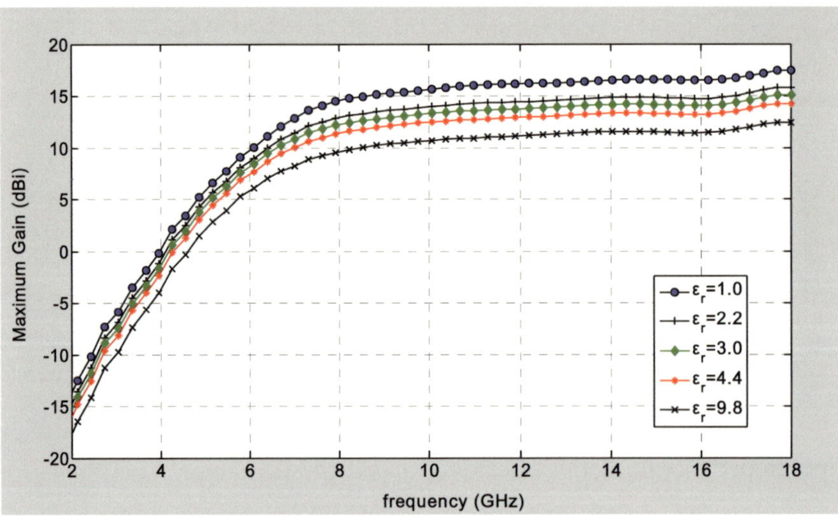

Fig. 14. Maximum gain for various flare angles and ε_r=3.0.

4. Conclusion

In this Chapter, we present a FDTD code in spherical coordinates implemented in MATLAB in order to simulate the radiation characteristics of conical antennas. MATLAB provides an interactive environment for algorithm development, data post-processing and visualization. The spherical FDTD equations can be found using a modified Yee cell in spherical coordinates. Spherical Berenger's perfectrly matched layer (PML) is applied as absorbing boundary condition where a parabolic conductivity profile in the spherical PML-region is used.

The code is used to design and simulate a conical antenna covered by a spherical dielectric structure and placed above a large ground plane. This quasi-planar antenna is mechanically stable and, relative easy to build and integrate with the planar circuits. Parametric studies lead to the optimum values of cone's arm length ℓ =45 mm and flare angle θ_0=47^0 for 50 Ω matched impedance. This design achieves an impedance bandwidth from 5.5 to 17 GHz, with stable radiation patterns over this bandwidth. The radiation patterns are monopole-like and their frequency dependence is small in the whole UWB frequency band. A time domain study has shown that the antenna distorts the excitation pulse in a moderate way.

It is observed that, the ultra wide-band characteristics of the antenna are not sensitive to the variation of dielectric constant ε_r of the spherical cover. Consequently, a wide range of dielectric materials can be used to construct the spherical cover of the antenna.

Our study suggests that a spherical dielectric covered conical antenna holds sufficient potential as a low-profile antenna with very wideband characteristics. A very important need is to verify more of the simulation results with experimental measurements which will be reported in a future communication.

5. Acknowledgment

The author wishes to thank his former graduate students G. Kyritsis and D. Touzloudis (now First-Lieutenants at Hellenic Air-Force) for improving and testing the first version of FDTD-code as well as some post-processing MATLAB-codes during their diploma thesis.

6. Appendix

```
==========================================================================
tmax=16384; % we use 2^{14} steps!
k=0; mu_0 = 4*pi*1e-7; eps_0 = 1e-9/(36*pi);
impedance_free=120*pi; c = 3e+8; Zline=50;
% =================== Define the antenna dimensions ======================
ant_length= 15;         % ant_length in units (dr) (mm).
ant_angle = 48;         % flare angle:'ant angle'Add (+1)for Matlab
e_rel=3.0;              % relative dielectric constant of substrate
tan_loss=0.0009d0;      % tangent loss of dielectric substrate
sub_length=ant_length;  % defines dielectric substrate length
e_sub=e_rel*eps_0;
impedance_medium=impedance_free/sqrt(e_rel);
radial_view=121; % give the position (r,theta) to view the far-fields
theta_view=46;
% ================== Definitions and Constants ===========================
dr = 0.003;             % radial step
```

```
dth = 1.0*pi/180;       % angular step in radians
dt = 0.2e-12;           % time step in sec
tsample=0.2e-12;
radial_max =201;        % simulation space radius
theta_max = 91;         % simulation space angle
b = 0.006;              % coaxial feed-line outer radius
a = 0.003;              % coaxial feed-line inner radius
fc = 6.5e+9;            % central frequency of the spectrum
% Define the parameters of the Gaussian sine-modulated driving pulse.
td = 64e-12; t0 = 4*td; once = 0; Vmax = 0.1; Rs = 50; Zin = 0;
R0 = 1e-14;   % select the desired zero-angle reflection.
Npml = 20;  % select number of PML layers
sigma_space = - eps_0*c*log(R0)/16*dr*Npml^3;% free space conductivity
sigmaM_space = mu_0*sigma_space/eps_0;        % impedance matching condition
% calculate final conductivity for parabolic profile
sigmaPML(Npml) = 24*sigma_space*Npml^2;
sigmaMPML(Npml) = mu_0*sigmaPML(Npml)/eps_0;
for I=1:(Npml-1)
sigmaPML(I) = sigmaPML(Npml)*(I/Npml)^2;
sigmaMPML(I) = mu_0*sigmaPML(I)/eps_0;
end
for I = 1:Npml %Initialize the PML domain for magnetic field
   for J=1:theta_max
   Hpr(I,J) = 0;
   Hpt(I,J) = 0;
   end
end
% =============  Set up the conducting antenna surface ====================
sigma_cu = 5.8d+7; % conductivity of Cu:5.8e+7 mhos/m
sigmaM_cu = mu_0*sigma_cu/eps_0;
sigma_epsilon = 2.d0*pi*fc*e_sub*tan_loss; %dielectric substrate losses
 sigmaM_epsilon = mu_0*sigma_epsilon/e_sub;
for I =1:radial_max
for J= 1:theta_max
    if (J==ant_angle)
        if (I <= ant_length)
            sigma(I,J) = sigma_cu;
            sigmaM(I,J) = sigmaM_cu;
            elseif (I < radial_max-Npml+1)
            sigma(I,J) = sigma_space;
            sigmaM(I,J) = sigmaM_space;
        else
sigma(I,J) = sigmaPML(I + Npml - radial_max);
sigmaM(I,J) = sigmaMPML(I + Npml - radial_max);
end
elseif (I < ant_length)
    if (J < ant_angle)
       sigma(I,J) = sigma_space;
       sigmaM(I,J) = sigmaM_space;
    else
       sigma(I,J) = sigma_space;
       sigmaM(I,J) = sigmaM_space;
    end
else
if (I< radial_max-Npml+1)
    sigma(I,J) = sigma_space;
    sigmaM(I,J) = sigmaM_space;
```

```
else
sigma(I,J) = sigmaPML(I + Npml - radial_max);
sigmaM(I,J) = sigmaMPML(I + Npml - radial_max);
  end
end
if ((I <=sub_length) & (J > ant_angle )& (J< (theta_max-1)))
       sigma(I,J)= sigma_epsilon;
       sigmaM(I,J)= sigmaM_epsilon;
    end
    end
end
for I = 1:radial_max %initialize, zero the fields for all free nodes
    for J= 1:theta_max
if ((I >= ant_length)|(J >= ant_angle))
    Er(I,J) = 0; Et(I,J) = 0;  Hp(I,J) = 0;
    end
  end
end
g1 = dt/(2*mu_0);   g2 = dt/(2*eps_0);
g3 = dt/(dr*eps_0); g4 = dt/(dr*mu_0);
I_factor = 2*pi*b;
V_factor = (log(sin(ant_angle*pi/180))-log(1-cos(ant_angle*pi/180)))/log(2);
%========================= Begin of time iterations ====================
t = 0;
fid=fopen('Etime.dat','wt');
while (t < (tmax*dt))
t = t + 0.5*dt; % For the first half time-step, update the H-field.
for I = 3:(radial_max-Npml)
  for J = 2:(theta_max-1)
    if ((I >= ant_length)|(J >= ant_angle))
    g5 = sin(J*dth)/sin((J-1)*dth);
    Da = (1-sigmaM(I,J)*g1)/(1+sigmaM(I,J)*g1);
    Db = g4/(1+sigmaM(I,J)*g1);
    ER1 = (g5*Er(I,J+1)-Er(I,J))/((I-1/2)*dth);
    ET1 = (I/(I-1))*Et(I+1,J) - Et(I,J);
    Hp(I,J) = Da*Hp(I,J) + Db*(ER1 - ET1);
    end
  end
end
J = theta_max; % H-field at the ground plane
for I = 3:(radial_max-Npml)
Da = (1-sigmaM(I,J)*g1)/(1+sigmaM(I,J)*g1);
Db = g4/(1+sigmaM(I,J)*g1);
ET1 = (I/(I-1))*Et(I+1,J) - Et(I,J);
Hp(I,J) = Da*Hp(I,J)- Db*ET1;
end
for I = ant_length:(radial_max-Npml)
Hp(I,1) = Hp(I,2); % H-field along the line of symmetry
end
layer = 1; % Update the H-field in the PML region
for I = (radial_max-Npml+1):radial_max
Dar = (1-sigmaMPML(layer)*g1)/(1+sigmaMPML(layer)*g1);
Dbr = g4/(1+sigmaMPML(layer)*g1);
Dat = Dar; Dbt = Dbr;
for J = 2:(theta_max-1)
g5 = sin(J*dth)/sin((J-1)*dth);
ER1 = (g5*Er(I,J+1)-Er(I,J))/((I-1/2)*dth);
```

```
if(I == radial_max)
ET1 = 0;
else
ET1 = (I/(I-1))*Et(I+1,J)- Et(I,J);
end
Hpr(layer,J) = Dar*Hpr(layer,J) - Dbr*ET1;
Hpt(layer,J) = Dat*Hpt(layer,J) + Dbt*ER1;
Hp(I,J) = Hpr(layer,J) + Hpt(layer,J);
end
layer = layer + 1;
end
J = theta_max; % Update H-field in the PML along the ground plane
layer = 1;
for I = (radial_max-Npml+1):radial_max
Dar = (1-sigmaMPML(layer)*g1)/(1+sigmaMPML(layer)*g1);
Dbr = g4/(1+sigmaMPML(layer)*g1);
Dat = Dar;
if(I == radial_max)
   ET1 = 0;
else
   ET1 = (I/(I-1))*Et(I+1,J) - Et(I,J);
end
Hpr(layer,J) = Dar*Hpr(layer,J) - Dbr*ET1;
Hpt(layer,J) = Dat*Hpt(layer,J);
Hp(I,J) = Hpr(layer,J) + Hpt(layer,J);
layer = layer + 1;
end
t = t + 0.5*dt; % For the second half time-step, update the E-fields.
Vsource= Vmax*exp(-((t-t0)/td)^2)*sin(2*pi*fc*(t-t0));
Vin = 0; Iins = 0;
for J = ant_angle:theta_max
    Iin = I_factor*sin((J-1/2)*dth)*Hp(3,J);
    Vdrv = Vsource- Rs*Iin;
if ((t >= tsample) & (J > ant_angle))
   Vin = Vin + b*Et(3,J)*dth;
   Iins = Iins + Iin;
   if(J == (theta_max-1))
     Iins = Iins/(theta_max - ant_angle -1);
     exVin = Vin; exIin = Iin;
   end
end
Et(3,J) = Vdrv*(1/(b*log(2)))/sin((J-1/2)*dth);
end
k=k+1;
piVin(k)=Vin;
piIin(k)=Iin;
for I = 4:(radial_max-Npml) % Step E-fields for free nodes
    for J = 2:(theta_max-1)
    if ((I >= ant_length)|(J >= ant_angle))
    g6 = sin((J-1/2)*dth)/sin((J-3/2)*dth);
    Ca = (1 - g2*sigma(I,J))/(1 + g2*sigma(I,J));
   Cb = g3/(1 + g2*sigma(I,J));
    HPHI1 = (g6*Hp(I,J)- Hp(I,J-1))/((I-1/2)*dth);
    HPHI2 = Hp(I-1,J)-((I-1/2)/(I-3/2))*Hp(I,J);
    Er(I,J) = Ca*Er(I,J) + Cb*HPHI1;
    Et(I,J) = Ca*Et(I,J) + Cb*HPHI2;
    end
```

```
    end
end
% ================ Introduction of spherical dielectric cover ==============
for I = 4:sub_length
   for J = ant_angle:theta_max-1
        g6 = sin((J-0.5)*dth)/sin((J-1.5)*dth);
        g2_sub = 1/(1*e_sub/eps_0);
        g3_sub = 1/(1*e_sub/eps_0);
        Ca = (1 - g2_sub*sigma(I,J))/(1+ g2_sub*sigma(I,J));
        Cb = g3_sub/(1 + g2_sub*sigma(I,J));
        HPHI1 = (g6*Hp(I,J)- Hp(I,J-1))/((I-0.5)*dth);
        HPHI2 = Hp(I-1,J)-((I-0.5)/(I-1.5))*Hp(I,J);
        Er(I,J) = Ca*Er(I,J) + Cb*HPHI1;
        Et(I,J) = Ca*Et(I,J) + Cb*HPHI2;
    end
 end
J = theta_max;E  % Compute the fields at the ground plane
for I = 4:(radial_max-Npml)
Ca = (1 - g2*sigma(I,J))/(1+ g2*sigma(I,J));
Cb = g3/(1 + g2*sigma(I,J));
HPHI2 = Hp(I-1,J) - ((I-1/2)/(I-3/2))*Hp(I,J);
Er(I,J) = 0;
Et(I,J) = Ca*Et(I,J) + Cb*HPHI2;
end
J = theta_max; % Compute the E-fields for the substrate domain
 for I = 4:sub_length
     g2_sub = 1/(1*e_sub/eps_0);
     g3_sub = 1/(1*e_sub/eps_0);
     Ca = (1 - g2_sub*sigma(I,J))/(1+ g2_sub*sigma(I,J));
     Cb = g3_sub/(1 + g2_sub*sigma(I,J));
     HPHI2 = Hp(I-1,J) - ((I-1/2)/(I-3/2))*Hp(I,J);
     Er(I,J) = 0;
     Et(I,J) = Ca*Et(I,J) + Cb*HPHI2;
end
for I = ant_length:(radial_max-Npml) %E-field along line of symmetry
    Ca = (1 - g2*sigma(I,1))/(1 + g2*sigma(I,1));
    Cb = g3/(1+g2*sigma(I,1));
    HPHI1 = (Hp(I,2) - Hp(I,1))/((I-1/2)*dth);
    Er(I,1) = Ca*Er(I,1) + Cb*HPHI1;
    Et(I,1) = 0;
end
layer = 1; % Update the E-fields in the PML region
for I = (radial_max-Npml+1):radial_max
   for J = 2:(theta_max-1)
   g6 = sin((J-1/2)*dth)/sin((J-3/2)*dth);
   Car = (1 - g2*sigmaPML(layer))/(1 + g2*sigmaPML(layer));
   Cbr = g3/(1 + g2*sigmaPML(layer));
   Cat = Car; Cbt = Cbr;
   HPHI1 = (g6*Hp(I,J) - Hp(I,J-1))/((I-1/2)*dth);
   HPHI2 = (Hp(I-1,J) - ((I-1/2)/(I-3/2))*Hp(I,J));
   Er(I,J) = Cat*Er(I,J) + Cbt*HPHI1;
   Et(I,J) = Car*Et(I,J) + Cbr*HPHI2;
   end
layer = layer + 1;
end
layer = 1; %E-field in the PML region at the ground plane
J = theta_max;
```

```
for I = (radial_max-Npml+1):radial_max
Car = (1 - g2*sigmaPML(layer))/(1 + g2*sigmaPML(layer));
Cbr = g3/(1 + g2*sigmaPML(layer));
HPHI2 = (Hp(I-1,J) - ((I-1/2)/(I-3/2))*Hp(I,J));
Er(I,J) = 0; Et(I,J) = Car*Et(I,J) + Cbr*HPHI2;
layer = layer + 1;
end
Etheta(k)=Et(radial_view,theta_view);
Radial_view=151; tt=t/1e-12;
for sJ=1:theta_max-1
    EthetaT(sJ,k)=Et(radial_view,sJ);
end
end
fclose(fid);
table=[tt; Et(radial_view, theta_view)];
%========== Spherical to rectangular coordinates transformation ===========
for I=1:radial_max
  for J=1:theta_max-1
  x= radial_max +round((I*sin((J-1)*dth)));
  x2 = (2*radial_max+1) - x; y = 1 + round((I*cos((J-1)*dth)));
  Ecart(x,y) = Et(I,J); Ecart(x2,y) = Et(I,J);
  end
end
for I=1:(2*radial_max-1)
   for J = 1:radial_max
   EcartNew(I,J) = Ecart(I,J);
   end
end
Imin = 2; Imax = 2*radial_max - 2; Jmin = 2; Jmax = radial_max-1;
for I = Imin:Imax
   for J = Jmin:Jmax
      if ((Ecart(I,J)=0)&(radial_max*cos((I-radial_max)*dth*91/151)+25>= J))
      ItempLo = I-1; ItempHi = I+1;
      while ((Ecart(ItempLo,J) == 0) & (ItempLo > 1))
        ItempLo = ItempLo-1;
      end
      while ((Ecart(ItempHi,J) == 0) & (ItempHi < 2*radial_max -1))
        ItempHi = ItempHi + 1;
      end
      M = Ecart(ItempLo,J); N = Ecart(ItempHi,J);
      if(M == 0)
        temp1 = N;
      elseif(N == 0)
        temp1 = M;
      else
        temp1 = sign(M+N)*sqrt(abs(M*N));
      end
      JtempLo = J-1; JtempHi = J+1;
      while ((Ecart(I,JtempLo)= 0) & (JtempLo > 1))
       JtempLo = JtempLo-1;
      end
      while ((Ecart(I,JtempHi)= 0) & (JtempHi < radial_max))
      JtempHi = JtempHi + 1;
      end
      M = Ecart(I,JtempLo); N = Ecart(I,JtempHi);
      if(M == 0)
      temp2 = N;
```

```
        elseif(N == 0)
        temp2 = M;
       else
       temp2 = sign(M+N)*sqrt(abs(M*N));
       end
       if (temp1==0)
       EcartNew(I,J) = temp2;
       elseif(temp2 == 0)
       EcartNew(I,J) = temp1;
       else
       EcartNew(I,J) = sign(temp1+temp2)*sqrt(abs(temp1*temp2));
       end
   end
   end
   EcartNew(1,radial_max)=1.0; EcartNew(2,radial_max)= -1.0;
end
%======================== 3D time evolution of E-field =====================
I=1:2*radial_max-1; J=1:radial_max;
x(I) = I; y(J) = J;
surfl(y(J), x(I), EcartNew(I,J))
xlabel('Y-axis cm'), ylabel('X-axis cm')
zlabel('Etheta V/m')
shading interp; colormap bone
%==========================  Frequency-Domain Analysis =====================
t_val=0.2e-12:0.2e-12:0.2e-12*tmax;
dt = t_val(2) - t_val(1); t0 = t_val(1); V_val=piVin; I_val=piIin;
iplot = 1; ipad = 0; omega_plot_max =2*pi*10e+9; omin=2; omax=61;
central_f=14; % omega (14)corresponds to frequency 6.5 GHz!
Vft_power,Vft,omega,iflag] =
get_Fourier_transform(dt,t0,V_val,iplot,ipad,omega_plot_max);%Call FFT
iflag=0; N=length(Vft);
[Ift_power,Ift,omega,iflag] = ...
 get_Fourier_transform(dt,t0,I_val,iplot,ipad,omega_plot_max);
Z_FT=complex(zeros(1,N),zeros(1,N)); cutoff=1e-25;
for m=1:N
    if(abs(Ift(m)< cutoff))
        Z_FT(m)=0;
    else
        Z_FT(m)=Vft(m)/Ift(m);
    end
end
j=1:N; Z=Z_FT(j); % Impedance Matrix
imath=sqrt(-1); phase=exp(-imath*0.5*omega*dt);
ZTR1=Vft./Ift; ZTR=ZTR1.*phase;
Re=real(ZTR); Im=imag(ZTR); Zabs=abs(ZTR);
plot(omega(omin:omax)/(2*pi*1e9),Re(omin:omax),'k-.')
xlabel('frequency (GHz)'); ylabel('Impedance (Ohms)');
GAMMA=(ZTR-Zline)./(ZTR+Zline);       % Reflection coefficient
RLoss=20*log10(abs(GAMMA));           % Input Return Loss in (dB)
VSWR=(1+abs(GAMMA))./(1-abs(GAMMA)); % Voltage standing wave ratio
plot(omega(omin:omax)/(2*pi*1e9),VSWR(omin:omax),'k-.')
xlabel('frequency (GHz)'); ylabel('VSWR');
FeedPower=0.5*real(Vft.*conj(Ift)); % Input Power versus frequency
omeg=omega(central_f);
plot(omega(omin:omax)/(2*pi*1e9),RLoss(omin:omax),'k-.')
xlabel('Frequency (GHz)'); ylabel('Return Loss (dB)');
```

```
% ========================Directivity & Gain ============================
iflag=0; % used in the FFT-routine
for J=2:theta_max-1
    itime=1:k;
    iplot_new=0;
    Etheta_val=EthetaT(J,itime);
    EthetaJft_power,EthetaJft,omega,iflag] = ...
    get_Fourier_transform(dt,t0,Etheta_val,iplot_new,ipad,omega_plot_max);
    Gain=(2*pi/impedance_medium)*EthetaJft_power./FeedPower;
    Gain_theta(J,:)=Gain; Gain_Max(J)=max(Gain(:));
    Directivity(J,:)=EthetaJft_power;
end
J=2:theta_max-1; itime=1:k;
Gain_elevation=Gain_theta(J,itime);
     for itime=omin+1:omax;
         GMax_F(itime)=max(Gain_elevation(:,itime));
     end
plot(omega(omin:omax)/(2*pi*1e9),10*log10(GMax_F(omin:omax)),'k.')
xlabel('Frequency (GHz)'); ylabel('Maximum Gain (dBi)');
for itime=1:k;
    step=1; arg=2:(theta_max-1);
    f=Directivity(arg,itime);%Directivity as a function of θ and time-step
g=sin(arg.*pi/180); fun=f*g;
table = cumtrapz(fun)*step*pi/180; % Integration over angle theta
integral=table(theta_max-2)-table(1); intg(itime)=integral;
end
%====================== Power Radiation Pattern =========================
theta_max=91; radial_max=0;
rmin=-20; rticks=10;
line_style='-';
theta1=1:theta_max-1;
FFP= Directivity(theta1,central_f);
D11=10*log10(FFP./max(FFP));
th1=[1:length(D11)]';
hpol = polar_dB(th1,D11,rmin,radial_max,rticks,line_style);
hold on;
th1=[1:length(D11)]';
hpol = polar_dB(360-th1,D11,rmin,radial_max,rticks,line_style);
```

Table 1. FDTD simulation of a dielectric covered conical uwb antenna in MATLAB.

7. References

Berenger J.P. (1996). Perfectly Matched Layer for the FDTD Solution of Wave-Structure Interaction Problems. *IEEE Transactions on Antennas &Propagation,* Vol.44, No. 1, pp. 110-117

Brocato, R. W. (2004). *FDTD simulation tools for UWB antenna analysis,* Sandia Report, SAND2004-6577, Sandia National Laboratories.

Fusco M. (1990). FDTD Algorithm in Curvilinear Coordinates. *IEEE Transactions on Antennas & Propagation,* 38, pp. 76-89

Harrison C. W., Jr. & C. S. Williams, Jr. (1965). Transients in Wide-Angle Conical Antennas, *IEEE Transactions on. Antennas & Propagation,* Vol. AP-13, pp. 236-246

Gentili G. B., Cerretelli M. and Cecchi L. (2004). Coated conical antennas for automotive application. *Journal Electromagnetic Waves & Applications*, Vol.18, No.1, pp. 85-97

Katz, D.S., Thiele, E.T & Taflove, A. (1994). Validation and extension to three dimensions of the Berenger PML absorbing boundary condition for FDTD meshes. *IEEE Microwave & Guided Wave Letters*, Vol, 4, No.8, pp. 268 - 270

Kliros G. S., Kyritsis G. & Touzloudis D. (2010), Dielectric-EBG covered conical antenna for UWB applications. *COMPEL: Internationlal Journal for Computation & Mathematics in Electrical and Electronic Engineering*, Vol. 29, no. 4, pp. 1134-1143

Kliros G. S., Kyritsis G. & Touzloudis D. (2010). FDTD Analysis of a Conical Microstrip Antenna on EBG–substrate. *Journal of Applied Electromagnetism (JAE)*, Vol. 12, No.1, pp.1-8, ISSN: 1109-1606

Liang X. & Wah M. C. Y. (2000). Low-profile broadband omni-directional monopole antenna. *Microwave & Optical Technology Letters*, Vol. 25, No. 2, pp.135–138

Liu G. & Grimes C. (1999). Spherical-coordinate FDTD analysis of conical antennas mounted above finite ground planes. *Microwave & Optical Technology Letters*, Vol.23, pp.78-82

Lu M., Bredow J., Jung S. & Tjuatja S. (2007). A Quasi-Planar Wide Band Conical Antenna. In: *Ultra-Wide Band Short-Pulse Electromagnetics*, Baum, C. E., Stone, A. P., Tyo, J. S. (Eds.), pp. 25-32, Springer, ISBN 978-0-387-73045-5, New York

Ma J., Yin Y.Z., Zhou S.G. & Zhao L.Y. (2009). Design of a new wideband low-profile conical antenna. *Microwave & Optical Technology Letters*, Vol.51, No.11, pp. 2620–2623

Maloney J. G. & Smith G. S. (1993). Optimization of a conical antenna for pulse radiation: an efficient design using resistive loading. *IEEE Transactions on Antennas & Propagation*, Vol. 41, No.7, pp.940-947

Minin, I. (Ed.). (March 2010). *Microwave & Millimeter Wave Technologies Modern UWB antennas and equipment*, InTech, ISBN 978-953-7619-67-1, Croatia

Molisch A.F. , Foerster J. R. & Pendergrass, M. (2003). Channel models for ultrawide-band personal area networks. *IEEE Wireless Communications*, Vol. 10, pp. 14–21

Palud S., Colombel F., Himdi M., Le Meins C. (2008). Compact multi-octave conical antenna. *Electronics Letters*, Vol. 44, No. 11, pp 659-661

Sandler S. & King R.W.P. (1994). Compact conical antennas for wide-band coverage. *IEEE Transactions on Antennas & Propagation*, Vol.42, No.3, pp 436-439

Sibille A., Roblin C., Bories S. & Lepage A. C. (2006). A Channel-Based Statistical Approach to Antenna Performance in UWB Communications. *IEEE Transactions on Antennas & Propagation* Vol. 54, No. 11, pp. 3207-3215

Stuzman W. A. & Thiele G. L. (1997). *Antenna theory and Design*, 2nd ed., John Wiley & Sons, ISBN: 0-471-02590-9, New York

Taflove A. & Hagness S. C. (2005). *Computational electrodynamics: the finite-difference time-domain method*, 3nd ed., pp. 411-472, ISBN 978-1-58053-832-9, Artech House, Boston

Yee K. (1996). Numerical solution of initial boundary value problems involving Maxwell's equations in isotropic media. *IEEE Transactions on Antennas and Propagation*, Vol.14, pp. 302–307

Yu Y. K. & Li J. (2008). Analysis of electrically small size conical antennas. *Progress in Electromagnetic Research Letters*, Vol. 1, pp. 85-92

Zhou S., Ma J., Deng J., & Liu Q. (2009). A low-profile and broadband conical antenna. *Progress in Electromagnetic Research Letter,* Vol.7, pp. 97-103

Wiesbeck W., Adamiuk G. & Sturm C. (2009). Basic properties and design principles of UWB antennas. *Proceedings of the IEEE,* Vol. 97, No.2, pp.372-385

10

Variable Ballast Mechanism for Depth Positioning of a Spherical Underwater Robot Vehicle

Bambang Sumantri[1] and Mohd. Noh Karsiti[2]
[1]Electronic Engineering Polytechnic Institute of Surabaya,
[1,2]Universiti Teknologi Petronas
[1]Indonesia,
[2]Malaysia

1. Introduction

A spherical shape of a submerged body with closed frame provides uniform drag at all direction along its surface. In this chapter, the shape of a spherical URV that is used in this book-chapter is presented. The vertical motion equation is also derived. The forces that affect the dynamics of the system are also described. In order to control vertical motion due to control depth position of the URV, a variable ballast mechanism is used. This mechanism controls the weight of URV's body. This chapter also presents detail mechanism of the variable ballast system and describes detail of the used parts and design of the mechanism. Kinematic and dynamic model of the variable ballast system are also derived.

2. Design of URV

The shape of spherical URV used in this book is shown in Figure 1. As a sphere body, the location of center of buoyancy (COB) of URV's body is at the center of sphere or the intersection point between vertical and horizontal diameter. The variable ballast tank is located at the top inside the hull. Location of the tank is adjusted so that the position of center of mass (COM) is aligned vertically with COB. Mechanism of the variable ballast and detail of its parts are explained in section 4.3. At the upper side of the hull above the tank, there are some holes as the way of water to enter into and exit from the tank. The space below the movable plate inside the hull is waterproofed so that the water can not enter this space.

In order to make the URV stable in equilibrium condition, the hull of URV must be designed with bottom heavy that is the center of mass is located at under of the equator or at underside hemisphere. To make the hull in bottom heavy, fixed ballast is located at the bottom of the hull. The location of COM of the hull must be aligned vertically with COB of the hull thus in equilibrium condition, the position of the ballast tank is at the top of the URV's hull exactly. This condition is important when the URV is provided with horizontal propulsion in order to give ability to the URV to move in horizontal plane.

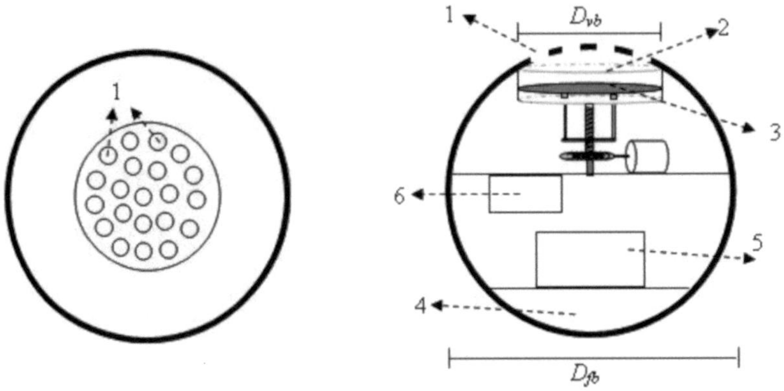

(a) Top view

(b) Side view

1. holes for the way of water in and out of the tank.
2. variable ballast tank.
3. movable plate..
4. fixed ballast.
5. battery.
6. cpu and electronics components.

Fig. 1. Shape of spherical URV and its parts

3. Vertical motion equations

Since the URV moves in vertical plane without any propeller, so it just depends on the gravitational force, buoyant force and other forces that appear because of its motion.
By assuming there are no external forces that can disturb the motion of URV, the forces acting on the URV can be shown in Figure 2. Let F_B is buoyant force, W is gravitational force, F_D is drag force, f_a is force that appear because of the availability of the acceleration, m_a is added mass, and m_t is total mass of the URV's body which is constant then forces equation act at URV are given as (Rajput, 2003)

$$W = F_B + F_D \tag{1}$$

and,

$$W = m_t g\ , \tag{2.a}$$

$$F_B = \rho_w V_{fb} g\ , \tag{2.b}$$

$$F_D = sign(v)\frac{1}{2}C_D A_{fb} \rho_w v^2\ . \tag{2.c}$$

The direction of gravitational force and buoyant force are opposite to each other when W is downward and F_B is upward. From Eq. 2.c, it can be seen that the direction of the drag force depends upon the direction of the velocity. If the URV moves downward, the velocity is positive so that the drag force is positive and it direction is upward. The drag force and velocity are negative if the URV moves upward.

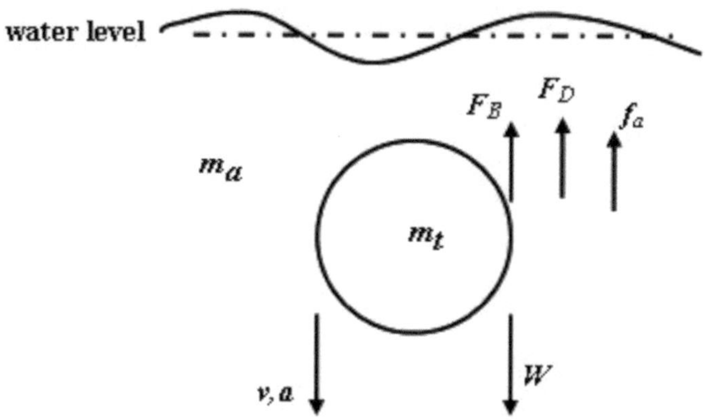

Fig. 2. Forces acting at URV's body

Substituting Eq. 2 into Eq. 1, then the force equation can be represented as

$$m_t g = \rho_w V_{fb} g + sign(v)\frac{1}{2}C_D A_{fb}\rho_w v^2 . \tag{3}$$

Since dimension of URV, V_{fb} and A_{fb}, are constant, then the velocity v, is also constant. This velocity is known as *terminal velocity*, which is expressed as

$$v = sign(m_t g - \rho_w V_{fb} g)\sqrt{\left|\frac{2(m_t g - \rho_w V_{fb} g)}{C_D A_{fb}\rho_w}\right|}, \tag{4.a}$$

$$|v| = \sqrt{\left|\frac{2(m_t g - \rho_w V_{fb} g)}{C_D A_{fb}\rho_w}\right|} . \tag{4.b}$$

From Eq. 4.a, it can be seen that the vertical motion of the URV depends on the gravitational force and the buoyant force. If $W > F_B$, then the URV moves downward and it will move upward if $W < F_B$. If $W = F_B$, the URV will stay at its position. Since volume of URV's hull, V_{fb}, g, and ρ_w are constant, the buoyant force is also constant. So, the motion of URV depends on the total mass of URV's body, m_t. By controlling m_t, the vertical motion of the URV can be controlled.

Since equilibrium condition is occurred when $W = F_B$, then $v = 0$ and $m_t = m_s$ which is initial total mass of the URV. If the total mass changes as much as Δm from the initial total mass, m_s, then the total mass of URV is expressed as

$$m_t = m_s + \Delta m . \tag{5}$$

Thus, the associated velocity will be change. The change of the velocity depends upon whether Δm is a variable or simply a constant. If Δm is a variable, the acceleration, a, occurs. This acceleration, besides accelerates mass of URV itself, m_t, also accelerates mass of surrounding water which is known as *added mass*, m_a.

Due to this acceleration, the force f_a will occur and it is expressed as

$$f_a = (m_s + \Delta m + m_a)a \ . \tag{6}$$

Considering this last force, f_a, Eq. 1 can be rewritten as

$$W = F_B + F_D + f_a \ . \tag{7}$$

Substituting Eq. 2 and Eq. 6 into Eq. 7, yields

$$m_s g + \Delta m g = F_B + sign(v)\frac{1}{2}C_D A_{fb}\rho_w v^2 + (m_s + \Delta m + m_a)a \ . \tag{8}$$

Recalling equilibrium condition,

$$W = F_B ,$$

$$m_t = m_s ,$$

$$v = 0 ,$$

$$a = 0 \ . \tag{9}$$

From Eq. 5 obviously we have $\Delta m = 0$.
By substituting Δm and Eq. 9 into Eq. 8, yields

$$m_s g = F_B \ . \tag{10}$$

Since m_s and F_B are constant, then by the change of Δm, Eq. 8 becomes

$$\Delta m\, g = sign(v)\frac{1}{2}C_D A_{fb}\rho_w v^2 + (m_s + \Delta m + m_a)a \ . \tag{11}$$

Since $\Delta m\, g = \Delta W$, then Eq. 11 is written as

$$\Delta W = sign(v)\frac{1}{2}C_D A_{fb}\rho_w v^2 + (m_s + \frac{\Delta W}{g} + m_a)a \ . \tag{12}$$

By solving for the acceleration, a, the dynamic equation for vertical motion is given as (Xu and Smith, 1994)

$$a = \frac{\Delta W}{(m_s + m_a + \frac{\Delta W}{g})} - \frac{sign(v)C_D A_{fb}\rho_w v^2}{2(m_s + m_a + \frac{\Delta W}{g})} \ . \tag{13}$$

And, if the depth position of the URV can be measured as z, then by differentiating z respect to time t, the velocity of URV in vertical plane can be expressed as

$$v = \dot{z} \ . \tag{14}$$

4. Variable ballast system

The common design of variable ballast uses tank as chamber for controlling amount of water in URV's body in order to control buoyancy/weight of the URV. The space or volume of the used tank is fixed so that if the amount of water in the tank is not full, there will be a space which is not filled by water. This condition can make water move freely around the space of the tank if the tilt of URV is unstable such as illustrated in Figure 3(a). This motion can produce a moment that can disturb the stability of the URV. If tilt of URV's body is change (as shown in Figure 3(b)) the center of mass, C_M, will also change. This condition sometime is undesired. Therefore, a variable-ballast with variably volume of chamber of the tank is designed in this book, in order to make water always fulfill the space in the tank but variably in term of volume.

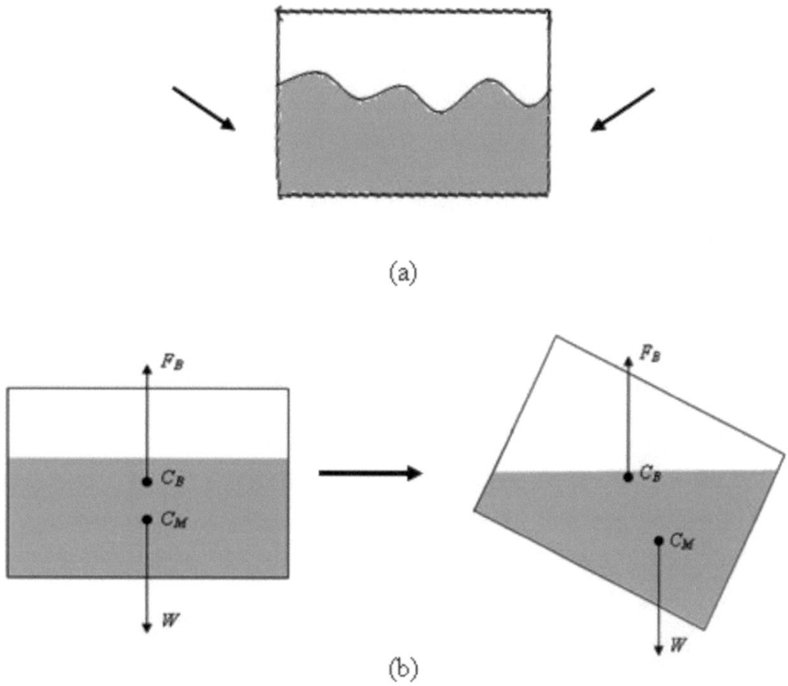

Fig. 3.(a) Surface of water in ballast tank when the URV's body is shaking; (b) Position center of mass and center of buoyancy of water in the tank when tilt is change.

4.1 Variable ballast design

In order to make water always fill space in the ballast tank, even if the volume of water is different, then the volume of the tank itself must be adjustable which is illustrated in Figure 4. The shape of the variable ballast's tank is cylinder which is opened at the top side. This part is connected directly to the water environment therefore water can always fulfill the space in the tank (as shown in Figure 1(b)).

To make variably volume of the tank, a movable plate is located at the bottom of the tank. The space below the movable plate is waterproofed, so that water can not enter this space. If the movable plate is moving upward, the space of the tank will be decreased as well as the volume of water in the ballast tank. If the movable plate is moving in opposite, downward, the space of the tank will be increased and also the volume of water in the ballast tank. Therefore, in any volume of water in the ballast tank there is no empty space in the ballast tank that is not filled by water.

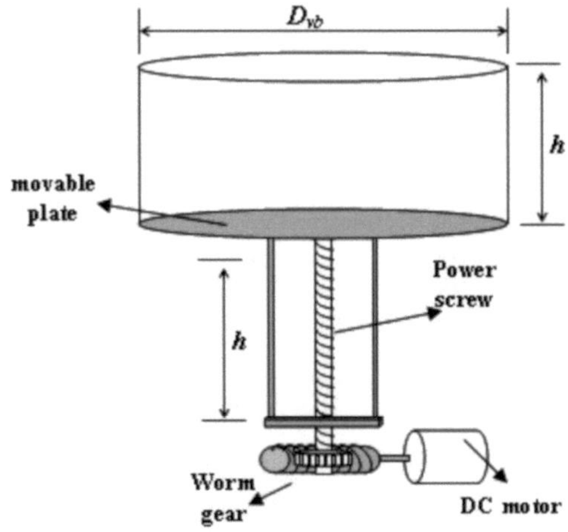

Fig. 4. Mechanism of variable ballast system

In order to change position of the movable plate, a DC motor is used to drive the movable plate through power screw and worm gear coupling. This variable ballast mechanism is analyzed in this chapter. The analyzing involves kinematics analysis and dynamics analysis.

4.2 Kinematics analysis

The movable plate of variable ballast system is coupled to the nut of power screw. This nut can be moved up and down by turning the screw.

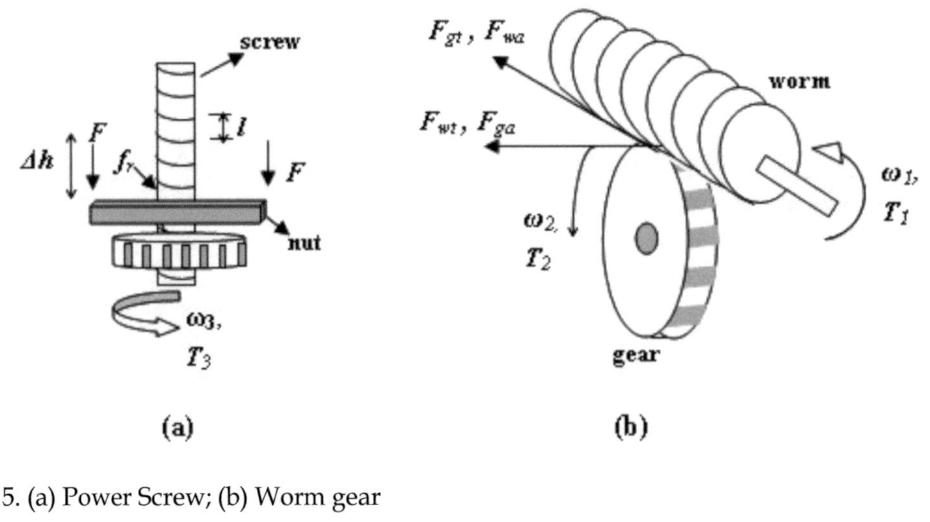

Fig. 5. (a) Power Screw; (b) Worm gear

So, the screw converts the rotation motion into linear (vertical) motion. This coupling can be seen in Figure 5(a). Based on Figure 5(a), l is lead of screw per revolution, Δh denotes change of nut position, ω_3 is angular velocity of screw. If Δt is the time needed by screw to change nut position at Δh regarding angular velocity ω_3, then their relation can be written as

$$\frac{\Delta h}{\Delta t} = \frac{l\omega_3}{2\pi}. \tag{15}$$

To turn the power screw, a DC motor is used and coupled with worm gear as illustrated in Figure 5(b). The worm has number of thread per revolution equal to N_w, and the gear has number of teeth equal to N_g. If the worm is coupled directly to the motor which turns in velocity ω_m, then the gear will turn in velocity ω_2 which is expressed as

$$\omega_2 = \frac{N_w}{N_g} \cdot \omega_m. \tag{16}$$

As shown in Figure 5(a), the gear and screw is ally so that its angular velocity is the same,

$$\omega_2 = \omega_3. \tag{17}$$

By substituting Eq. 17 and Eq. 16 into Eq. 15, the change of nut position can be rewritten as

$$\frac{\Delta h}{\Delta t} = \frac{lN_w}{N_g 2\pi}\omega_m,$$

$$\Delta\dot{h} = \frac{lN_w}{N_g 2\pi}\omega_m,$$

$$\omega_m = \frac{N_g 2\pi \Delta\dot{h}}{lN_w}. \tag{18}$$

4.3 Dynamics analysis

The dynamic of variable ballast mechanism is analyzed by considering torques and forces acting in the system. The forces and torques involved in the mechanism come from internal mechanism those are from the DC motor and the transmission system, and also come from external that is from the surrounding as hydrostatic pressure.

4.3.1 Power screw

As illustrated in Figure 5(a), T_3 is input torque that is required to operate the screw to move the nut which is coupled with movable plate, can be expressed as

$$T_3 = T_F + T_{fr}, \tag{19}$$

where T_F is torque required to overcome force F, and T_{fr} is torque required to overcome friction between screw and nut. To evaluate these terms, the equilibrium conditions are applied such as illustrated in Figure 6.

Figure 6(a) illustrates coupling between nut and screw and also its parameters that must be considered. There is an additional useful geometric relationship between lead angle, α, and lead, l. Suppose the triangular segment of a plane wrapped around the screw is considered in such a way that slanted edge lies along the helix and follows it for one revolution, obviously we have

$$\tan\alpha = \frac{l}{\pi d_m}. \tag{20}$$

Figure 6(b) illustrates a force P which is applied at a mean radius r_m which causes the load to be raised. The reactive forces act at point O on the screw thread surface. The reactive force F_n acting normal to the surface has the following components:
OD = f_r which is the friction force opposing movement up the thread surface
OA = is equal and opposite to the force being lifted. (F)
OB = is the vector sum of OD and OA and forms an angle θ_n with vector F_n
Summing the forces in the vertical direction results in

$$F_n \cos\theta_n \cos\alpha = F + f_r \sin\alpha\ . \tag{21}$$

If coefficient friction of screw surface is μ_s, then friction force is expressed as

$$f_r = \mu_s F_n\ . \tag{22}$$

By substituting Eq. 22 into Eq. 21, yields

$$F_n = \frac{F}{\cos\theta_n \cos\alpha - \mu_s \sin\alpha}. \tag{23}$$

By considering forces in horizontal direction, obviously we have

$$P = f_r \cos\alpha + F_n \cos\theta_n \sin\alpha\ , \tag{24}$$

and by substituting Eq. 22 into Eq. 24, yields

$$P = F_n(\mu_s \cos\alpha + \cos\theta_n \sin\alpha)\ . \tag{25}$$

By equating F_n at Eq. 25 and Eq. 23, force P applied on screw in order to lift force F can be expressed as

$$P = F\left(\frac{\mu_s \cos\alpha + \cos\theta_n \sin\alpha}{\cos\theta_n \cos\alpha - \mu_s \sin\alpha}\right). \tag{26}$$

By analyzing again Figure 6(b), it also can be concluded that:

$$BC = AE = OA\cdot\tan\theta = OB\cdot\cos\alpha\tan\theta\ ,$$

$$\tan\theta_n = \frac{BC}{OB} = \cos\alpha\tan\theta\ . \tag{27}$$

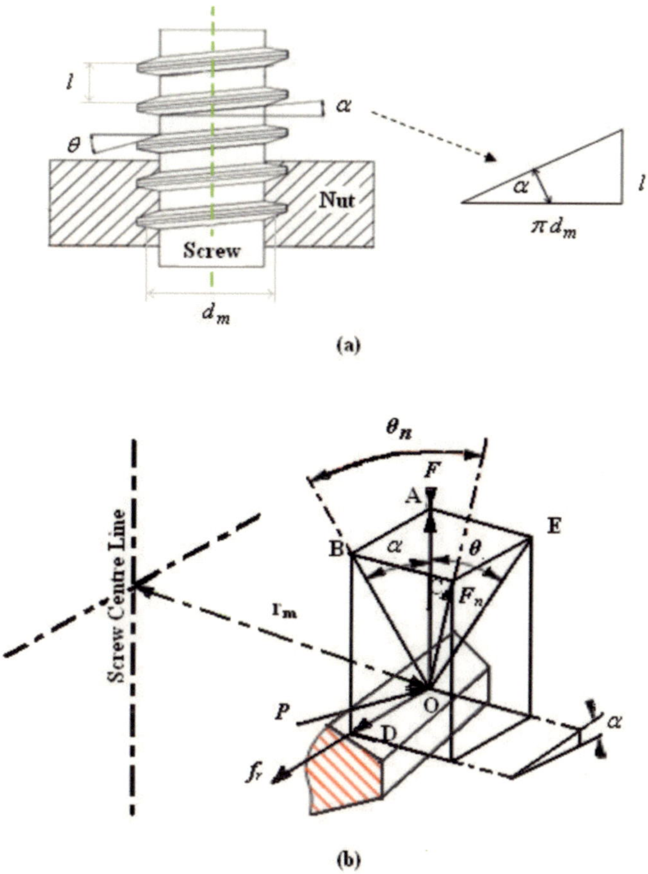

Fig. 6. (a) Screw and nut coupling; (b) Detail of forces working in the power screw (roymech.co.uk, 2008)

If lead angle α is small, then $\cos\alpha \approx 1$, so we have

$$\tan\theta_n \approx \tan\theta ,$$

$$\theta_n \approx \theta . \tag{28}$$

Substituting Eq. 28 into Eq. 26, yields

$$P = F\left(\frac{\mu_s \cos\alpha + \cos\theta \sin\alpha}{\cos\theta\cos\alpha - \mu_s \sin\alpha}\right),$$

$$P = F\left(\frac{\mu_s + \cos\theta \tan\alpha}{\cos\theta - \mu_s \tan\alpha}\right). \tag{29}$$

Again, by substituting Eq. 20 into Eq. 29, force P applied on screw to lift load F can be rewritten as

$$P = F\left(\frac{\pi\mu_s d_m + l\cos\theta}{\pi d_m \cos\theta - \mu_s l}\right). \tag{30}$$

In order to lift load F, a torque, T_{3U}, must be applied to the screw. If the screw has mean diameter d_m, then the torque applied to the screw can be expressed as

$$T_{3U} = P\frac{d_m}{2}. \tag{31}$$

Substituting Eq. 30 into Eq. 31, the applied torque required to lift load F can be expressed as

$$T_{3U} = \frac{d_m}{2}F\left(\frac{\pi\mu_s d_m + l\cos\theta}{\pi d_m \cos\theta - \mu_s l}\right). \tag{32}$$

In order to lower load F, a torque must be applied to the screw in reverse direction with T_{3U} and it is named as T_{3L}. Applying torque in reverse direction will also deliver force P in reverse direction. By using same procedure in deriving T_{3U}, the torque required to lower load F can be expressed as

$$T_{3L} = \frac{d_m}{2}F\left(\frac{\pi\cdot\mu_s\cdot d_m - l\cdot\cos\theta}{\pi\cdot d_m \cos\theta + \mu_s\cdot l}\right). \tag{33}$$

4.3.2 Worm-gear set

Conceptually in worm-gear set, the worm can be analogous to the screw power, and worm gear or gear can be analogous to the nut, see Figure 7. The forces resolution for power screw may therefore be directly applied to the case of a worm by observing that screw lead angle α is equivalent to worm lead angle λ_w, and power screw normal angle θ_n is equivalent to normal pressure angle φ_n for the worm gear. Illustration of these forces, based on Figure 6(b), can be seen in Figure 8.

Fig. 7. Worm gear (www-mdp.eng.cam.ac.uk, 2008).

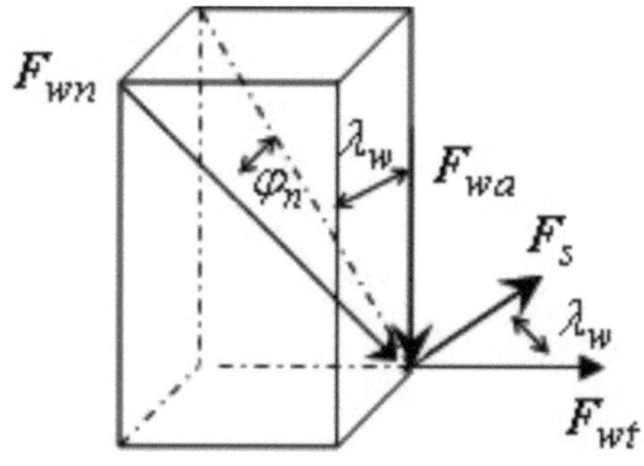

Fig. 8. Detail of forces on worm gear.

If worm has lead l_w per revolution and diameter d_w, then worm lead angle λ_w can be determined by

$$\tan\lambda_w = \frac{l_w}{\pi d_w}. \tag{34}$$

Based on Fig. 8, by summing the forces in vertical direction obviously results in

$$F_{wa} = F_{wn}\cos\varphi_n\cos\lambda_w - F_s\sin\lambda_w, \tag{35}$$

where F_{wa} is axial force of worm, F_{wn} is reactive force on worm, and F_s friction force of worm. If coefficient friction of worm surface is μ_w, then the friction force F_s is expressed as

$$F_s = \mu_w F_{wn}. \tag{36}$$

If Eq. 36 is substituted into Eq. 35, then the reactive force F_{wn} is written as

$$F_{wn} = \frac{F_{wa}}{\cos\varphi_n\cos\lambda_w - \mu_w\sin\lambda_w}. \tag{37}$$

If forces in horizontal direction are considered, then by summing of these forces will result

$$F_{wt} = F_{wn}\cos\varphi_n\sin\lambda_w + F_s\cos\lambda_w, \tag{38}$$

where F_{wt} is tangential force of worm.

By substituting Eq. 37 into Eq. 38, the tangential force of worm can be expressed as (Collins, 2003).

$$F_{wt} = F_{wa}\left(\frac{\cos\varphi_n\sin\lambda_w + \mu_w\cos\lambda_w}{\cos\varphi_n\cos\lambda_w - \mu_w\sin\lambda_w}\right),$$

$$F_{wt} = F_{wa}\left(\frac{\cos\varphi_n\tan\lambda_w + \mu_w}{\cos\varphi_n - \mu_w\tan\lambda_w}\right). \tag{39}$$

Then, by substituting Eq. 34 into Eq. 39, yields

$$F_{wt} = F_{wa}\left(\frac{l_w \cos\varphi_n + \pi\mu_w d_w}{\pi d_w \cos\varphi_n - \mu_w l_w}\right),$$

$$F_{wa} = F_{wt}\left(\frac{\pi d_w \cos\varphi_n - \mu_w l_w}{l_w \cos\varphi_n + \pi\mu_w d_w}\right). \tag{40}$$

From Figure 5(b), it is shown the relation of forces working at gear and worm. Forces on gear are related by equilibrium to forces on the worm as

$$F_{gt} = F_{wa}, \tag{41.a}$$

$$F_{ga} = F_{wt}, \tag{41.b}$$

where F_{gt} and F_{ga} are tangential and axial force working at gear respectively. If T_2 is torque applied on gear with diameter d_g, then this torque T_2 is expressed as

$$T_2 = \frac{d_g}{2} F_{gt}. \tag{42}$$

By equating Eq. 40 and Eq. 41.a and substitute into Eq. 42, yields

$$T_2 = \frac{d_g F_{wt}}{2}\left(\frac{\pi d_w \cos\varphi_n - \mu_w l_w}{l_w \cos\varphi_n + \pi\mu_w d_w}\right). \tag{43}$$

To actuate this mechanism, the worm is coupled directly to the shaft of a DC motor. If T_m is motor torque applied on worm to result tangential force F_{wt} which is expressed as

$$F_{wt} = \frac{2}{d_w} T_m, \tag{44}$$

then by substituting Eq. 44 into Eq. 43, torque applied on gear is expressed as

$$T_2 = \frac{d_g T_m}{d_w}\left(\frac{\pi d_w \cos\varphi_n - \mu_w l_w}{l_w \cos\varphi_n + \pi\mu_w d_w}\right). \tag{45}$$

Reviewing Figure 5 again, obviously can be seen that the gear and power screw are allied in same shaft so that torque required to actuate the gear, T_2, will be equal to the torque required to turn power screw, T_3. Since $T_3 = T_2$, then $T_{3U} = T_{2U}$ and T_{3U} is torque needed by screw to lift up the load F. In order to produce torque T_{3U} on the screw or T_{2U} on the gear, the DC motor must produce torque T_{mU}. If $T_3 = T_{3U}$, $T_2 = T_{2U}$, and $T_m = T_{mU}$ then by equating Eq. 32 and Eq. 45 yields

$$\frac{d_g T_{mU}}{d_w}\left(\frac{\pi d_w \cos\varphi_n - \mu_w l_w}{l_w \cos\varphi_n + \pi\mu_w d_w}\right) = \frac{d_m}{2} F\left(\frac{\pi\mu_s d_m + l\cos\theta}{\pi d_m \cos\theta - \mu_s l}\right),$$

$$T_{mU} = \frac{d_m d_w F}{2d_g}\left(\frac{\pi\mu_s d_m + l\cos\theta}{\pi d_m \cos\theta - \mu_s l}\right)\left(\frac{l_w \cos\varphi_n + \pi\mu_w d_w}{\pi d_w \cos\varphi_n - \mu_w l_w}\right). \tag{46}$$

By using the same analogy for calculating T_{mU}, then the torque of the motor required to lower the load F which is known as T_{mL}, can be expressed as

$$T_{mL} = \frac{d_m d_w F}{2d_g}\left(\frac{\pi\mu_s d_m - l\cos\theta}{\pi d_m \cos\theta + \mu_s l}\right)\left(\frac{l_w \cos\varphi_n + \pi\mu_w d_w}{\pi d_w \cos\varphi_n - \mu_w l_w}\right). \tag{47}$$

From Eq. 46 and Eq. 47, it can be shown that many coefficients, which are constant, are involved in the equation, so that if the constants are simplified then we have

$$\frac{d_m d_w}{2d_g} = k_{pr},$$

$$\left(\frac{\pi\mu_s d_m + l\cos\theta}{\pi d_m \cos\theta - \mu_s l}\right) = k_{TU},$$

$$\left(\frac{\pi\mu_s d_m - l\cos\theta}{\pi d_m \cos\theta + \mu_s l}\right) = k_{TL},$$

$$\left(\frac{l_w \cos\varphi_n + \pi\mu_w d_w}{\pi d_w \cos\varphi_n - \mu_w l_w}\right) = k_{wg}, \tag{48}$$

where k_{pr} is coefficient of power transmission ratio between worm gear set and power screw, k_{TU} and k_{TL} are coefficient of power screw in lifting and lowering load mechanism respectively, and k_{wg} is coefficient of worm gear set. Hence, Eq. 46 and Eq. 47 can be simplified into

$$\begin{aligned} T_{mU} &= k_{pr} k_{TU} k_{wg} F \\ T_{mL} &= k_{pr} k_{TL} k_{wg} F \end{aligned} \tag{49}$$

or it can be written as

$$T_m = k_m F, \tag{50}$$

where $k_m = k_{mU} = k_{pr} k_{TU} k_{wg} \Rightarrow T_m = T_{mU}$ and $k_m = k_{mL} = k_{pr} k_{TL} k_{wg} \Rightarrow T_m = T_{mL}$.

From Eq. 50, it can be seen that torque T_m is the input, and F is the output. Although not explicitly stated, it does not mean that if $T_m = 0$ then F must be zero. Because of friction, a certain value of F must be reached to make it *self-locking*, before power screw start rotating and allow the load lift or lower, and it's called *overhauling*. To guarantee the screw will be self-locking, a condition based on the geometric parameter and coefficient of friction must be fulfilled (Collins, 2003).

4.3.3 External forces analysis

Torque and force which are provided by the motor and its mechanics system are used to overcome the load F in order to control amount of water in the ballast tank. Load F itself is total force working on the movable plate of variable ballast system which is coming from inside and outside of URV's hull. The illustration of forces working on the movable plate is shown in Figure 1.

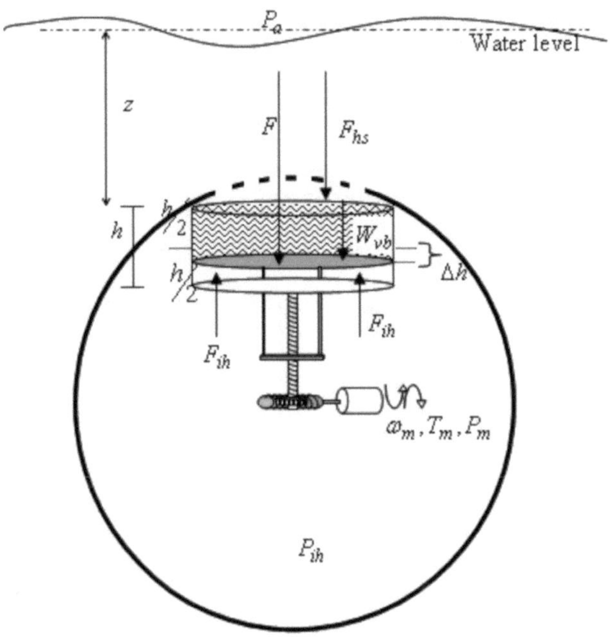

Fig. 1. External forces working on variable ballast system.

If Figure 1 is analyzed, the force coming from inside hull, F_{ih}, is caused by the change of air pressure inside the hull, P_{ih}, due to the change of space inside the hull. As explained before, the variable ballast mechanism is used to control weight of URV by controlling volume of water in ballast tank. To control volume of the water, a mechanism like piston is designed. In this mechanism, a movable plate which is base of space in the tank that can be filled by water is used. By controlling position of the movable plate which is height of the tank, the volume of water in the tank can be controlled. Since space under movable plate is impermeable, by the change of position of movable plate, the volume of space inside URV's hull is also change. This change impacts to the air pressure inside the hull.

As known that relation between pressure and volume, V_{ih}, in closed space is expressed as (Moran and Shapiro, 1998)

$$P_{ih} V_{ih} = \text{constant} . \tag{51}$$

So, if the volume of air inside URV's hull is changed, then its pressure is also changed. In initial condition or in equilibrium condition, the pressure inside the hull is equal to the pressure of the air at water surface, P_a. By assuming the air pressure at water surface and temperature inside URV's hull are constant then since the volume of space inside the hull is constant, the pressure inside the hull is also constant. If volume of the space inside the hull is changed because of the change of position of movable plate, the pressure P_{ih} is also change and will cause a force act at movable plate surface, known as F_{ih}. The relation of P_a, P_{ih}, and F_{ih} is expressed as

$$F_{ih} = \left(P_{ih} - P_a\right) A_{vb}, \tag{52}$$

where A_{vb} is projected area of movable plate which is base of variable ballast tank.

In initial condition, where $P_{ih} = P_a$, volume of the air or empty space inside URV's hull is V_{ih}, and the position of movable plate is at the middle of full height of the tank, so if the maximum height of the tank is h then the position of movable plate is at $0.5h$ from the top of the tank, which is known as initial position. At this position, Δh, which is the change of movable plate position, is equal to zero ($\Delta h = 0$). So that if position of movable plate is upper than initial position ($< 0.5h$) then $\Delta h < 0$ and if lower than initial position then $\Delta h > 0$. By the change of Δh, the volume of the air or space inside the hull will change as ΔV. The relation is expressed as

$$\Delta V = \Delta h\, A_{vb}. \tag{53}$$

From Eq. 53, it is seen that the change of volume of the air inside the hull is equal to the change of volume of water in the ballast tank.

By the change of volume of the air, the pressure is also change from its initial condition and expressed as

$$P_a V_{ih} = P_{ih}\left(V_{ih} - \Delta V\right),$$

$$P_{ih} = \frac{P_a V_{ih}}{V_{ih} - \Delta V}. \tag{54}$$

By substituting Eq. 53 into Eq. 54 and substitute the result into Eq. 52, then force acts on movable plate's surface due to change of volume of the air inside hull is expressed as

$$F_{ih} = \frac{\Delta h \left(A_{vb}\right)^2 P_a}{V_{ih} - \Delta h\, A_{vb}}. \tag{55}$$

From Figure 1, it can be shown that load F is resultant of F_{hs}, ΔW, and F_{ih}, and the relation is expressed as

$$F - W_{vb} + F_{hs} - F_{ih}, \tag{56}$$

where W_{vb} is weight of the water in the ballast tank and F_{hs} is hydrostatic force on surface of movable plate. Weight of water in the ballast tank depends on volume of the water in this tank. In equilibrium or initial condition, the volume of water is half of maximum volume of the tank, $W_{vb} = W_{bs}$. By the change of position of movable plate in Δh, the weight of water in ballast is also will change in ΔW from initial weight. So that at any condition, W_{vb} can be expressed as

$$W_{vb} = W_{bs} + \Delta W \,. \tag{57}$$

Hydrostatic force, F_{hs}, is force acting on surface of immersed body caused by the height of liquid (water) above of it, or in other word it can be said that hydrostatic force is weight of the liquid above immersed surface. In this system, the height of liquid above is equal to the depth position of the URV. If depth position of URV is measured form water surface to top part of URV's body known as z, then F_{hs} acting on surface of movable plate is expressed as (Rajput, 2003)

$$F_{hs} = \rho_w \, g \, A_{vb} \, z \,, \tag{58}$$

where ρ_w and g are density of water and gravitational acceleration respectively.
Substituting Eq. 55, Eq. 57, and Eq. 58 into Eq. 56, load F can be expressed as

$$F = W_{bs} + \Delta W + \rho_w \, g \, A_{vb} \, z - \frac{\Delta h \left(A_{vb}\right)^2 P_a}{V_{ih} - \Delta h \, A_{vb}} \,, \tag{59}$$

and the change of water in the ballast tank is expressed as

$$\Delta W = \Delta h \, A_{vb} \, \rho_w \, g \,,$$

$$\Delta h \, A_{vb} = \frac{\Delta W}{\rho_w \, g} \,. \tag{60}$$

Substituting Eq. 60 into Eq. 59, then the load F can be rewritten as

$$F = W_{bs} + \Delta W + \rho_w \, g \, A_{vb} \, z - \frac{\Delta W \, A_{vb} P_a}{\rho_w \, g \, V_{ih} - \Delta W} \,. \tag{61}$$

Recalling Eq. 50 and substitutes Eq. 61 into this equation, then torque of the motor that is required to change position of movable plate in order to control amount of water in ballast tank is expressed as

$$T_m = k_m \left(W_{bs} + \Delta W + \rho_w \, g \, A_{vb} \, z - \frac{\Delta W \, A_{vb} P_a}{\rho_w \, g \, V_{ih} - \Delta W} \right). \tag{62}$$

In order to change position of the movable plate, the DC motor must provide power P_m and rotates at angular velocity ω_m in order to produce torque at T_m, and can be expressed as

$$P_m = T_m \, \omega_m \,. \tag{63}$$

By substituting Eq. 18 and Eq. 62 into Eq. 63, obviously yields

$$P_m = k_m \left(W_{bs} + \Delta W + \rho_w \, g \, A_{vb} \, z - \frac{\Delta W \, A_{vb} P_a}{\rho_w \, g \, V_{ih} - \Delta W} \right) \frac{N_g \, 2\pi \, \Delta \dot{h}}{l N_w} \,. \tag{64}$$

If $\frac{N_g 2\pi}{l N_w} = k_{gc}$ is known as coefficient of velocity reduction of power screw and worm gear couple, then Eq. 64 can be rewritten as

$$P_m = k_m\, k_{gc}\, \Delta\dot{h}\left(W_{bs} + \Delta W + \rho_w\, g\, A_{vb}\, z - \frac{\Delta W\, A_{vb} P_a}{\rho_w\, g\, V_{ih} - \Delta W} \right). \tag{65}$$

From Eq. 60, if A_{vb} , ρ_w , and g are simply constant, then by differentiating this equation results

$$\Delta\dot{h} = \frac{\Delta\dot{W}}{\rho_w\, g\, A_{vb}}, \tag{66}$$

where $\Delta\dot{h}$ is rate change of position of movable plate and $\Delta\dot{W}$ is rate change of weight of water in the ballast tank.

By substituting Eq. 66 into Eq. 65 and solving $\Delta\dot{W}$, then the rate change of weight of water in the ballast tank is obviously expressed as

$$\Delta\dot{W} = \frac{\rho_w\, g\, A_{vb}\, P_m}{k_m\, k_{gc}\left(W_{bs} + \Delta W + \rho_w\, g\, A_{vb}\, z - \frac{\Delta W\, A_{vb} P_a}{\rho_w\, g\, V_{ih} - \Delta W} \right)}. \tag{67}$$

5. Simulation of open loop system

In order to know responses of the system resulted from the modeling process, the simulation using Simulink in MATLAB is built. The Simulink model is built in block by block system based on the mathematic models. Some input models are tested in order to analyze responses of the model.

5.1 Simulink model

From Eq. 67, Simulink model of rate change of weight in the ballast tank, $\Delta\dot{W}$, is shown in Figure 2. From Figure 2, it can be seen that value of k_m depends on power input, P_m, which results torque T_m to change amount of water in the ballast tank. If $P_m > 0$ then $T_m = T_{mL}$ therefore $k_m = k_{mL}$, otherwise $k_m = k_{mU}$.

The rate change of weight in the ballast tank, $\Delta\dot{W}$, has saturation values ($\pm\Delta\dot{W}_{sat}$). This saturation value depends on the maximum angular velocity of the DC motor that drives this mechanism both in counterclockwise and clockwise direction. Then, the change of weight in the ballast tank, ΔW, can be obtained by integrating $\Delta\dot{W}$ which is shown in Figure 3. ΔW also has saturation values ($\pm\Delta W_{sat}$) which depends upon the maximum volume of the ballast tank.

Output of this model is acceleration of the URV. In order to obtain velocity of URV's vertical motion, v, an integration block diagram is used. In order to get the depth position of the URV, this velocity is integrated. The Simulink model is shown in Figure 5. The condition of depth position and velocity are depth position always be positive ($z \geq 0$) and for $z = 0 \Rightarrow v \geq 0$.

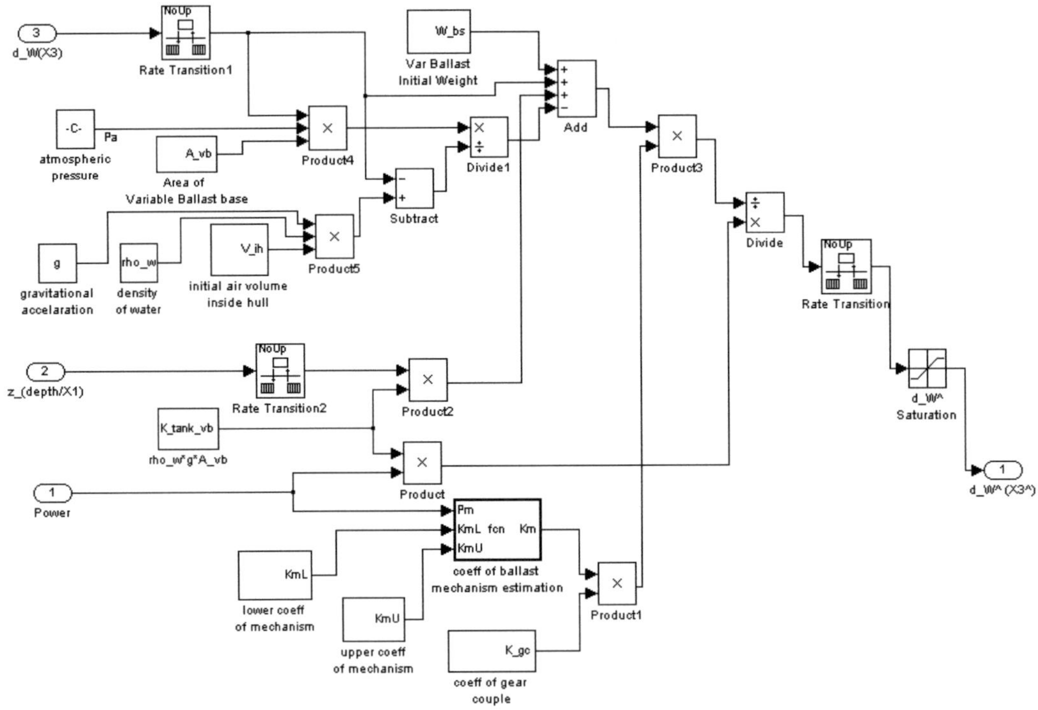

Fig. 2. Model for rate change of weight in the ballast tank.

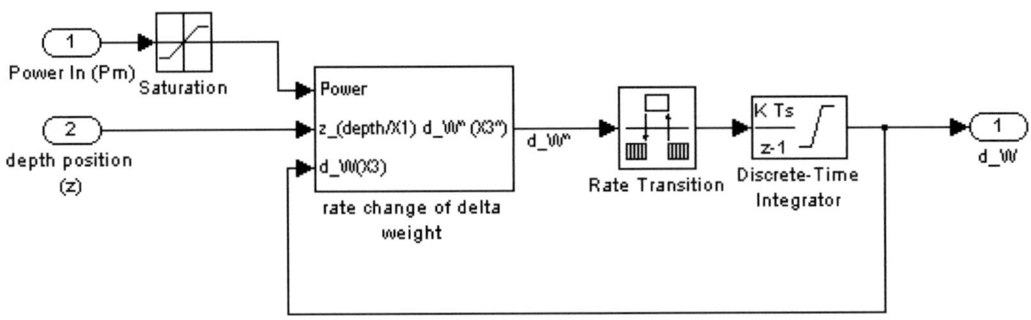

Fig. 3. Model for the change of weight in the ballast tank.

The Simulink model of URV motion in vertical plane which is taken from Eq. 13, is shown in Figure 4. By combining all models, obviously Simulink model for depth positioning of the spherical URV is shown in Figure 6.

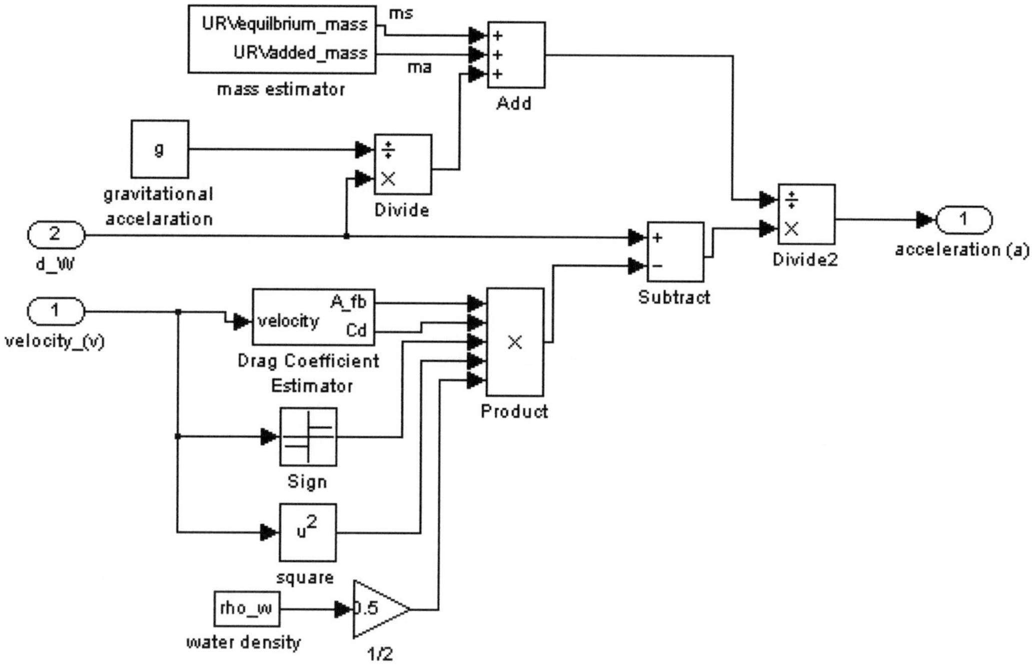

Fig. 4. Model for vertical motion acceleration of URV.

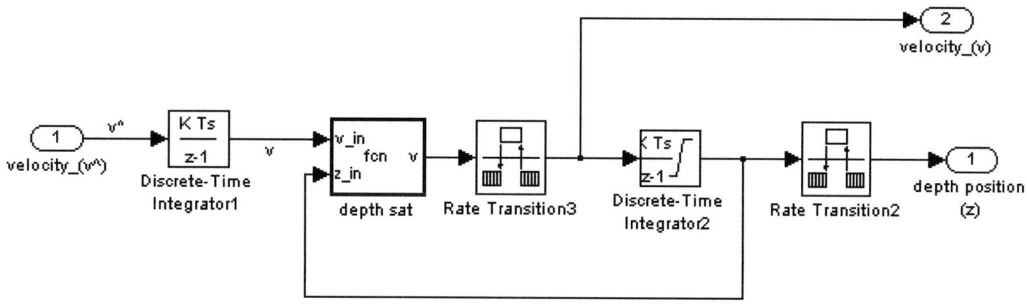

Fig. 5. Model for velocity and depth position of URV.

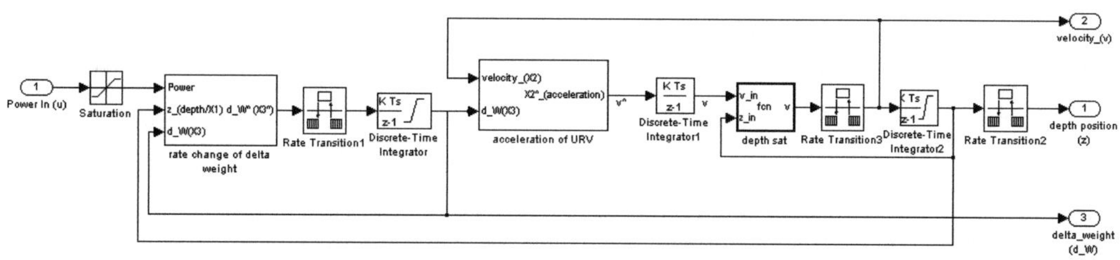

Fig. 6. Model for depth positioning of a spherical URV.

From Figure 6, it can be shown that the power input, P_m, has saturation values that is $\pm P_m$ max. This power depends upon the power provided by the DC motor.

5.2 Simulation result

The dynamic model for depth positioning of the spherical URV involves many constants and parameters both for URV and it ambient. The assumption of these constants and parameters used in the simulation are presented in Table 1.

Parameters	Symbols	Values
Ambient parameters:		
Atmospheric pressure at water surface	P_a	1 atm
Density of water	ρ_w	998 kg/m^3
Dynamic viscosity of water	μ	10^{-3} Ns/m^2
Gravitational acceleration	g	9.81 m/s^2
URV's hull:		
Initial mass of URV	m_s	22.39 kg
Added mass of URV	m_a	11.2 kg
Diameter of URV	D_{fb}	0.35 m
Projected area of URV	A_{fb}	0.09616 m^2
Initial volume of empty space inside URV's hull	V_{ih}	50 % of V_{fb}
Variable ballast system:		
Diameter of variable ballast tank	D_{vb}	0.18 m
Projected area of base of variable ballast tank	A_{vb}	0.0254 m^2
Maximum height of variable ballast tank	h	0.08 m
Initial weight of water in ballast tank	W_{bs}	9.96 N
Transmission ratio of worm gear and power screw	k_{gc}	8.164x10^4 rad/m
Coefficient of worm gear and power screw couple for downward moving	k_{mL}	4.601x10^{-5}
Coefficient of worm gear and power screw couple for upward moving	k_{mU}	1.122x10^{-4}
Power saturation resulted by DC motor	$\pm P_{m\_max}$	±100 Watt
Angular velocity saturation of DC motor	$\pm \omega_{m\_max}$	±157 rad/s

Table 1. Parameters of URV and the ambient.

Some types of input are tested to analyze response of the model. The first input tested in the open loop simulation is a single pulse input. The responses of the model are shown in Figure 7. The given power input from the DC motor, P_m, is a single pulse with amplitude at 50 Watt. The origin position of URV is at 0 meter from surface. Since this input is applied, the URV is descent from surface.

From Figure 7, it is also seen when the power is applied to the motor as positive value, the weight change, ΔW, is increased and reaches saturation around 10N, as maximum value of ΔW. When the power is reset to zero, ΔW still remain at the last value, and the URV still moves with velocity v, which is proportional to ΔW. The depth position of URV, z, will increase since the velocity is available as positive.
If the velocity is negative, the URV is ascending as shown in Figure 8. The increment of ΔW depends on the total power given by the motor to actuate the variable ballast and also depends on the depth position of the URV. If the power given is small then the increment of ΔW is also small, and since the power is available, ΔW will keep increasing till reach saturation. If same power is given to the system but in different depth positions, the increment of ΔW at deeper position is lower than shallower position. This is caused by the availability of hydrostatic force.

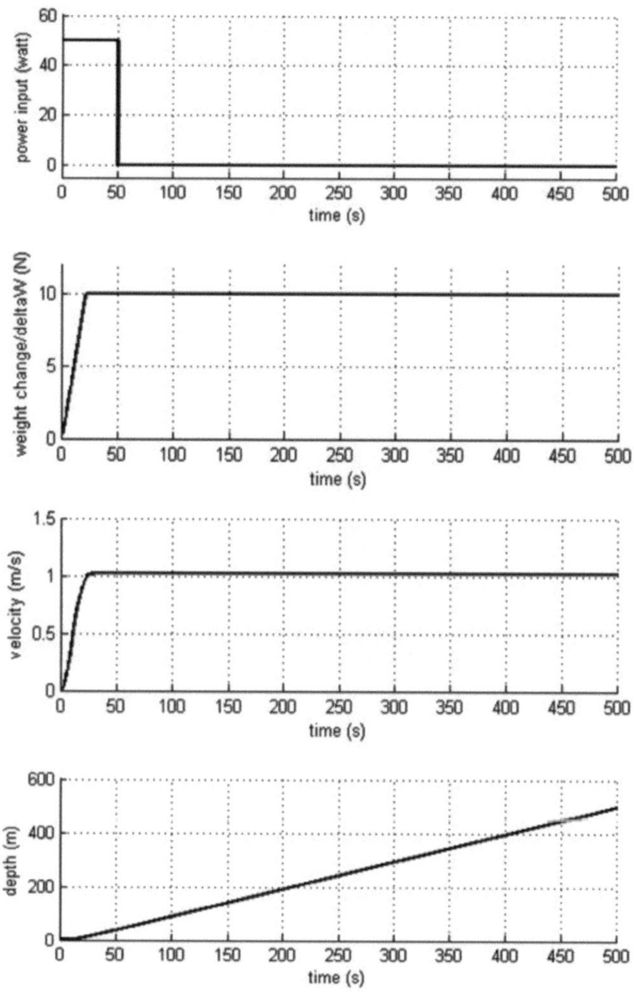

Fig. 7. Response of the system for single pulse input.

When the power is zero, ΔW remains at its last value as well as velocity v. The velocity will remain constant until ΔW change and velocity in this condition is known as *terminal velocity*. This is the advantage of using variable ballast as vertical motion actuator, even the zero power is given to the actuator, the URV still moves therefore it will save the power usage. If $\Delta W = 0$, then the zero velocity occurs. The depth position of URV, z, will remain at its last position, and this condition is called *equilibrium point*. The equilibrium point occurs at any depth position since v and ΔW is equal to zero.

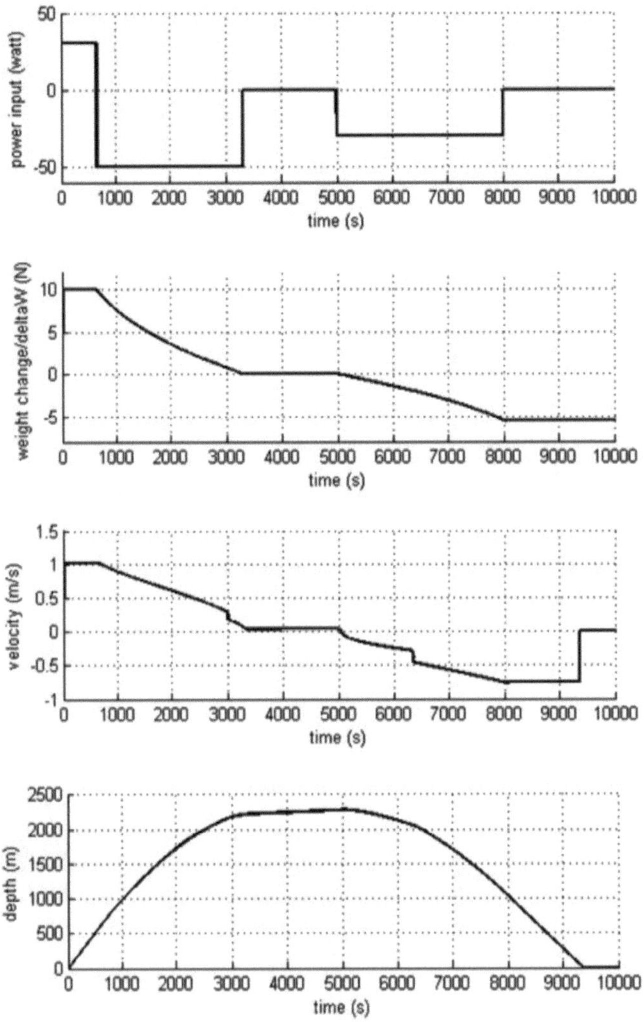

Fig. 8. Response of the system for pulse input in different amplitude.

If ramp input is applied, then the response of the system is shown in Figure 9. By looking to the response, obviously the nonlinearity of the weight change of the URV's body and the velocity in vertical motion are shown. By the increment of P_m, v and ΔW also increase until both of these reach saturation. Depth position, z, keeps increasing since $v > 0$.

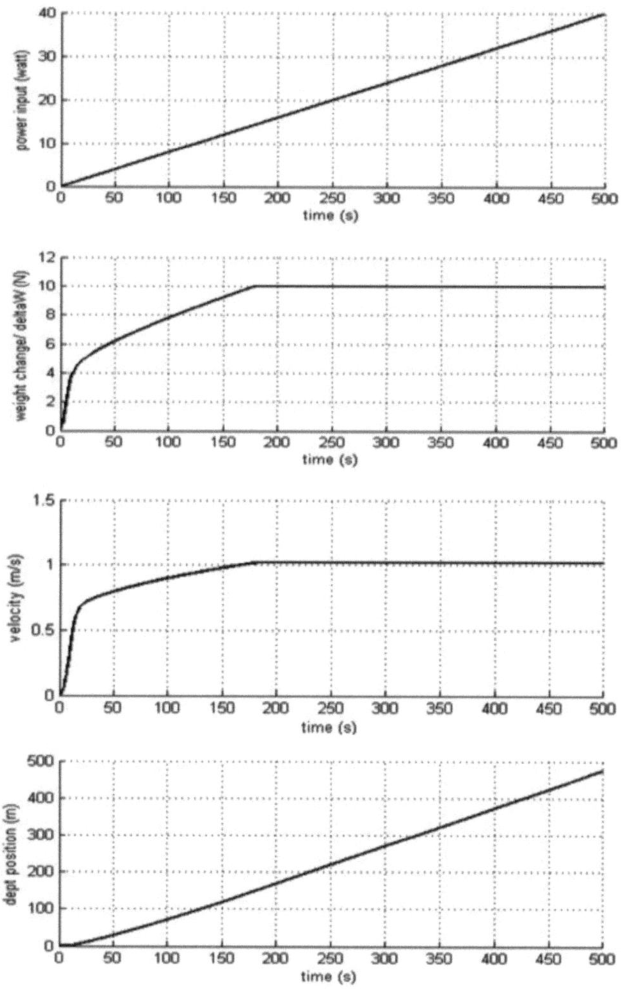

Fig. 9. Response of the system for ramp input.

6. Conclusion

The dynamic model of depth positioning of a spherical URV is obtained by considering the physical laws involve in this system. The dynamic model presented in this chapter is nonlinear. Some inputs are tested to see the responses and characteristics of this system. In the next chapter, the control systems will be designed in order to control the depth position of this spherical URV.

7. References

Collins, J. A. Mechanical Design of Machine Elements and Machines: a Failure Prevention Perspective. New York: John Wiley & Sons Inc, 2003.

Moran, M. J., and H. N. Shapiro. Fundamentals of Engineering Thermodynamics, 3rd ed. Chichester-England: John Wiley & Sons Inc, 1998.

Rajput, R. K. R. K. Rajput, A Textbook of Fluid Mechanics and Hydraulics Machines in SI Units. New Delhi: S. Chand and Company, 2003.

http://www.roymech.co.uk/Useful_Tables/Cams_Springs/Power_Screws_1.html. 2008.

http://www-mdp.eng.cam.ac.uk/resources/2.007/Lead Screws, Gears, and Power Budgets.pdf. 2008.

Xu, M., and S. M. Smith. "Adaptive Fuzzy Logic Depth Controller for Variable Buoyancy System of Autonomous Underwater Vehicles." Third IEEE Conference on IEEE World Congress on Computational Intelligence. Orlando, Fl, USA, 1994.